Cold War Olympics

Cold War Olympics

A New Battlefront in Psychological Warfare, 1948–1956

HARRY BLUTSTEIN

McFarland & Company, Inc., Publishers
Jefferson, North Carolina

ISBN (print) 978-1-4766-8687-5
ISBN (ebook) 978-1-4766-4523-0

LIBRARY OF CONGRESS AND BRITISH LIBRARY
CATALOGUING DATA ARE AVAILABLE

Library of Congress Control Number 2021054430

Front cover: (top) Sprinters at the start of the men's 100 meter final
in the 1952 Summer Olympics in Helsinki, Finland
(Sports Museum of Finland); bottom images © 2022 Shutterstock

Printed in the United States of America

*McFarland & Company, Inc., Publishers
Box 611, Jefferson, North Carolina 28640
www.mcfarlandpub.com*

For CAROL

and in loving memory of my father-in-law,
WALLY LAWSON (1935–2018)

Table of Contents

Acknowledgments

Many people helped me with this book.

I am particularly indebted to Svetlana Chervonnaya, a talented Cold War historian who helped with the research. She tracked down documents, many obscure, from Soviet-era archives, educated me on the finer points of Soviet politics during the 1950s, translated key passages and provided me with insights into what life was like in Moscow during the 1950s. She also provided invaluable feedback on the manuscript and much to my shame picked me up for lapses in some finer points of English grammar.

A special thanks to Janos Zoltan and Karel Hynie, talented filmmakers who generously provided me with footage of their interviews with Olympic athletes.

I had a lot of help translating the foreign-language sources. Foremost was László Kónya who, over chamomile tea and cookies, patiently waded through a large number of Hungarian sources. László had been an athlete who lived in Hungary during the communist period, and his knowledge of that time was invaluable. Janna Hilbrink helped me with Dutch sources, Dana Klimova and René Vodstrcil with Czechoslovak sources and Peter Inzenhofer and Christine Schuler with German ones.

I had considerable help from Tony Foley and Marina Zovko from RMIT University's Document Delivery Service, who tracked down the most obscure newspapers and books that I needed for this book, Bruce Coe for uncovering invaluable papers among Wilfrid Kent Hughes's papers, and Peter Wolcott for ferreting out papers from American archives.

In Budapest I received great help from László Menyhard from the Vonnegut Antikvárium bookshop, who went to great lengths to track down Hungarian books and documents I needed for my research.

I would like to thank all the Olympic athletes who spent time sharing their experiences. All their remarkable stories deserved to be written about and it was only for lack of space that I've had to omit some of their stories. I would particularly like to thank Eugene Hamori for his hospitality while I was in Budapest, Martin Lauer for his insights on what it was like to compete in the combined

German team, and Cecilia Burke and Ivan Gaal for sharing their experiences of life in pre-revolutionary Hungary. Thanks also go to Maria Cabeliza and Leon Wiegard, who helped put me in touch with Australian Olympic athletes. I would also express my appreciation to Vlasta Sustek, who attended the 1948 slet in Prague and shared with me her recollections and documents.

I would particularly like to thank Jean Roberts for reading through the manuscript and providing valuable feedback and for her suggestions on the finer points of grammar, not one of my stronger suits. Peter Duras, Rudi Michelson, Paul Maher, Paul Liistro and Jim Wilson also read parts of the manuscript and the comments helped improve it immeasurably.

With apologies to those I might have forgotten, I'd also like to thank Francine Carraro, Thomas Domer, Ian Pfennigwerth, Richard Mills, Klaus Huhn, Marjolein te Winkel, Pat Butcher, Michael Kenn, Christopher Heathcote, Lionel Hogg, William Lucas, David McKnight, Ray Smee, Terry Claven, Steve Rosen, John Cann, Bob Dent, Lindsay Gaze, Judith Kopacsi Gelberger, Rainer János, Simon Geissbühler, Adam Connolly, John Bell, Kurt Rietmann, Charmaine Janson, Phillip Deery, Les Hody, Mal McCormick, Greg Leon, Johanna Mellis, and Charles Gireth. Special thanks go to Danny Epstein, who educated me on the finer points of ice hockey and promised to take me to a game when I next visit him in Toronto. Paul Hoffman also looked out for Australian slang that I unconsciously had used and made useful suggestions on how to replace them for my American readership.

As much of the book was written in the writer-friendly café at the Fairfield Boathouse, I'd like to thank the staff for making sure that my pot of tea was constantly filled up.

While I have been able to tap into the collective expertise wisdom of the many people who provided input into this book, needless to say any errors of fact, of omission or commission, are my responsibility alone.

Author's Note

Often I have resorted to using a superseded name for security organs of the USSR and Hungary because this is what they were known as at the time by the protagonists who populate this book. In 1950, the Hungarian security organ changed its name from the *Államvédelmi Osztálya*, universally known as the ÁVO, to the *Államvédelmi Hatóság*, or ÁVH. While its official title may have changed, Hungarians continued to refer to it as the ÁVO, as I have in this book. During the period covered by this book, the sections of the security service of the USSR that were active in policing Soviet athletes traveling overseas (referred to as "security police") were part of broader security organs. These were known as NKVD (1936–46), MGB (1946–53), MVD (March 1953–March 1954), and KGB (1954–91). As events in this book often cover several of these periods, I have generally referred to the security agency as NKVD, MGB, or KGB.

The name of the Red Army (*Raboche-krest'yanskaya Krasnaya armiya* or RKKA) was officially changed to the Soviet Army (*Sovetskaya Armiya*) in February 1946. After this date, it continued to be referred to as the Red Army, which I use in this book.

Germany was divided in 1949. The German Democratic Republic (GDR) was governed by East Berlin, and the Federal Republic of Germany (FRG) was governed by Bonn. At the time they were mainly known as East and West Germany, and I generally follow this convention. Similarly, in 1949, at the end of the civil war in China, the communists created the People's Republic of China with its capital in Beijing, then commonly called Peking. At the time, it was known as "Communist China," "Mainland China," and often "Red China." The nationalists fled to the island of Taiwan (also known as Formosa), where they created the Republic of China with its capital in Taipei. At the time, this was referred to as "Taiwan." In Chapter 6, the Classical Theater of China is also referred to as the Peking Opera, as that name was often used by the company when it toured overseas.

One of the main characters in this book is Nikolai Romanov. For most of the period covered by this book, he was the chairman of the Soviet All-Union Committee on Physical Culture and Sport. It was the supreme policy-making body and reported to the Central Committee of the Communist Party. It acted much like a sports ministry, and, for simplicity, Romanov is referred to as the sports minister. The same convention is followed for Gyula Hegyi, who held the equivalent position in Hungary.

The Soviet ship the *Gruzia* translates to the "Georgia," but it has not been translated in the text.

The convention with Hungarian names is for the surname to go first. Rather than follow this convention in this book, I place surnames last.

For many sporting events described in this book, there is no single reliable account. My descriptions of contests are based on multiple accounts contained in contemporary newspapers and from eyewitnesses.

Preface

After the Second World War the two ideological blocs engaged in a global Cold War which permeated many areas of political, cultural, and civic life. So it should come as no surprise that the Olympic Games were caught in its thrall.

Once they were armed to the teeth with nuclear weapons, the two superpowers and their allies put most of their energies into nonlethal strategies, what the Americans called "psychological warfare," and the communists, who were less coy, called "propaganda." I use these terms interchangeably.[1]

This book looks at how the players evolved and tailored strategies and psychological operations to make use of the unique environment of the Olympics.

Psychological warfare was not new, having been employed during the Second World War against Axis powers to sap the enemy's morale. What changed during the Cold War was its aim: to win the hearts and minds of unaligned countries, and to reassure allies and their own populace that they had the strength and determination to prevail. Divided by the Cold War, countries like the two Germanys and the two Chinas used the Olympic Games to assert their legitimacy as the sole representative of both parts of their countries.

During the Cold War, the Olympics were among the few, and certainly one of the most high-profile global stages on which psychological warfare was waged. Using this lens has revealed new insights into the Cold War and its impact on the Olympic movement.

The Soviet Union was the first to fully appreciate the Olympics' propaganda potential, with the United States a latecomer. While the USSR did not compete in its first Olympics until 1952, its preparations started in 1945, which is the starting point of *Cold War Olympics*. However, most of this book is devoted to the first three post-war Olympiads where Cold War politics intruded.

It was during these early Olympic Games that strategies were tested and refined. And while the Cold War ended after the fall of Soviet communism between 1989–1991 the playbook has been revived and adapted in the twenty-first century by a new generation of superpowers, who still see the value of exploiting the Olympics for political advantage.

1

What made the Olympic Games so attractive to Cold War warriors was that for sixteen days, the stadiums, swimming pools, gymnasia, and playing fields of the host city were symbolically and ritually excised from their geographic locality to become a global commons. As a result, the Olympics were highly visible around the world, making them an ideal stage for launching psychological operations.

Another feature of the Olympics that made it an opportune stage for propaganda was that it "crosses language barriers and slices through national boundaries, attracting both spectators and participants to a common lingua franca of passions, obsessions and desires," according to social scientist Toby Miller.[2] The beauty of using sport was that spectators were often unaware that a particular performance contained propaganda messages.

While the Olympic movement nurtured friendly competition between athletes of all nations as a way to promote amity, understanding, and peace, both sides of the Cold War cynically riffed on these values to serve their political interests.

This book describes how psychological warfare was translated into performances at Olympic venues. These performances manifested themselves in many ways, depending on the objectives and the actor, and the opportunities presented during the Olympics. Some were carefully choreographed, others spontaneous. Nor were states the only actors. For example, disaffected athletes from Eastern Europe saw sport, and the Olympics in particular, as a way to criticize communism, and denounce Soviet oppression of their countries.

Sporting events and Olympic ceremonies were not the only occasions to launch psychological operations. Host cities also organized cultural programs to coincide with the Games, which provided additional opportunities to stage political performances.

In researching *Cold War Olympics*, I found that many of the files held by the CIA and Russian archives were highly classified, and inaccessible, despite the considerable passage of time since the events described in this book. Fortunately, this was not the case when I asked for files held by the Australian Security and Intelligence Organization (ASIO), which were provided to me by the National Archives of Australia, with few redactions. I was also helped in my research by the Eisenhower Library and some private archives, whose assistance is greatly appreciated.

Interviews with athletes provided another invaluable source of information. Their vivid memories bring to life what it was like for them, particularly those from behind the Iron Curtain, with many surprises. Their recollections and contemporary accounts allowed me to imbue the narrative with human warmth, and their voices are heard in the pages of this book.

Much of the material in *Cold War Olympics* was published in Australia by

Echo Books in 2017[3] and was tailored to that audience. Parts of this international edition have been rewritten, with new material, including a description of the Cold War games played at the 1948 London Olympics. There is also an account of the tour of Australia by the Peking Opera. This opera company planned to perform in Melbourne during the Olympic Games but was stopped by the Australian government, which feared that the tour would achieve what its communist sponsors hoped: to win hearts and minds before a global audience. The book has also been substantially restructured, closely following the chronology of the first three post-war Olympiads.

My interest in the early Olympics was piqued not as a sporting event but as an expression of globalization, an aspect that is often overlooked by historians. This book is a companion to *Games of Discontent*,[4] in which I explored how discontents at the 1968 Olympic Games in Mexico were able to use the global platform offered by the Olympics to reach a large audience. These books, which cover a nongovernmental global movement, complement my earlier book, *Ascent of Globalisation*,[5] in which I describe the emergence of international governmental institutions that created the rules and norms that gave globalization its structure.

CHAPTER 1

Let the Cold War Olympics Commence

Peace That Is No Peace

On July 17, 1948, Maria Angelakopoulou put the final touches on home-made white robes fashioned from borrowed cloth and held together with pins. The night before, she had agreed to perform the role of an ancient Greek priest-ess and ignite the Olympic Flame in a ceremony at the Temple of Hera. Aleka Mazaraki, a well-known actress from Athens, had initially been cast in the role, but she was unable to travel to Olympia. As well as being tall and statuesque, Angelakopoulou had the necessary qualification of living nearby, in the town of Pyrgos, just 10 miles (16 kilometers) away.

This was not the only hitch that made this ceremony, which marked the start of the XIV Olympiad, far from normal.

King Paul also had not arrived in Olympia, even though he was presi-dent of the Hellenic Olympic Committee and would have been expected at the ceremony.

By tradition, the ceremony is held at dawn when the sun's first rays are focused by a parabolic mirror until dry twigs from an olive tree catch fire. The sacred Flame is then transferred to a 2,400-year-old bowl-shaped lamp. This was the first time the ceremony had been delayed.

At noon, twenty young men in black shorts and showing off bare muscular torsos formed a semi-circle around Angelakopoulou and knelt as she brought the Olympic Flame to life.

Konstantinos Dimitrelis then stepped forward. A commando, he was sta-tioned near Olympia. Before he approached the altar, he put his rifle to one side, removed his steel helmet, and divested himself of his uniform and boots. Now stripped to his running shorts, he lit a torch and proudly held it up above his head. Then, barefooted and barechested, Dimitrelis started on the first leg of the relay, which would take the torch to London for the first post-war Olympic Games.

5

The torch ceremony is part of the Olympic experience that distinguishes the Games from other international sporting events. While technically secular, the Olympic movement cloaks itself in faux religious rituals and symbolism that celebrate social peace, friendship, and fair play.

As much as the Olympic movement hoped that the post-war Games would promote tranquility and amity, politics conspired to make this difficult as two hostile blocs emerged under the leadership of the United States and the Soviet Union.

In 1945, in a prescient article, George Orwell worried that each bloc possessed "a weapon by which millions of people can be wiped out in a few seconds." And because each was now "unconquerable," the world had been plunged into "a permanent state of 'cold war,'" which was an indefinite period of *"peace that is no peace."*[1]

With a hot war between the two superpowers posing an existential threat to themselves and the world, the USSR and United States each looked for new avenues to best the other. A strategy that would become one of the mainstays of the Cold War was for the two superpowers to engage in proxy wars, supporting allies with arms, funding, and technical advice. And it was the first proxy war of the Cold War that disturbed the Olympic torch ceremony.

Since 1946, civil war had raged in Greece between communist insurgents and the right-wing Greek government, supported by Great Britain and U.S. military and economic aid. Seeing the Olympics as a global platform on which they could draw attention to their struggle, communist guerrillas attempted to disrupt the ceremony at Olympia.

It was the night before the start of the torch relay. In a taverna in the port of Katakolon, a group of naval officers and journalists were enjoying a bottle or two of local wine. Their evening was interrupted by automatic gunfire. After a short gun battle with local gendarmes, the communist guerrillas escaped after killing a policeman.

As well as the attack at the taverna, the Olympic organizers had to deal with other unwelcome exigencies. King Paul did not attend the ceremony because he might be put in harm's way. Aleka Mazaraki could not travel to Olympia because traffic on the Corinth Canal access road was threatened by guerrilla activity. And to prevent the torch from being captured by communist guerrillas, troops were deployed in the low hills around Olympia, and overhead Spitfire fighters and reconnaissance planes patrolled.

There were other precautions. The traditional escort of children who usually followed the first runner, chanting passages from Euripides, was canceled. Instead, armed soldiers lined the route.

The heavy presence of the military around Olympia undermined the powerful symbolic act by Corporal Dimitrelis of divesting himself of his military identity so that he could personify the Olympic message of universal peace: Pax Olympia.

Finally, organizers canceled most of the first leg of the relay, which would have taken the Flame to Athens and then back to the southwest coast, a trip of 470 miles (750 km). Instead, the torchbearers made a beeline for the coast, 22 miles (35 km) away, where the Greek destroyer *Hastings* was waiting to take the torch to Corfu. Next, it was then taken aboard the British frigate HMS *Whitesand Bay*, which had landed at Bari in Italy. Runners then carried the torch across continental Europe.

On July 29, the Flame arrived in London, which still showed evidence of the aftermath of the war. The city was shabby. Bombed-out buildings pockmarked the cityscape. Housing was in short supply, and the population was still complaining about rationing, a topic that they alternated with grumbling about the weather. In anticipation of food shortages, some countries brought their own food supplies for their athletes.

Under Sunny Skies

On this particular day, however, there was nothing to complain about. The sky was clear and the weather very warm as an estimated 82,000 spectators streamed into Wembley Stadium for the opening ceremony.

It was hard to be pessimistic on a day like this. After a hiatus of twelve years everyone looked to the London Olympics to show that the world was returning to normality. Czechoslovak long-distance runner Emil Zátopek, who would win a gold and a silver medal in London, recalled those times. "After all those dark days of war, the bombing, the killing, and the starvation, the revival of the Olympics was as if the sun had come out," he said. "Men and women who had lost five years of the full life were back again."[2]

A fanfare by the trumpeters of the Household Cavalry marked the start of the opening ceremony.

In the shimmering heat, the stadium was a blush of bright color: women were dressed in gay blues, pinks and yellows, and many men had taken their jackets off, adding a splash of white to the stands; the well-tended infield was vivid green with a red cinder track around its perimeter; and the Brigade of Guards marched into the stadium wearing scarlet jackets, dark blue trousers, and tall bearskin headgear. The English's well-known reserve evaporated as spectators cheered, stamped their feet, and clapped their way through the ceremony. The contrast with dour London would not have been starker.

Another fanfare heralded the arrival of King George VI, who entered the stadium on a walkway shaded by a green and white striped canopy. He was followed by a small party of minor royals, aristocrats, and other VIPs, including the Maharaja Sir Yadavinder Singh in a blue turban. With the temperature tipping 93°F (34°C), the stiff upper lips of these bluebloods had a sweaty sheen on them. The King then walked down to the infield, where he was welcomed by officials from the International Olympic Committee (IOC), many of whom wore morning suits and black silk top hats.

A popular part of the ceremony was the Parade the Nations, with national teams entering the stadium in eye-catching outfits. As the home of the ancient Olympics, Greece had the honor of leading the parade. As they marched past the King, their heads turned sharply to their right and their standard bearer dipped the Greek standard as a sign of respect to the host. After that, countries entered in strict alphabetical order from Afghanistan to Yugoslavia, with the host, Great Britain, coming last.

After British Guiana marched into the stadium, Bulgaria should have been next. However, it and Romania had pulled out of the Games days before the opening ceremony. No official reason was given by Bulgaria, while the Rumanian People's Sports Organization explained that they were protesting the inclusion of "war criminals" and representatives of fascist governments on the IOC.[3] Their outrage was confected. Both countries had competed in the Winter Olympics in St. Moritz six months earlier when the same "war criminals" were in charge of the IOC. The real reason was probably less righteous or principled. Neither had won medals at those Games. A repetition would not only reflect poorly on their countries but also jeopardize the careers of communist sports officials. There may have also been a practical reason. Both countries were short of hard currency and they probably could not afford to attend. Nevertheless, it set a precedent followed by other countries in subsequent Cold War Olympics, who used boycotts (even faux boycotts) to pursue political ends.

Despite these absences, other eastern European countries participated, belying the notion that the communist bloc was unified when it came to the Olympics. Poland, Czechoslovakia, Hungary, and Yugoslavia had a long and affectionate relationship with the Olympic movement, and their teams were pleased to be part of the parade.

Yugoslavia had been part of the communist bloc up to June 1948, when it was expelled following a feud between its leader, Marshal Josip Tito, and Joseph Stalin. This dispute did not have an immediate impact on the Yugoslavian team in London. "At that time, it was not yet clear whether we would break up with Russia," explained sprinter Marko Račič.[4]

Following the London Olympics, the consequence of the rift became evident on sport when Yugoslavia was frozen out of competition with other communist countries. Artur Takač, who had managed the Olympic athletics team in London, was summoned to a meeting with Yugoslavian leaders. "Artur, Stalin turned his back on us, and at the moment we have no contact with the West. You'll get money and a plane. Travel and connect us with sporting agencies in the West. Stalin must see that we are not alone."[5] Takač traveled to Paris and used his contacts in the Olympic movement to arrange friendly sporting competitions with Western countries and secure new sporting equipment supplies.

Once the Soviet Union joined the Olympics, its rivalry with Yugoslavia would be fierce, a proxy for the enmity between their leaders. This may have been a sideshow during the Cold War. Still, it was important because it exposed a fissure in the unity of the communist bloc, which the West was keen to exploit.

East and West Germany were not in London. They had not been invited, which was understandable as memories of the war were still fresh. They did, however, participate in subsequent Olympics, with each insisting it was the sole representative of the German people.

For the Polish team, its appearance in London was particularly poignant, as the sports newspaper *Przegląd Sportowy* explained. "After years of terrible suffering, the team of our country, which had been ravaged during the havoc of war, marched amongst other nations."[6]

As the countries appeared in alphabetical order, the United States should have marched behind the Union of Socialist Soviet Republics. The USSR, however, did not appear because it had not yet joined the Olympic movement.

The king then was invited up to the microphone, where he officially opened the games. "I proclaim open the Olympic Games of London celebrating the XIV Olympiad of the modern era." It was also the unofficial opening of the first Cold War games.

Psychological Warfare

In anticipation that they would eventually participate in the Olympics, the Kremlin had sent ten officials to the London Games to assess whether the Soviets could beat the Americans on the medal table. The Kremlin had also sent observers to the winter Olympics in St. Moritz five months earlier, after which they concluded that "since there is no such firm confidence in achieving first place, we consider participation in the Olympic Games inappropriate."[7]

Since 1945, the Kremlin was considering using sport as part of its propaganda war against the West. The Communist Party enshrined this strategy in policy a year after the London Olympics by committing the Soviet Union to "winning world supremacy in all the major sports in the immediate future."[8] There was no better platform for implementing this policy than the Olympic Games. By showing its superiority on the sporting field, the Soviet Union hoped to demoralize its enemies, win the hearts and minds of unaligned nations, and consolidate the loyalty of allies. This last objective was vital for the Soviet Union, which had recently drawn Eastern European countries into its orbit.

The presence of Soviet officials in London showed that the USSR was keen to add sport to its propaganda armory. The United States, however, was oblivious to the threat. This would change. In the run-up to the Helsinki Olympiad, held in the summer of 1952, the United States began to engage the Soviet Union in "psychological warfare" as international sport became a new front of the Cold War.

Lieutenant-General Gleb Baklanov, head of the Physical Culture and Sports Directorate of the Soviet Army, had been carefully selected by the Kremlin to lead this mission to London. Baklanov, however, was puzzled why he had been chosen. "Everyone knows, including in the West, that I am a military man, a general. How will it look?" The Kremlin was astute in its choice. "You can leave your uniform in Moscow and change into civilian clothes," he was told. "Treat this like a combat mission and then report to the leadership on what needs to be done."[9] The Kremlin viewed sport as a form of war, which is why it entrusted this mission to a military man who would provide a dispassionate assessment of the chances of Soviet athletes at future Olympics.

With the Soviet Union choosing not to compete, sportswriters predicted that the United States would easily top the medal table, not unreasonably so as it had no serious challengers. Besides, the Americans well-fed athletes had a distinct advantage over their European opponents, many of whom were still suffering the privations of post-war rationing.

When the Americans marched into Wembley Stadium, they were all smiles, and there was a swagger in their step; some were even chewing gum.

The *New York Times* reported that "applause for the Americans was not as enthusiastic as that for some other nations, possibly in part because they did not dip colors."[10] The United States was the only country to ignore this IOC rule, which required each team to show respect by dipping its flag as it marched past the host. Seeing itself as the only superpower, the Americans did not much care for global opinion. This would change as the United States realized that winning hearts and minds was important to winning the Cold War. Dipping the Stars and Stripes, though, was not negotiable, as they argued that the United States would not bow before "earthly kings,"[11] and Americans were willing to wear the opprobrium.

After the Parade of Nations concluded, athletes gathered in the center of the infield where they heard the Olympic oath read by British hurdler Donald Finlay. Then white pigeons, a symbol of peace, were freed from cages located around the perimeter of the infield. The organizers claimed that 7,000 pigeons had been released. This number was disputed by American sports journalist Red Smith, who unkindly suggested that "the brass didn't dare turn loose that many squab in this hungry nation."[12]

British athlete John Mark then ran into the stadium to thunderous applause, holding the torch aloft, trailing sparks behind him. The Flame, kindled in Olympia twelve days earlier by Maria Angelakopoulou, had arrived. After completing a circuit of the track, Mark stopped before a cauldron at the east end of the stadium. He raised the torch high above his head and then plunged it into the bowl, where the Olympic Flame flared up to announce the official start of the XIV Olympiad. Watching this ceremony was future one mile world record holder Roger Bannister, who recalled: "I had the feeling that we were witnessing sacred rights performed in an open air Cathedral."[13]

After unseasonably hot weather for the opening ceremony, the days that followed were cool and frequently wet. This gave everyone the opportunity to do some serious grumbling.

Because of delays obtaining visas and then trouble securing a flight to London, Baklanov and his team only arrived five days before the closing ceremony and were only able to look in at a few events.

There was a second objective of General Baklanov's mission. To be admitted to the Olympic movement, the Soviet Union needed to join international sporting organizations that covered Olympic events. As many associations held their congresses in London during the Games, it was an ideal opportunity for Baklanov to lobby them for membership.

As a superpower, the Soviet Union had demands that it insisted be met. In this, Baklanov's diplomatic skills would be tested. The USSR wanted Russian accepted as an official language. Most of these associations communicated only in English and French, as did the IOC. The Soviets also insisted that Soviet representatives be appointed to the governing bodies of each association. Finally, the Soviet Union wanted fascist Spain expelled. Knowing that this last demand was untenable—being nakedly political, which went against these associations' rules—Baklanov did not pursue it with any enthusiasm.

Baklanov was disappointed by the lack of support he received from representatives from Soviet satellite countries, many of whom were executive members of these associations. "We were unable to develop a unified plan with members of people's democracies [Eastern European countries] in the congresses of international sports associations," he complained.[14] When it came to sport, Baklanov would discover that sports officials from Eastern Europe showed disturbing independence from Moscow.

None incurred Baklanov's ire more than Czechoslovakia's Marie Provazníková, who was on the executive of the Fédération Internationale de Gymnastique. When he tried to set up a meeting with her, she refused to attend.

There was a good reason why Provazníková had no intention of meeting with a representative of the Kremlin. On February 25, 1948, the Soviet Union helped the Czechoslovak Communist Party stage a coup. This takeover upset

Provazníková. "Today, democracy perished in Czechoslovakia."[15] Noncommunist president Edvard Beneš had been allowed to remain in his position after the coup. Still, on June 7, after watching the Stalinization of Czechoslovakia gather pace, Beneš resigned. He was replaced by hardline communist, Klement Gottwald.

The communist takeover posed a personal risk to Provazníková because apparatchiks from the new regime feared that she would organize anti-communist protests at a sporting and cultural festival, called a slet, which would be held in Prague a month before the Games.

Slets were held every six years. They were organized by Sokol, a voluntary patriotic association. Through sporting, fitness, and cultural programs, Sokol wanted to create a vibrant and vigorous Slavic identity based on democracy, social equality, team spirit, moral strength, fair play, and women's emancipation. When these values were attacked by the Nazis during their occupation of Czechoslovakia, Sokol went underground and provided the backbone of the resistance. Many of its leaders were hunted down, tortured, and executed.

In Eastern Europe, many sporting organizations had deep roots in their communities, and sport would become a popular avenue to vent discontent with communism during the Cold War. There was no better example than Sokol, and its slet would provide a platform where opposition to the communist coup would be expressed.

The main festival took place from July 1 to 8, when the resignation of Beneš was still fresh in people's minds.

Before an estimated quarter of a million spectators, spectators, in the center of the Strahov Stadium Sokol members (or in English, Falcons) performed mass synchronized exercises, gymnastic exhibitions, and folk dancing. These mass displays of bodies personified the spirit of unified and independent Czechoslovakia, which were an anathema to the Stalinists who now ruled the country.

Provazníková organized the girls' and women's components of the slet. "No festival had ever been prepared with so much love and sacrifice as this one," she explained.[16] Determined to go out on a high note, the climax of the women's performance was an exuberant composition, involving 30,000 women, call the "*Rej*" [whirl]. Believing that the communists would eventually infiltrate Sokol and destroy its democratic ideals, Provazníková saw this slet as a final hurrah. It would be a joyous requiem, a memory that would keep the spirit of Sokol alive through the coming days of darkness.

The first sign of protest was during a performance of Soviet gymnasts. After their routine, a helicopter hovered over the stadium and dropped two bouquets of red roses, which were gathered by the gymnasts. As they sang *Song of Labor*, they presented the flowers to President Klement Gottwald and fellow hardline communist, Prime Minister Antonín Zápotocký. As the gymnasts approached the VIP stand, they could not have missed the booing from the stands.

Mass gymnastics performance at the IX Slet at the Strahov Stadium in Prague. The slet took place from 19 to 27 June 1948 (John Tiernry).

Next, a troupe of 750 Yugoslavian sailors formed, in enormous letters, "Tito," to which spectators chanted "Tito, Tito." This reaction was significant as it was only days after the rift between Stalin and Tito, when the Yugoslavian leader asserted his country's independence from Soviet hegemony.

During the slet spectators called out "Beneš," even though he was not in the stadium. In one performance, young girls formed a giant "B" in the stadium in front of President Gottwald and other communist worthies. In another incident, twenty young men, after they had finished participating in a mass athletics performance, pointedly turned their backs on the VIP box where President Gottwald was sitting and waved the Czechoslovak flag, to the delight of spectators. And during her welcoming address, Provazníková did not refer to the president by name, a deliberate snub.

After a day of protests, Provazníková was detained and questioned by government security agents. She was eventually released at 1 a.m. after being warned that she would be held responsible for any further demonstrations. Following her detention, she was followed by secret police for the remainder of the slet.

As part of the slet, Falcons paraded through Prague on July 6.

The night before the procession, Gottwald hosted a reception in Prague Castle. Before the reception started, he ushered Sokol officials into a private room. Worried there would be more protests during the procession, he attacked Sokol for encouraging these demonstrations. "If anyone thinks they can hurt me they're mistaken. Stuff yourselves here and leave." After this tirade, they turned their backs on Gottwald and stormed out of the reception without eating, further embarrassing Gottwald in front of his guests, many of them foreign diplomats.[17]

The procession lasted from 8:30 a.m. to 2 p.m., and over 75,000 Falcons 9,000 overseas visitors, and 933 riders on horseback paraded through central Prague to the sound of bands. Some older members wore the traditional outfit of red shirts, black calf-length boots, and *čapky*, small black caps, the sort that bell-hops used to wear, adorned with a feather. Sokol and Czechoslovak flags hung off balconies in the main thoroughfares.

Communist supporters had draped communist flags outside some build-ings, which were noteworthy because they were few in number. They chanted pro-government slogans, but they were drowned out by Falcons singing patri-otic songs.

The parade marched along Pařížská Street and then entered the old town square where Gottwald viewed the march from a grandstand. As Falcons marched past, many pointedly turned their heads away. They also chanted: "Long live President Beneš!"; "You can't dictate who we should love"; "We will sweep communism and Gottwald from the Republic"; and "A fist to the face for all com-rades." Gottwald looked on, stony-faced.[18]

Later that evening, after the procession ended, around 3,000 Falcons gath-ered on Wenceslas Square. This time, when they chanted anti-government slogans, police moved in and arrested 200 protesters. In the months that fol-lowed, 11,000 officials were expelled from Sokol, and some were imprisoned on trumped-up charges.

After the slet, Provazníková left for London, but not without drama. See-ing her as a troublemaker, the government held up her passport until after the British Embassy closed, hoping that she would miss out on receiving a visa to London. When the British became aware of her plight, they dealt with her appli-cation after hours. With little time before the gymnastics competition, Provaz-níková could not book a seat on a commercial flight. Again, help came from the British Embassy staff, who found her a seat on a foreign carrier that left from Prague's Ruzyně Airport (now Václav Havel Airport Prague).

When Provazníková arrived in London she was greeted with bad news. The team had been on an earlier flight, and while on the plane one of her gymnasts, Eliška Misáková, complained of headaches and nausea. By the time the plane landed in London, she had a high temperature and was suffering from back pain. At the hospital the doctors discovered that she had polio. Because it was an incur-able disease and highly infectious, Eliška was transferred to Uxbridge Isolation Hospital. "We visited Eliška," teammate Věra Růžičková recounted, "but the doc-tors did not let us in. She could only be seen through the glass. She lay encased by an iron lung. She couldn't speak, and her hands and feet were paralyzed."[19] It was particularly hard for Eliška's sister, Miloslava, who was also a team member.

At the grandstand, in the Old Town Square in central Prague, Falcons marched past President Gottwald (circled) without respectfully turning their heads right. They were protesting to communist coup that had taken place in February 1948 (Národní muzeum—Historické muzeum).

Once Provazníková arrived in London the Czechoslovak government had her followed, worried that she might defect. Her shadow was Miroslav Klinger, a former Olympian. While he was a member of Sokol, he was a loyal servant of the Communist Party.

The competition began on August 12, and the Czechoslovak gymnasts were emotionally drained. "Before the competition, we sat down and said to ourselves that we would fight for Eliška," recalled Růžičková. "And if we won, Eliška would also win."[20]

The Czechoslovak team was in second place before the final event, 0.5 points behind Hungary.

As Provazníková stood waiting for the final event to commence, she received an urgent message. Miloslava needed to rush to the hospital as the doctor believed her sister might have just hours to live. Provazníková waited until the final was over before she passed on the news. A little after midnight, Miloslava rushed to the hospital. Eliška died at 7:30 a.m. without regaining consciousness.

Because the competition had finished late, the medal ceremony was held on August 14, the last day of the Olympics. By then, all the gymnasts knew that

Eliška had died. On the victory podium they were in tears. When the Czechoslovak flag was raised it was draped in black crepe. In a first, Eliška Misáková was awarded a gold medal posthumously.

On the day Eliška died, Provazníková received a message from Miroslav Klinger, informing her that she was expected to fly home after the closing ceremony. Now worried that government agents might try and kidnap her, Provazníková moved to the home of Josef Janek, president of the London division of Sokol.

Eliška was cremated in London, after which a small service was held, attended by her teammates. Before the service, Provazníková met privately with the gymnasts and told them she would not be returning to Czechoslovakia. Two of the girls wanted to stay with her in London, but she persuaded them to return home. At the funeral, communist officials tried to sideline Provazníková. However, she insisted on giving the eulogy.

On August 18 Provazníková attended a press conference during which she announced that she was "a political refugee and proud of it." She went on to say: "There is no freedom in Czechoslovakia now—no freedom of speech, or of the press, or of assembly."[21]

Other East European athletes did not return home. They were Jiří Kovář, Jiří Linhart, Josef Schejbal, and Oszkár Czuvik. Others overstayed, but eventually returned home. None of these competitors declared that they were seeking political asylum. The only genuine defector was Provazníková, making her the first in Olympic history.

Nevertheless, U.S. newspapers identified all of them as defectors and argued that they had chosen freedom over slavery, a familiar Cold War trope of the time. "Communist leaders fear dissatisfaction among their people if they see that conditions in the free countries are far better than in their own land," argued an editorial in the Palladium-Item.[22] The Arizona Republic's editorial claimed that defecting athletes "decided that they would forgo the plaudits of the crowds at home and stay in a free country. To forsake friends and family and all home ties for the sake of liberty, requires a high order of courage."[23] Columnist Robert Ruark wrote that for defectors, "the idea of forgoing in the future the delights of life under Communist regimes may have been inspired partially by the discovery that athletes from the 'decadent' democracies didn't look or act at all like slaves of the capitalistic system."[24]

Provazníková (who later shortened her name to Provaznik) used her profile to attack the Czechoslovak communist regime on the BBC in a broadcast in primetime on Christmas Day. Transcripts of her broadcast were smuggled into Czechoslovakia and circulated among Sokol members. After Provazníková moved permanently to the United States, she continued her anti-communist campaign with weekly broadcasts on Voice of America and Radio Free Europe.

The Olympics came to an end on August 14. The weather was again warm, although not quite as hot as the first day. Wembley Stadium was packed as spectators looked forward to the closing ceremony.

At precisely 6 p.m., flagbearers paraded on the field as guardsmen played *March of the Gladiators.*

During the closing ceremony, IOC president Sigfrid Edström addressed athletes who would participate in the next Games in Helsinki. "May they display cheerfulness and concord so that the Olympic torch may be carried on with ever greater eagerness, courage and honour for the good of humanity throughout the ages."[25] These words are a formula read out during every closing ceremony. In London, these sentiments were particularly incongruous as the London Games were a prelude to the intrusion of Cold War politics into the Olympics.

The Flame, which had been carried across Europe from Olympia, was then extinguished, bringing the celebration of the London Olympic Games to a close with the solemnity worthy of the grand occasion.

After the Soviet observer team returned to Moscow, General Baklanov prepared his report. He concluded that the Soviet Union would have been second only to the United States on the medal table.[26] Nevertheless, the United States was beatable, as there were a number of sports in which its world ranking was far from the top, including water polo, wrestling, football, distance events in track and field, and fencing. Another major vulnerability was that the United States did poorly in most women's events.

This report was critical to whether the Soviets would participate in the next Olympics, and those reading the report were only interested in how it helped the Soviet Union exploit the Games for Cold War propaganda, as sports journalist Stanislav Tokarev explained:

> For the best friend of Soviet athletes [Stalin], it was not who was running and jumping and how: all he cared for was victory—as further evidence of [quoting Pushkin] "obedient to me, strong is my realm," and failure would be taken as a travesty of the entire system. That meant that sport had become an instrument of big-league politics.[27]

The Soviet Union's journey towards joining the Olympic movement, though, would be unsteady and fraught.

CHAPTER 2

Red Road to Olympus

The Start of the Journey

Nikolai Romanov should be giving credit for convincing Stalin to seek membership of the Olympic movement. Joseph Stalin was not much interested in sport, but he was interested in opening up a new front in the Cold War, one which the Soviet Union would dominate. To this end, Romanov had to reorganize sport in the Soviet Union so it could produce athletes who would be capable of not just participating in the Olympic Games but winning.

When Romanov was appointed chairman of the Soviet All-Union Committee of Physical Culture and Sport in 1945, in effect his country's sports minister, he became obsessed with turning the Soviet Union into a sporting superpower.

If anyone had the qualities to succeed in this ambitious endeavor, it was Romanov. Having come up through the Soviet bureaucracy as secretary of the youth wing of the Communist Party, the Komsomol, he knew his way around the Kremlin and how to traverse the treacherous labyrinths of political power. Whereas five of his six predecessors were shot during purges, Romanov survived by dent of his competence, dedication, and astute judgment—qualities appreciated by members of the ruling Politburo. It was his longevity—he retired as chairman in 1962—that allowed him to execute his long-term plan of transforming Soviet sport.

Thin-lipped and solidly built, with a three-packs-a-day cigarette habit, Romanov was a cultured man, smart, and had a cheerful disposition. But he could be tough when needed. A talented functionary with an impressive knowledge of a large number of sports, he was respected by sportspeople for being plain-spoken and for encouraging them to experiment with tactics that might give them a winning edge. During his time as chairman, he invested heavily in sports science, making the Soviet Union a pioneer in this field, which helped athletes manage their training loads and improve their techniques. In a remarkably short time, Romanov was able to bring Soviet elite athletes to the point where they could compete with the world's best.

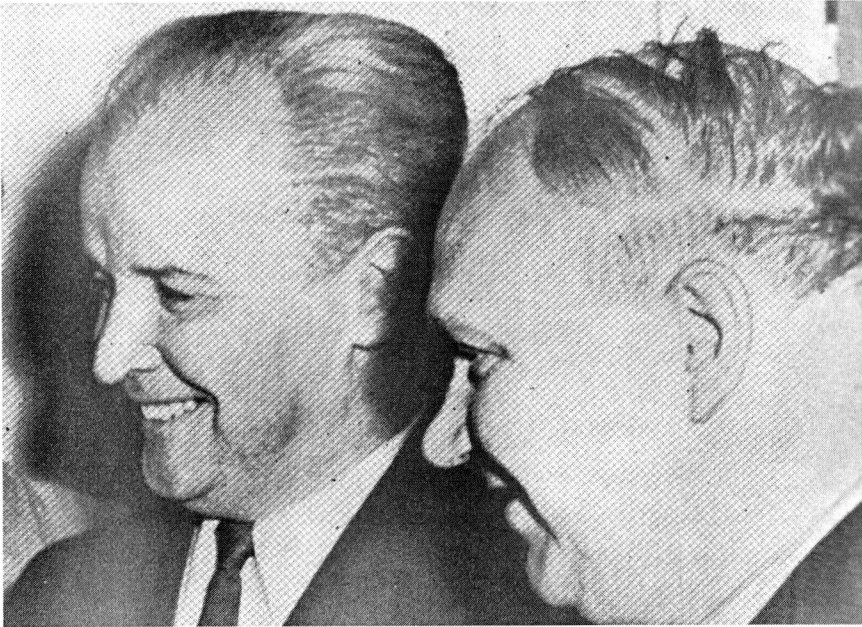

Nikolai Romanov, Soviet Minister of Sport (left), with an unknown sports official.

At the start of his campaign Romanov faced formidable challenges. After the 1917 revolution the country's ideologues had rejected elite competitive sport as "bourgeois" and eschewed the Olympic Games because they were designed to "deflect workers from the class struggle and to train them for new imperialist wars."[1] His other problem was that many Olympic sports were unknown in the Soviet Union.

Romanov did, however, have strong foundations on which to build. Since the 1920s the Soviet regime had invested considerable resources in *fizkul'tura* (physical culture). This program was designed for the masses. It included cross-country running and skiing for fitness. There were large-scale gymnastics displays for discipline and solidarity. And weightlifting and wrestling built brawn needed to defend the Motherland from imperialist invaders. *Fizkul'tura* also gave equal attention to women's athletics, arguing that "well-developed young women will also produce healthy and robust children."[2]

Fortunately for Romanov's plans, *fizkul'tura* had not completely eliminated competitive sports, and football in particular quickly gained a passionate following after it was introduced in the early 1920s. So while the Soviet state was not always able to provide sufficient bread to its population, it did permit more than a few circuses.

If the USSR was to compete at the Olympics, Romanov realized its athletes would need to be tested against international competition. The logical choice was football because the domestic competition was robust, leading Romanov to believe that a quality Soviet team would be competitive with the world's best.

The perfect opportunity opened up soon after VE Day, when the English Football Association, on behalf of Great Britain, invited the Soviet Union to send Moscow Dinamo[3] to play a series of Friendlies. The British populace harbored warm feelings towards its Soviet ally, which had suffered enormous losses to defeat the Nazis, and this was a chance to show its appreciation.

Dinamo dominated the football competition in Moscow, and it was the obvious choice for the tour. Created in 1923 by the State Political Directorate, Dinamo was among the oldest sports clubs in the USSR, and during the Soviet period was sponsored by the security police organs, the NKVD.

Before the team left for Great Britain, Stalin called a meeting which was attended by the players and management. Lavrentiy Beria, the head of the NKVD as well as being president of Dinamo, was also present. Stalin commanded them not to lose to "bourgeois Capitalist football sides."[4]

On the evening of November 4, 1945, with the light fading, two planes arrived unexpectedly at Northolt Aerodrome. No one was waiting to greet them because Moscow had failed to notify British officials when Dinamo would be arriving. Once football officials received a phone call informing them that the Soviet planes had landed, they rushed to the aerodrome to welcome their guests: players, trainers, officials, journalists, and presumably secret police from the NKVD. They were wearing royal blue overcoats adorned with red hammer and sickle insignias.

Once they were on British soil, the press had no hesitation in passing judgment before the first kick-off. The Cold War had not quite started, yet the English sports journalists were distinctly frosty towards Dinamo. Paul Irwin from the *Sunday Express* casually dismissed the Dinamo team. "Do not expect much from this bunch of factory workers." And Tom Morgan wrote in *People* magazine, "These pale boys are far too slow for the top drawer."[5]

Nine days after they arrived, Dinamo played its first game against Chelsea. English fans had been starved of football during the war years, and when the gates closed at 2:30 p.m., the Stamford Bridge ground had filled to overflowing. Spectators were even standing on the edge of the pitch, while others perched on the roofs of the stands.

Charming their English hosts, the Dinamo players presented their opponents with large bouquets before the match but omitted the traditional greeting between Russian men—a kiss on the lips—which might have been a little too friendly for the English players.

Once the game started, the visitors treated spectators to a splendid feast of slick passes, speed, and clever positional play. As a result, Dinamo dominated

Programs for a series of Friendlies between Dinamo and British football teams.

the early stages, but not on the scoreboard, failing to convert numerous scoring opportunities. Chelsea's attacks, on the other hand, were more efficient, and at half-time it led 2–0.

In the first 20 minutes of the second half, Dinamo missed a penalty and then had a goal disallowed because it had bounced off one of the spectators standing on the edge of the playing field. Then came a long Soviet goal, followed by another seven minutes later, leveling the score, 2–2. Two more goals followed in quick succession, one to Chelsea and then one to Dinamo. Although the Soviets' last goal was clearly offside, the English referee let it stand for "diplomatic reasons."[6]

Fans accepted that the final score of 3–3 was a fair reflection of the quality of play on the field, and, in a show of appreciation, hundreds of spectators ran onto the pitch lifting the Dinamo players aloft.

In a live broadcast to Moscow, sports journalist Vadim Siniavskii preened, "We have passed our first exam with honours."[7] Winning (or at least not losing) was also crucial to Romanov if he was to convince Stalin to send more sporting teams to foreign climes to gain valuable international experience.

Having given a good account of itself, Dinamo was keen to test itself against one of the best sides in the world. "To come to London and not play Arsenal would be like visiting Cairo without seeing the pyramids," said Coach Mikhail Yakushin.[8]

The game was played—unusually for an Arsenal match—at White Hart Lane. The ground was shrouded by a pea souper, and Arsenal's manager begged the Russian referee to abandon the game. He refused, and 54,000 spectators struggled to see the match through the thick fog. Then light rain fell as the match started.

It is hard to know what exactly happened that day, although quite a few irregularities were alleged. Players scored from offside. Others sent off returned immediately, undetected in the fog. And the Russians may have played with twelve men for 20 minutes. Dinamo won, 4–3, and while the game was played under deplorable conditions, the class of the Soviet players shone through.

In the next two games, Dinamo thrashed Cardiff City 10–1 and drew with Glasgow Rangers 2–2.

At the end of the tour, in a remarkable about-face, the English sports journalists now showered the Soviet team with compliments. *The Times* (London), for example, acknowledged Dinamo's "superiority in collective ball control … and their amazing speed in the midfield."[9] Another sports journalist purred, "Not a single team has shown a higher class of football." And a third gushed, "It is the cleverest team I have had the opportunity of seeing."[10] Rather than being a second-rate side, Dinamo showed that the USSR could produce world-class footballers.

Moscow closely followed the matches, and the results were used for propaganda. For example, coach Yakushin boasted that the team's successes were the product of the socialist approach to football in which "we put collective football first" rather than relying on brilliant individuals.[11] The *Daily Worker* pointed out that in Britain, the working class had only the street to kick a football. In contrast, in the USSR, all citizens had access to training, equipment, and everything they needed to participate in sport.[12] *Krasnyi sport* trumpeted, "It is a triumph for our school of football, which is based on collectivism, organization and the unbending will for victory, the characteristic qualities of Soviet man."[13] The unavoidable conclusion was that Dinamo's successes owed everything to the communist system.

The success of this tour convinced the Kremlin of the propaganda power of international sport, provided they were able to dominate.

Throughout the Cold War, the USSR would continue to use its sporting victories to show the world how the communist system had perfected a new genus of humankind, *Homo Sovieticus*, who was physically superior to athletes from the decadent West. To unaligned nations, the message was that communism was on the ascent. For its satellites in Eastern Europe, it was a reminder that the USSR was better in every way.

These propaganda objectives needed a large stage to demonstrate Soviet superiority over the capitalist West, and there was no larger stage than the Olympic Games. However, Romanov realized that much still needed to be done before the Soviet Union was ready to take on the world.

Sporting Clubs

Despite the initial success of the tour of Great Britain, Romanov faced huge problems in preparing the Soviet Union for the Olympics. He wanted to select his country's best athletes and test them against the best in the world, but he often faced political interference, particularly in football, where powerful politicians not only sponsored sporting clubs but used the success of their clubs to project their power within the Kremlin.

Dinamo was undoubtedly the best football side in the Moscow league in 1945. However, it owed its dominance to foul play by Lavrentiy Beria, head of the NKVD, the club's most enthusiastic supporter and patron.

Before the war, Beria was determined to see Dinamo dominate the Moscow championship. But standing in his way was Spartak, whose success was mainly due to the brilliance of Nikolai Starostin, who managed and coached the side, together with his three brothers.

In 1939, Spartak defeated Dinamo Tbilisi in the semi-final for the Soviet Cup. Beria intervened, and the teams were ordered to replay the match. An indication that he would not countenance another defeat became obvious when, before the rematch, the original referee was arrested by the secret police. Ignoring the real risk of crossing Beria, Spartak won again.

Beria waited a few years before exacting his revenge. In 1942 his secret police arrested the Starostin brothers. They spent the next two years in Lubyanka prison, where they were brutalized to extract confessions. They were convicted of a raft of charges: embezzlement of funds, facilitating draft evasions, and pro–German feelings. They were sentenced to ten years' hard labor and interred in Butyrka prison before being transferred to camps in the Gulag.

To Starostin's astonishment, the Gulag was not the hell it was made out to be, at least not for talented sportspeople. "With the passage of time, I am no longer surprised that the camp bosses, responsible for the fates of thousands and thousands of people, perpetrators of the inhumanities and horrors of the gulag, responded positively to anything having to do with football," he wrote in his memoir. "Their unlimited power over people was nothing compared with the power of football over them."[14]

In return for coaching the camp's football team, Starostin enjoyed comfortable accommodation outside the barracks, good food, and privileges, like visiting the local cinema and public spa in a nearby town. What he could not avoid was the stench of rotting bodies in winter when the icy ground was too hard to bury them. Instead, they piled up in the camp's makeshift morgue, which was overrun by well-fed rats.

In 1948 Starostin was in a camp in Khabarovsk on the Amur River, in the far east of the country. In the middle of the night the First Secretary of Komsomolsk Communist Party arrived at the camp and went immediately to Starostin's hut. "Get dressed," the official blurted out, still breathless. "You urgently need to call Stalin!" Half an hour later, he was at the local Party headquarters and was handed a black phone. "Hello, Nikolai, this is Vasili Stalin," came a surprisingly high-pitched voice over the phone.[15] Vasili was the feckless son of Joseph Stalin and a lieutenant-general in the air force, which had its own football team, VVS (Voenno-Vozdushnye Sily). He told Starostin he wanted him in Moscow to coach his side.

His father, no angel himself, described Vasili as a "spoilt boy of average abilities, [a] savage."[16] Despite his many failings, Vasili had been promoted well beyond his ability and spent most of his days inebriated. His main passion was sport—particularly football and later ice hockey. Vasili also believed he could improve his political standing within the Kremlin by turning VVS into a sporting powerhouse that would challenge Beria's Dinamo.

Even though Beria had been replaced as head of the NKVD by Sergei Kruglov in December 1945, he retained his influence over the secret police and Dinamo.

In 1946 VVS had been promoted into the first division but languished at the bottom of the standings. To improve the club's fortunes, Vasili built the club excellent facilities and recruited talented footballers. But he still needed a manager who could take the club to glory in the Moscow Championship.

An air force plane picked up Starostin from his labor camp and flew him to Moscow, despite his objections. He seriously doubted that Vasili would be able to protect him from Beria. Starostin was sure that he would be picked up by the secret police and returned to the Gulag under conditions much less convivial than he had been enjoying.

A day after he arrived in Moscow, Starostin was woken by two NKVD colonels who ordered him to leave Moscow within 24 hours. Unwilling to lose his prize coach, Vasili moved Starostin into his mansion at 7 Gogolevskii Boulevard to better protect him. "I immediately saw the tragicomic situation in which I found myself, under the personal protection of the son of a tyrant," Starostin wrote in his memoir. "We were doomed to be inseparable. We went everywhere together: the Air Force headquarters for training, his dacha. We even slept in the same big bed. And when we went to bed, Vasili Iosifovich placed his revolver under his pillow."[17] He also witnessed Vasili's prodigious thirst, which started at breakfast with three slices of watermelon washed down by prodigious quantities of vodka.

After two months under Vasili's protection, Starostin had had enough of his boorish, short-tempered, and drunken host. Wishing to visit his family, he escaped out of a window while Vasili was in a stupor. At 6 a.m. the next day the doorbell rang and two NKVD men were waiting for him. They took him to the railway station and put him on a train to a camp in Krasnodar, near the Black Sea. But at a stopover in Oryol, an air force plane arrived and took Starostin off the train and brought him back to Moscow. After a few days in hiding, Starostin finally persuaded Vasili to allow him to travel to Krasnodar. For the next two years he moved between several labor camps.

After Joseph Stalin died, Starostin wrote to First Secretary Nikita Khrushchev, who allowed him to return to Moscow. By the time he arrived back home, Beria had been executed. And Vasili Stalin had been arrested, tortured, and was serving eight years in Vladimir Central Prison.

Soon after, Starostin was back managing Spartak with considerable success. They were runners up in 1954 and 1955 and won the competition in 1956, just in time to form the core of the football team that competed in the Melbourne Olympic Games.

Thankfully, most other sports did not suffer from politics to anywhere near the same degree as football. Still, there were other challenges that Romanov faced.

Tripped Up

In readying the Soviet Union to join the Olympic movement, Romanov was aware that Stalin would not tolerate losses. This posed a problem for the sports minister. To prepare his athletes for the Olympics, he needed to expose them to high-quality international competition. But that raised the possibility that they could lose, and Romanov knew that it was unwise to disappoint Stalin. "Responsibility for the final result was high, and the consequences of defeat were very harsh," Romanov recalled.[18]

And so, to reach the summit of Olympus, Romanov had to step delicately along the narrowest of ridges, with steep drops into a chasm below should he stumble. Athletes and coaches also approached international competitions with trepidation. They also knew that losses would attract "consequences" for their careers, and quite possibly their liberty.

Fortunately for Soviet sport, several Eastern European countries with strong sporting reputations had become virtual vassals of the USSR after the war. This allowed Romanov used teams from Hungary, Bulgaria, Czechoslovakia, and East Germany to help train Soviet athletes and provide them with high-standard international competition.

But this was not enough, and Romanov took considerable risks pitching Soviet athletes against sporting teams from the West in international championships, although he took care to select events that he judged his athletes had a good chance of winning.

In August 1946 Romanov sent a small team to the European Athletics Championships in Oslo, the Soviet's first official foray into international athletic competition. The Soviets walked away with six gold, fourteen silver, and two bronze medals. Next, Soviet weightlifters traveled to Paris for the World Championships, held in October 1946. Coming face to face with the United States for the first time, they won five medals, the same as the United States. Successes followed. In the spring of 1947, the USSR won all six basketball matches at the FIBA EuroBasket Championship. While the United States did not compete, everyone was surprised at how these relative newcomers had done so well.

But there were also setbacks. In 1947 USSR finished second at the European Wrestling Championships in Prague. This was a sport in which the Soviets were highly rated. Afterward, Stalin reproved Romanov, "If you're not ready, then there's no need to participate."[19] As a result, just before the European Amateur Boxing Championships, the USSR team withdrew suddenly when its coach decided that the competition was too strong.

In February 1948 Romanov showed fine judgment by opposing sending speed skaters to the European Championships in Norway. However, he was overruled by Politburo member Marshal Kliment Voroshilov, who argued that arrangements were too well advanced to pull out. When the male skaters failed to gain a place, Romanov and Voroshilov were summoned into Stalin's presence. The coaches and athletes were also present, and understandably they were in a panic; one of the athletes, Ivan Anikanov, wondered whether he should have packed his suitcase. Turning to Voroshilov, Stalin roared, "None of the skaters are going abroad until they learn to skate and beat all world records."[20] At the meeting, Romanov diplomatically did not mention that Voroshilov had overridden his decision not to participate.

Skating on Thin Ice

Another Olympic sport that demanded Romanov's attention was ice hockey. The game was usually referred to as "Canadian hockey" because it had been invented in that country, and Canada dominated most international competitions before the war. This sport had never been popular in the USSR. Instead, Russians enjoyed a local game called *hockei s myachom*. Played with a small ball instead of a puck, it more or less followed the rules of field hockey. Popular in northern Europe, outside the USSR the game was called bandy.

In the winter of 1946 Romanov created a domestic competition, which consisted of six foundation teams. It soon developed a following and was played in Moscow, Leningrad, Riga, Kaunus, and Archangel. When the first championship was played between Dinamo and the army's team, TsSKA, around 30,000 fans turned up to watch.

Despite his success in getting ice hockey off the ground, Romanov ran into trouble. In January 1948 an article in *Komsomolskaya Pravda* accused Romanov of the unforgivable sin of replacing Russian hockey, meaning *hockei s myachom*, with "Canadian" hockey. A vigorous riposte was published in *Sovetskiy Sport*, a newspaper controlled by Romanov, titled "Unnecessary Resistance."[21] This drew a counterattack that was even more vehemently nationalistic, titled "Restore the Rights of Russian Hockey."

By labeling ice hockey "Canadian" hockey, Romanov feared that his enemies would tap into the xenophobia surging through the Kremlin.

In this struggle, Romanov faced a powerful enemy, as *Komsomolskaya Pravda* was the official newspaper of the youth wing of the Communist Party, the Komsomol. To shore up support, Romanov invited Marshal Voroshilov to a game. Fortunately, Voroshilov thoroughly enjoyed himself. He particularly liked the inclusion of the two-minute penalty, which did little to discourage the ferocious play that made the game exciting. At half-time they bumped into Nikolai Mikhailov, First Secretary of the Komsomol. As a former editor of *Komsomolskaya Pravda*, he probably had a hand in the campaign against ice hockey. Baiting Mikhailov, Voroshilov asked him, "What is this hockey called?" to which Mikhailov contemptuously replied, "Canadian hockey." "No," Voroshilov protested. "It should henceforth be called Russian hockey because it suits the Russian character: it requires courage, split-second reactions, resourcefulness, and great endurance. And if necessary, you can fight."[22] Voroshilov ended this conversation by announcing that he intended to introduce the sport to the army. Soon after, articles appeared in *Komsomolskaya Pravda* supporting ice hockey.

After two years, Romanov realized that his ice hockey players needed help. They had been learning their craft from Canadian books, translated into Russian, on technique and tactics. After the 1948 communist coup in Czechoslovakia, Romanov had access to one of the world's best teams, which had won silver at the Winter Olympics, four years earlier. Romanov coopted the Czechoslovaks, and he filmed their training from every angle. The Soviets' equipment was makeshift—helmets that looked like army surplus, football pads, and leather gloves. After examining the Czechoslovak's equipment, the Soviets were able to replicate it. Now its players looked like they were part of a real ice hockey side.

In February and March 1948, a Soviet national side played Czechoslovakia's premier team, LTC Praha. The Soviets won the first 6–3, lost the second 3–5, and drew the third 2–2. After these games, the Czechoslovak captain Vladimír Zábrodský predicted of the Soviet side that "in a short time it can become the strongest in the world."[23]

Marriage of Convenience

In May 1948 Romanov was replaced by Colonel General Arkady Apollonov and demoted to his deputy. This was probably a power play by Beria to put one of his people into this key position. As the former deputy chief of the MVD, the

Soviet security police, Apollonov's appointment also acted as a warning to athletes: if they failed to win international competitions they might face dire consequences to their careers, and perhaps even a trip to the Gulag.

Apollonov turned out to be ineffective. Not particularly interested in sport other than football, he used his position to promote Dinamo in the national competition. Fortunately for Romanov, he was given a free hand preparing the Soviet Union to enter the Olympic Games. However, he decided they were not ready to participate in the 1948 Olympiads.

The next opportunity for the USSR to enter the Olympic Games was in 1952, with the Winter Games held in Oslo and the Summer Games in Helsinki.

The IOC was not certain whether the USSR was serious about participating in the Olympics. Assuming that they would soon receive an application, IOC executive members were highly ambivalent about what to do. The IOC wanted the Olympic Games to be the world's premier sporting event, requiring all countries to participate, including the USSR. The problem was they were doubtful whether the Soviet Union would comply with its rules. In particular, there were serious doubts about whether it could form a National Olympic Committee (NOC) independent of the government and whether its athletes were genuine amateurs.

IOC vice-president Avery Brundage fired off a letter to his president, Sigfrid Edström, on December 7, 1950, warning that an application from the Soviet Union would be "loaded with dynamite." He added that "the IOC is going to be at the centre of the explosion when it develops if we are not careful." In his letter he fretted that the Soviet NOC would not be

Avery Brundage became president of the International Olympic Committee in 1952 (Rob Mieremet, National Archives of the Netherlands/Anefo).

independent of the government. His conclusion was "If we conform to fundamental Olympic principles and follow our rules and regulations we cannot possibly recognise any Communist Olympic committee."[24]

Brundage was a zealous protector of the other pillar the Olympic movement was built on: amateurism. Yet, it was strongly suspected that, in secret, the Soviet government financially supported its athletes. Many elite athletes were members of the Soviet armed forces and security police or held senior positions in unions or state-owned enterprises, with few other duties but to train. They were also supported by government-funded coaches and first-rate sporting facilities. And athletes who broke world records were surreptitiously slipped monetary rewards.

While Brundage strongly suspected that the Soviet Union was flouting IOC amateur rules, he conceded "that there would not be any means of ascertaining or not whether they were complied with." He went on to point out that "if the application for recognition was denied, it was apparent that there would be a noisy Communist outburst against the committee [IOC] which would be charged with violating its regulations against introducing politics into sport."[25] Edström was more candid. In a letter to IOC Chancellor Otto Mayer, he speculated that had the Soviet application been rejected, "the sporting world would be divided into two great camps—East and West."[26]

The threat Edström foresaw was credible. The USSR organized its own sporting festivals, called Spartakiads, which included athletes from communist youth clubs and unions. The first of these was held in Moscow in the summer of 1928, and in the following years they had spread through the Soviet republics. Competitors from communist sporting clubs and unions in other countries also participated. Might such sporting festivals be expanded to compete with the Olympic Games?

After China fell to the communists on October 1, 1949, there was a possibility almost half the world's population might turn their backs on the Olympic movement.

These fears were probably unfounded, as the Spartakiads had not been popular among those Eastern European countries that had a long history with the Olympic Games.

The mistrust was mutual. The USSR saw the IOC as an instrument of Western imperialism, with its members selected, almost exclusively, from countries in Western Europe and the United States. They had a particular reason not to be enamored with Edström and Brundage. They had both opposed boycotts of the 1936 Berlin Games and, even after the war, counted former Nazi Olympic officials among their friends.

While neither side liked nor trusted the other, a marriage of convenience looked inevitable.

On April 23, 1951, the IOC was forced to declare its hand when Petr Sobolev sent a telegram to the IOC seeking admission. He introduced himself as the executive secretary of the newly formed Soviet NOC, which was led by Konstantin Andrianov. Sobolev was a prominent sports journalist and writer, while Andrianov was Romanov's deputy and clearly a government functionary.

The application was considered at the IOC meeting in Vienna and formally accepted on May 7, 1951.

After the vote, Andrianov barged into the meeting, assuming he was now an IOC executive member. He was promptly told by Edström to wait outside the room. Under IOC rules, new members were chosen by the executive. Invariably, the IOC recruited members to join their ranks who were reliable chaps, like themselves—wealthy businessmen, aristocrats, retired military officers, and a smattering of royals—who could be trusted to protect the sacred traditions of the Olympics. Unfortunately, within the workers' paradise no such chaps existed anymore. So IOC members swallowed their collective pride and invited Andrianov, an ex-factory worker, back into the room as its newest minted member.

The USSR also had reason to enter a marriage of convenience. With the Cold War underway, Stalin was keen to use international sport for propaganda. Therefore the USSR needed the Olympics as much as the Olympic movement needed the USSR.

In August 1951, on Stalin's orders, Romanov replaced Apollonov. As the 1952 Winter Olympics approached, Stalin wanted someone in charge who was competent and whose judgment he trusted.

As the 1952 Winter Olympics approached, Romanov wrote a report for the Central Committee that concluded that there was no "firm certainty" that Soviet athletes would attain first place and therefore "participation in the Olympic Games was pointless."[27]

Romanov was more optimistic about the Soviet Union's chances at the Summer Games. To support the case for attending, he produced an analysis showing the Soviet team could win the medal count against the U.S.[28] This was a brave if not foolhardy prediction, as Romanov had patchy and unreliable intelligence on how good the U.S. team was, or, for that matter, on athletes from other Western countries who were medal contenders. After considering his report, the Council of Ministers accepted Romanov's recommendation to send a team to Helsinki.

In February of the following year, the wheels started to turn, readying members of the Soviet Olympic team. Food rations for athletes were increased, a small army of support staff was employed, and athletes were sent to training camps so that they could devote their time to their Olympic preparations. Romanov was also keen to keep a tight rein on propaganda and directed TASS, the official government news agency, to act as the sole conduit to the Western media on Soviet preparations for the Games.

On July 19, 1952, 295 competitors from the Soviet Union marched the Olympic stadium in Helsinki, changing the face of the Olympic movement.

CHAPTER 3

Dress Rehearsal

Sportsgrad Hospitality

Something was amiss; the American rowers were caught off guard. Coming face to face with their Soviet counterparts for the first time at Helsinki, they were surprised that they were not machine-like Ivans or muscle-bound Olgas spouting tracts from Marx and Lenin or bon mots from Stalin at them, as the newspapers at home had assured them that they would.

In the summer of 1952, when the Helsinki Olympics took place, Stalin was still in power, and the Cold War was very chilly indeed. However, for the American rowers training on Meilahti Bay, the Cold War seemed to be enjoying an unseasonably warm spell. Meeting their Soviet opponents for the first time, it was all smiles and bonhomie. And there was even some unexpected humor. When Dick Murphy was given a hammer and sickle badge, the Russian gift-giver warned, with a mischievous grin, "Should you wear this in the United States, they would put you on the electric stool."[1]

Such friendly encounters naturally disappeared when the rowers entered the water for the final of the coxed eights, and the highly fancied Americans were surprised when the Soviet rowers almost overtook them near the finishing line. The only thing that saved the Americans from an embarrassing defeat was their opponents' flawed technique.

After the medal ceremony it was all smiles again. The Americans were pleasantly surprised when their Soviet opponents invited them to dinner. It was held at the Soviets' Olympic Village in Otaniemi, jokingly called Sportsgrad by Western athletes.

Sportsgrad had been created when the Soviet government insisted that its athletes, and those from other Iron Curtain countries, be housed separately from the official Olympic Village.

The next evening, members of the U.S. rowing teams and officials hopped on a bus that took them south through winding country lanes shaded by pine and birch trees. After half an hour they crossed a bridge and reached a barrier, much

Soviet athletes standing outside the communist bloc Olympic Village at Otaniemi, on the outskirts of Helsinki (Helsingin kaupunginmuseo).

like a frontier checkpoint that you might read about in a John le Carré novel. Unlike a Le Carré novel, the uniformed sentry was not armed with a machine gun, just a smile. With only a cursory glance, he raised the red-and-white pole mounted on two white posts to allow the bus to pass.

The first thing the Americans noticed was that the fence surrounding the compound was topped with barbed wire, presumably to stop athletes from fleeing to the West. This was more like the world of the Iron Curtain that they had expected.

They then saw a large board, which had caused the IOC much angst because it kept score of medals won by the USSR and the United States. The IOC insisted the Olympics were about competition between athletes, not countries. Still, it was powerless to force Soviet officials to remove the board. Rather than a simple tally of medals won, points were allocated for places. Every day, newspapers published their own counts. So for the IOC, this was one horse that had most definitely bolted. The rowers saw that the United States was behind on the board, which no one in the West had predicted before the Games. Strong showings in early events, particularly women's track and field, and gymnastics, had helped the Soviet Union take the lead.

In the United States, journalists were also tuned in to the importance of winning the medal count. Six weeks before the Games commenced, sports journalist Arthur Daley wrote in the *New York Times* that the "Communist propaganda machine must be silenced so that there can't be even a distorted bleat out of it in regard to the Olympics."[2] Columnist Shirley Povich warned that a Soviet victory "would give the Russkis too much to brag about, and keeping them shy in that department could do much for the peace of the world."[3]

Winning was important to both sides because it acted as a proxy for which country had the superior political system. The Soviets believed that socialism produced exceptional athletes who would beat athletes produced by the moribund capitalist system. On the other hand, the Americans argued that freedom and individualism nurtured better sportspeople over their ideological foe's rigid collective system.

Victories abroad were also crucial for domestic consumption within the Soviet Union, as Dr. Viktor Matveyev, a former medical advisor to the All-Union Physical Culture Council, explained: "If Dinamo can beat a French team, obviously the French have even less bread and meat than we do."[4]

After a tour of the Village grounds, the American athletes were ushered into a large dining room where Soviet oarsmen greeted them. Benignly looking over the festivities were large images of Stalin and other comrades from the ruling Politburo, which hung in a neat row around the room. They were not hung flat against the wall but were angled slightly to create the impression that the leaders were looking down on the viewers.

Next came the gift-giving. The Americans handed over crew T-shirts, U.S. Olympic buttons, and chewing gum. The last gift caused some consternation for the Soviets, having never seen gum before. It was carefully inspected, smelt, and only then did a few rowers dare to put it into their mouths. The Americans were embarrassed when, in return, their hosts handed over gifts of cognac, cigarettes, tubs of caviar, and a red velvet banner: "From the Russian rowing team in the XV Olympics."

Afterward, photos were taken of Americans, arm in arm with pretty Russian girls; all so friendly. And in a Cold War world of "us" and "them," such photos showed that the Soviets were just like us, which was very much the purpose of the exercise.

As they sat down at a long table with a white tablecloth and vases of flowers, waiters in black tuxedos served them smoked sturgeon, black caviar, cold meats, and large platters of fruit. Nor were their glasses left empty, not even for an instant, as guests had a choice of cognac, wine, and, of course, fiery vodka. The athletes chatted amiably via interpreters and used sign language.

Later in the evening Vladimir Kuchmenko, chief of Soviet rowing, led the formalities with a toast to his guests: "We are happy for these friendships we have made on the water." Davey Manring responded on behalf of the Americans: "This has been a wonderful experience for all of us. We are glad to come here and meet your people and find they are just like us."[5] Always the polite guest, afterward Manring told United Press, "We went over there determined not to talk politics. We just wanted to know what made them tick. But they tried to get across the idea that the Russians really want peace and that it is the United States that is keeping the world on edge."[6]

According to a CIA report on the Games, Soviet athletes were "friendly and surprisingly gregarious" as part of a deliberate strategy "to lull world opinion into condoning Russian behavior in international affairs."[7]

The Soviet largesse—the lavish meal and handsome gifts—embarrassed the Americans, as it was probably intended to do. Responding to press reports of this dinner, an unnamed American official admitted: "We have troubles enough trying to raise money to send the team here, and we don't have any left for entertainment."[8]

In the run-up to the Olympics, the U.S. Olympic Committee was still $650,000 short. The situation was so dire that officials had to pay their way to Helsinki. In the world of Cold War propaganda, the support of the U.S. team looked threadbare and its hospitality miserly to the rest of the world, particularly to those unaligned countries that both sides of the Cold War were trying to court.

It was only at the last minute that the United States was saved from sending an undersized team to Helsinki. Coming to their rescue were Bob Hope and Bing Crosby. They hosted a 16-hour telethon to solicit donations to support America's Olympic campaign. As Hope and Crosby took time off from filming their fifth in the series *The Road to …* for the telethon, some wit dubbed the telethon *The Road to Helsinki*. Two television networks, NBC and CBS, carried the show live to an estimated 50 million viewers, who contributed $353,000 (US$3.5 million in 2021). Driving the telethon was the fear the USSR would defeat the United States. "I guess old Joe Stalin thinks he's going to show up our soft, capitalistic America," Bob Hope told his TV audience. "We've gotta cut him down to size."[9]

While there is no direct evidence the dinner for the rower, and others that followed, were part of a deliberate propaganda operation, it is inconceivable that the Central Committee of the Communist Party did not approve them. In Soviet times this supreme governing body decided all questions, from building new missiles to the smallest expenditures put before it by sports minister Nikolai Romanov. Moreover, it was implausible he had, on a whim, raided the provisions set aside for the athletes. They may have eaten well, but it is doubtful their daily staple included sturgeon, caviar, or vodka.[10]

Electing to wine and dine the rowing team may not have been a random choice. The USSR had been sensitive to the criticism that it flouted rules on amateurism. It was, therefore, an astute choice for them to host the American rowers, who were all members of the U.S. Naval Academy at Annapolis and were given time off to train. Almost certainly, the Soviets were subtly pointing out that the American government also sponsored its Olympians.

Soviet propaganda is seldom credited with subtlety. This is unfair as carefully staged gestures, like the well-publicized hospitality to the rowers, did much to counter the unsympathetic image cultivated by red-baiters in the United States. Offstage, though, the Cold War games were ruthlessly pursued.

Cold War Skirmishes

There was a heavy presence of security police in Sportsgrad, not just MGB (later known as the KGB) but also those from Eastern Europe. This was to prevent athletes from defecting to the West.

Five months before the Helsinki Games, senior officials of Olympic Committees from all communist countries met with members of their security services. The meeting was held in Moscow, where everyone agreed to vet the "political reliability" of athletes before the Games. They were determined to prevent defections, which would be exploited for propaganda by the West.[11]

Romanov was ruthless. Even athletes who were firm favorites for a gold medal were weeded out. There is no better example than Estonian Heino Lipp, a 225-pound, 6'4" (102 kilograms, 1.93 meters) blond giant, considered as one of the greatest decathletes of his day. Between 1945 and 1953 Lipp became the twelve-time USSR champion, and he broke thirteen national records. His crime was to come from a family who had supported an independent Estonia. It was only his fame as a sportsman that protected him from the fate that befell his brother, who disappeared into the Gulag, never to return. Lipp's absence from the Games was explained by the Soviet press as being due to "illness."[12]

In Hungary, its secret police, the ÁVO, identified twenty athletes who were flight risks. In this instance, the government was unwilling to suffer the opprobrium of banning popular athletes, particularly ones likely to do well. The result was that only five athletes, ones unlikely to win medals, were not allowed to go to Helsinki.

Defections had been weaponized and were used as high-caliber munitions in psychological warfare. They were a very public display by athletes of where they preferred to live—the communist East or capitalist West. After the 1948 London Olympics, when Czechoslovak Marie Provazníková and others from Eastern Europe defected, the West could claim that this was one front of the Cold War that it was winning. Extracting maximum value out of the situation, defectors were interviewed by Radio Free Europe and explained why it was much better living in the free West than under oppressive communism.

To amplify the voice of athlete-refugees, in May 1951 the U.S. government secretly funded the creation of the Union of Free Eastern European Sportsmen as part of its psychological warfare operations.[13] U.S. Cold War warriors believed such anti-communist propaganda, disseminated by "independent" organizations, was more credible than had it come from the U.S. government.

Representing the Union was Thomas de Márffy-Mantuano. On the eve of the Helsinki Games, he urged the IOC to allow exiles from communist regimes to compete. His submission was quickly dismissed. Had this request been granted, it would have severely embarrassed communist bloc governments. Competing against defectors was unacceptable, and the USSR and its allies would have little choice but to withdraw from the Helsinki Olympics.

Once the Games started, Sportsgrad became a battlefield between intelligence services. Colonel Arvo Erkki Lyytinen was appointed commandant at the Olympic Village because he spoke fluent Russian. He also had links with Western intelligence services and knowledge of Soviet counterintelligence, which allowed him to launch an operation in the Village to encourage athletes to defect to the West.

Working with the CIA, Colonel Lyytinen used the wives of Finnish officers as maids and cleaners to infiltrate Sportsgrad. Their targets were athletes from Estonia, Latvia, and Lithuania. These countries had recently been occupied by the Soviet Union, so Western intelligence agencies hoped to capitalize on their hostility to communism.

The Soviet Union had expected an operation of this sort. Sergei Fedoseyev from its counter-espionage department, the MGB, was ready and ordered his agents to keep a tight watch on athletes who might be tempted to defect to the West.[14]

The Soviets also tried to encourage Western athletes to defect. A prime target was sprinter McDonald Bailey. Born in Trinidad, he migrated to Great Britain. It is unclear why a Soviet agent targeted Bailey. Perhaps the MGB believed that he would be hostile to the British because he came from a British colony. Or maybe they assumed he was subject to racism.

During the Olympics Bailey was approached by a Soviet journalist, who introduced himself as Chekhenov. He explained that he was doing a feature on Western athletes and requested an interview. After a few preliminary questions, Chekhenov blurted out, "I think you should come back with us. It would be good for you. Don't worry about money, and don't worry about your family either, we'll bring them over too."[15] Encouraged when Bailey agreed to meet with him again, Chekhenov wined and dined the sprinter at a luxury hotel. Later that evening, Bailey phoned Chekhenov and told him that he was not interested. Chekhenov was not easily put off, and in the small hours of the morning the Russian knocked on Bailey's door bearing gifts of caviar and vodka. When Bailey told him again that he was not interested in defecting, Chekhenov became angry but eventually left.

While both sides tried hard, the scorecard on defection during the Helsinki Olympics was a nil-all draw.

Let the Count Begin

While these skirmishes were ultimately futile, Cold War warriors turned their attention to the actual competition, where each side hoped to use a win in the medal count for propaganda.

Romanov was under intense pressure. Before he left for Helsinki, he had to provide Stalin with a note assuring him that the Soviet Union would top the medal table. Romanov was only too aware that Stalin was not someone who took disappointments with good grace. And Romanov knew that Stalin was intensely interested in the results, insisting that his sports minister send him twice-daily reports from Helsinki.

Much to Romanov's relief, on the first day of competition, the USSR took an early lead in the unofficial points table with 23 points to America's 15 points. This was mainly due to a strong showing in the women's discus, in which Nina Ponomareva became the USSR's first gold medalist, with two other Soviet competitors taking out the other medals. At the victory ceremony, rather than being unemotional and machine-like, as expected in the Western media, Nina shed all-too-human tears of joy.

Nina was thrilled with the result but less than pleased with the reception she received when she visited the Olympic Village at Käpylä, where the athletes from non-communist countries were accommodated. "Foreigners thought we were almost cavemen, surprised that we didn't slurp soup with wooden spoons," she complained.[16]

The Western media were no kinder, often referring to Soviet female athletes like Nina as "Red Amazons,"[17] who were "big-hipped, broad-bicepted [*sic*]," as the *Washington Post* described them,[18] or "big strapping gals, built along the lines of a 10-ton truck," mocked columnist Pat Robinson.[19] Among their shortcomings, they "work side by side with men as miners, ditch diggers, stevedores, and in similar occupations where brawn is a primary requirement," Harry Schwartz wrote in the *New York Times*.[20] In post-war America, a woman's place was in the home.

In the Western press, unflattering photos of Soviet female athletes reinforced the impression they were dour and lacked femininity.

Unable to speak English (just as Western journalists could not speak Russian), Nina was not in a position to refute these stereotypes. Had journalists

Discus thrower Nina Ponomareva warming up before competition. She would become the Soviet Union's first gold medalist (PROV VPRS 10742/P0, item A151).

bothered to find out more about her they would have discovered a woman of great character who had triumphed through adversity, who was kind, who had a bubbly disposition, and a self-deprecating sense of humor. She was also a bit of a klutz, describing herself as "a clumsy little maid from the Land of Soviets."[21] She earned this reputation at the national championship in Kyiv when Nina's discus went further than the referee expected, forcing him to beat a fast retreat. Unfortunately, he was too slow, and the discus hit him. Distraught, Nina ran up to the poor man to apologize. He was not badly hurt and, not holding a grudge, he marked the throw from where it landed after bouncing off his back. As Nina was warming up at another competition, she lost her grip and released the discus, which hit one of the judges. This time she had to visit him in the hospital to beg forgiveness.

The celebration of Nina's achievement as the Soviet Union's first gold medal winner was surprisingly muted. The reason was that her biography was inconvenient. Born in 1929 to parents who were "class enemies," she spent the first six years of her life living in the cramped barracks in a prison camp near Sverdlovsk. They had to share a room in the dormitories with three other families, separated by a threadbare curtain. At night, bedbugs crawled over her body, feasting on her blood, and she was continually scratching scabs that had not healed. Her only toy was a rag doll made by her mother. "All that I remember of that time was the incredible hard labor the men were forced to do," she said.[22] And it wasn't just the men; her mother worked in the peat bogs, cutting fuel with a knife. Released in 1935, the family moved to Yessentuki, at the base of the Caucasus Mountains.

When the war came, like many young girls, Nina helped by plowing the fields, threshing wheat, and felling heavy white willow trees. Such physical activities may have helped build muscle, but she seldom had enough food, and her nickname was "sparrow."

In 1947 Nina became an accidental athlete. She worked in a co-op grocery store and was urged by co-workers to enter a cross-country race during the Komsomol Games. Nina did not have suitable gear to race in; she wore loose-fitting pants, held up with a rubber cord, and sandals. Nevertheless, she competed and came third. Soon, Nina was trying other sports, with some success, doing well in grenade throwing as well as more conventional sports like shot-put, javelin, and discus, which turned out to be her forte.

Nina's talent was quickly recognized and she joined Spartak sporting club. However, on just 500 roubles a month, she often went hungry. When an offer with a better stipend came from the army's sporting club, TsSKA, she moved. And she changed clubs again when Vasili Stalin's club, VSS, made an even better offer. She quickly realized that with success came extra food, called the "calorie allowance," and other rewards for winning events and setting records. Soon the sparrow filled out into a formidable athlete.

Whereas female talent like Nina's was nurtured and fêted in the USSR after the war, Americans were ambivalent about women taking up athletics. This was in stark contrast to the war years when American women were encouraged to join the workforce. Who could forget Norman Rockwell's "Rosie the Riveter," which presented an inspiring image of the independent woman, strong and capable. After the war, there was an abrupt U-turn. Like the Soviet Union's habit of airbrushing fallen political leaders out of photos, so male journalists, politicians, and sports officials erased from their minds strong, capable Rosie. Rockwell did the same. In the 1950s, he portrayed women on the covers of the *Saturday Evening Post* as decorative objects: beautiful for their husbands, competent homemakers, and caring mothers. When Rockwell occasionally showed girls involved in physical activities, there was only a handful he deemed suitable: tennis, swimming, and, best of all, cheerleading.

Nina bore an uncanny resemblance to Rosie the Riveter, as did many Soviet athletes. But fashions had changed in the United States. Rather than presented as a positive image, their features were no longer seen as admirable in a woman. They were the Red Amazons, as Ponomareva was described.[23]

The two superpowers' treatment of female athletes could not have been more different. In 1950, of the 10,230 athletes in the United States, five percent were women.[24] On the other hand, some 35 million women were involved in physical culture and sport in the USSR. There was, though, unwitting sexism among its male sports officials. "Soviet women do not play soccer or ice hockey, nor do they box or wrestle," said Vladimir Shteinbatch. "This is not anti-woman discrimination; it is a manifestation of concern for their health."[25]

In Helsinki, the superiority of Soviet women was clear. They gave the USSR an early lead over the United States by winning twenty-one medals, compared to the American women, who won just eight. Putting this in the context of the propaganda war, historian Susan Cahn pointed out "the weakness of women's track and field … stood out like a sore thumb and threatened American claims that, whether in politics, economics, or athletics, the United States could do it better."[26]

Once it was obvious that the Red Amazons were highly successful, the *Washington Post* downplayed their achievements, arguing that women's events had never been taken seriously "in this part of the world."[27] As a result, they received little coverage compared to men's events. Nothing illustrates this better than the coverage of that most masculine of sports—football.

Drama in Tampere

On the same day as Nina won gold in the discus competition, Yugoslavia met the USSR in the football elimination match, which took on Cold War significance. The game was played in Tampere Stadium, 100 miles (160 km) north of Helsinki.

Football was one competition in which there was not going to be a genuine confrontation between the USSR and the United States, as the inexperienced American team was bundled out of the competition by the Italian team, which humiliated it 8–0.

Uninterested in sport, Stalin's main interest in the Helsinki Games was that the USSR collect more medals than the United States. Yet football was one exception, not because Stalin was a devotee—he wasn't. However, playing Yugoslavia had profound political implications for Stalin because its leader, Marshal Tito, had broken away from the Soviet bloc in 1948. When Stalin called someone a "Titoist" it was usually a prelude to a long sojourn in a chilly corner of the Gulag. Stalin considered Yugoslavia as much a Cold War enemy as the capitalist West. Therefore, a loss at the Olympics would represent an unbearable loss of face and would erode Moscow's authority in its Eastern European Empire. Tito was equally hostile and accused Stalin of betraying Marxism and compared him to Hitler.[28]

So when the two teams met, the stakes could not have been higher.

The Soviet team went through its final preparation in Leningrad before traveling to Helsinki. Romanov accompanied the players, and during his address to the team he was at pains to remind them Stalin would be taking a personal interest in the outcome. This did nothing to inspire the players, and the goalkeeper, Leonid Ivanov, admitted it "unnerved" him. They were no longer football players but "gladiators," who were expected to "fight to the death."[29]

The pressure on the Yugoslavian players was not as intense. Nevertheless, they felt the expectations of their countrymen on them, according to Zlatko Tchaikovsky. "After this match, we'll be declared as either heroes or ... cowards!"[30]

Anticipating an epic struggle, 17,000 spectators packed into the stadium. Yugoslavia was the silver medal winner in London at the 1948 Olympics and had more international experience than its opponent. But knowing little about the Soviet side meant a victory was no certainty.

The day was warm, and the Yugoslavian player wore blue jerseys. The Soviet players were in red, with CCCP, in large white Cyrillic letters, emblazed on the front of their jerseys.

In the first 15 minutes, the Soviets had two shots on goal for no result. As the half wore on the Yugoslavs started to get on top and kicked three goals while the USSR remained scoreless.

Walking to the locker room at the break, the Soviet players would not have been human if they were not thinking about what Stalin would do to them if they did not win. And a win from 0–3 seemed just about impossible. Their mood was somber, heads bowed in despair, and even some barely suppressed tears. As the team's natural leader, Vsevolod Bobrov barked at his teammates, "They're getting tired; they can't keep it up."[31] The team relied heavily on Bobrov to score goals. His words of encouragement, however, failed to cheer them up as they watched the team doctor tighten the bandage around Bobrov's injured left knee and then inject him with the painkiller Novocain. They all knew he was playing on one leg, which made a win even more remote.

In the other locker room the Yugoslavian players were in a buoyant mood, confident they had the game won.

Within a minute of the resumption of play, Yugoslavia goaled. The score was now 0–4, and a rout was in the cards. With such a large lead, the Yugoslavs started to play defensively, content to run the clock down. On the other hand, the Soviet players took risks, with no other choice but to attack, attack, attack.

Bobrov hit the back of the net twice. More goals followed—one to Yugoslavia and a reply from the Soviets. Then Bobrov, running on adrenaline and Novocain, scored again, giving him a hat trick. He was on fire, inspiring the rest of the team, who played as if their lives depended on a win (as some of them probably thought it did). Still 4–5 down, and with 29 seconds to go, the Soviets took a corner. Every Yugoslavian player swarmed into the goalmouth. As the ball lobbed in, midfielder Aleksandr Petrov floated above the phalanx of players and headed the ball past the goalkeeper. Soon after, the game ended in a draw.

Spectators went crazy, knowing they had witnessed one of the greatest comebacks of all time and an extraordinary performance from one of the greatest players of the game: Bobrov. The Yugoslavian players stood around demoralized, wondering how they could have let the game slip away. Romanov and the coaches ran onto the field, hugging and kissing one another and the players.

But the game was not over. After a short break, the referee blew his whistle for 30 minutes of extra time in the hope of breaking the tie. Continuing the momentum, the Soviets launched wave upon wave of attacks. "We were completely empty. I couldn't even breathe, let alone run. Mentally completely empty," said Yugoslav forward Stjepan Bobek.[32] The ball hit the woodwork twice, but the Soviets couldn't break the tie. Without a winner, a rematch was scheduled for two days later.

The next day was hot, and the Soviet coach, Boris Arkadyev, perhaps panicked by the near loss, pushed his players in a hard training session.

After training and back in Sportsgrad, Romanov summoned the players and read them a two-page telegram he had received from Stalin. "We believe in you. You have to win." Rather than inspiring the players, it had the opposite effect, as Romanov unhappily recalled. "The cable further raised everyone's responsibility for the outcome of the match. Unfortunately, it had a powerful psychological impact on the players, and instead of instilling confidence, it created … nervousness."[33]

No less keen for victory, Tito wisely refrained from putting political pressure on his players. However, they knew that, as a keen football fan, he would be listening to the game on the radio. Having given up such a large lead in the previous game, the Yugoslavian players were plagued by self-doubt. As a result, they had trouble sleeping, and many lost their appetites.

The rematch started well for the Soviets. After six minutes, Bobrov conjured up some more magic when he fired the ball into the right-hand corner of the net for the first goal of the game. The goal seemed to spur on the Yugoslavs, who looked fresher. Dominating the center, the Yugoslavs scored two goals, leaving the Soviet goalkeeper slamming his fist into the turf in frustration. Going into the half-time break 2–1 up, the Yugoslavian players were almost certainly thinking about the earlier game when the Soviets staged a miraculous comeback.

In the second half, Soviet players were flagging badly. It was not just the heavy training session the day before, but many of the players were on old legs. Given the freedom to choose his own side, Coach Arkadyev might have chosen younger up-and-coming players, but he did not have that luxury. Before the Games he had been under intense pressure from the leaders of the security organs and generals to include their favorite (and older) players in the Olympic team.

At the 54-minute mark, Yugoslavia scored a lucky goal when a Soviet player inadvertently deflected the incoming ball, which slipped past the goalkeeper and into the net.

In the dying minutes of the game a political edge entered the game as one of the Soviet players yelled out to his opponent, "Nazi."[34] He returned the insult, shouting "capitalist" and predicting that he would soon find himself in Siberia. The final score was 3–1, with Yugoslavia the victor. "It was not a football match, it was a political game," said Yugoslav striker Stjepan Bobek. When he arrived home he recalled "seeing the headline: TITO 3 STALIN 1."[35]

In the final, Hungary met Yugoslavia. For Stalin, this game provided a chance of regaining some dignity should Hungary, a loyal friend of the USSR, beat the communist turncoat.

Hungary had a formidable team. Over the previous three years, it had played twenty-five international games for twenty wins, three draws, and just two defeats. It would continue to dominate international football until 1956 when many players escaped to the West after the revolution.

Soon after noon on game day, the Hungarian football manager Gusztáv Sebes received a phone call from Mátyás Rákosi, the Hungarian General Secretary. "He reminded me in no uncertain terms that defeat would not be tolerated," recalled Sebes. "I didn't relay the call to the players, but they knew what was at stake and there was great tension in the lead-up to kick-off."[36]

For the first 45 minutes it was an arm wrestle, with neither side getting the better of the other. There was also ill-feeling between the teams, and it was a physically tough game. At half-time neither team had scored. As the Yugoslavs started to tire in the second half, the Hungarians stepped up their attacks and won 2–0.

The Yugoslavian team may have only won silver, but its players were welcomed home as conquering heroes. Crowds danced and sang in the streets. In Pristina, the local military saluted the team with a round of artillery.

On the other hand, no Soviet newspaper published an account of the USSR–Yugoslavia game until after Joseph Stalin's death, nearly a year later. And all newsreel records of the game were destroyed.

Immediately after the game Romanov told Coach Arkadyev to leave Helsinki on the next flight out. The coach was certain he would be blamed for the loss to Yugoslavia, but he was not sure what that could mean to his career, or even his liberty. It would be days before he discovered his fate.

Depressed and fearful of what might await them, the players followed by train. On this journey they already saw that they were out of favor. Their ticket only took them as far as Leningrad, and they were told by an official that they needed to make their own way to Moscow. Fortunately, the local military took pity on them and provided them with food, travel documents, and tickets back to Moscow.

"Approaching Moscow, we were on edge," Yuri Nyrkov recalled. "We did not know where they would be taken from the station and how soon we would see our relatives. And when they realized that no one was meeting us, they were delighted and quickly went home."[37] They had further reason to relax when they were allowed to go back to their teams and play in the national league.

And the Winner Is…

The defeat of its Olympic football team was a severe blow to Soviet prestige. However, with two days to go, the Soviet Union was still ahead of the United States in the medal rankings. But the situation changed on the last day. The Americans hauled in five gold medals in boxing and four in swimming, with the Soviet Union winning none. As the U.S. points total rose, Romanov ordered the removal of the scoreboard outside Sportsgrad. Erected in its place was a noticeboard naming individual Soviet winners.

As the United States overtook the USSR, Romanov accused the referees of bias against Soviet athletes. At a press conference on the last day of the Games, Romanov said, "There is no doubt that had there been just refereeing in all types of sport, the athletes of the Soviet and of certain other countries would have received a significantly larger number of places."[38] Newspapers in Moscow took up the refrain. "It is no coincidence that by the end of the competitions, when it became clear that Soviet Union sportsmen were ahead of the Americans, some judges violated basic sports ethics by trying to help their transatlantic friends every possible way," opined the Soviet pictorial magazine *Ogonyok*. Betraying a streak of paranoia, the article reported that such "roguish tricks" were executed by "enemies of the proletariat."[39]

So who won? The answer was not immediately obvious because Romanov had devised his own points system, allocating points for gold medals and the next five places. Western newspapers used a different system that gave more points for a gold medal, which favored the United States. At first, Romanov claimed the USSR had narrowly won the Helsinki Olympics, 494 to 490.25.[40] A few days later he revised his score to a tie, 494 to 494. This led the author of a declassified CIA report to wryly conclude that "Romanov's calculation helped ensure his own well-being."[41]

A little over two weeks after the end of the Olympics, Georgi Malenkov, one of Stalin's chief lieutenants, summoned Romanov and some senior sports officials to the Kremlin to review the Soviet Union's performance in Helsinki. Also present were senior Politburo members, including Lavrentiy Beria, former head of the feared secret police.

At the meeting, Romanov made a brave effort to defend the performances of the Soviet athletes in Helsinki. No one at the meeting, though, was fooled by Romanov's effort to massage the final medal count to deliver a draw. With blame being liberally dispensed, Malenkov turned to Romanov and asked him a question to which there was no answer. "How could you deceive Comrade Stalin?" This attack on Romanov was blunted when a message arrived later that night from Stalin, who said "that the performance was not so bad, but some sports need to be significantly improved."[42]

The meeting also addressed, at length, the loss to Yugoslavia in football. When Malenkov asked whether the Olympic team was based on the army's team TsSKA, Romanov agreed, although he knew that only four of its members were from that side. Beria quickly nodded his agreement, even though five Dinamo players were also part of the team. Why did Romanov lie? He probably wanted to contain the damage by focusing on just one team. Also, he knew that Beria was a fanatical supporter of Dinamo and did not want to cross him. Once the focus turned on TsSKA, Beria made a veiled threat: "They have likely taken them to a wrong place"—meaning that they should not have been allowed to go home to Moscow but dispatched to the Gulag. It was finally decided the coach and TsSKA would be punished.[43]

After eight hours, the meeting ended at 6 a.m.[44]

After the meeting ended, Malenkov told Romanov that he couldn't allow the loss to Yugoslavia to go unpunished.

Unaware their fates were being decided, TsSKA players had resumed playing in the local competition and easily won its first three matches. Its next game was against Dinamo Kyiv. It was raining, but not enough to call off the game. Instead of seeing a bus waiting to take them to the ground, they were confronted by a grim-faced Romanov. Gathering around the sports minister, they heard TsSKA was disbanded. "You people are the military, you know—orders are orders," he explained.[45] Overnight the top league became fourteen teams, not fifteen, without any explanation to fans. Other punishments followed. Arkadyev was banned from coaching and stripped of his Merited Master of Sports title, as were three of his players. However, the hero of the first match, Bobrov, was not punished.

When interviewed many years later, Romanov admitted he was afraid. "In those days, I used to wake up at night, not knowing what would happen to me in the morning."[46]

Seven months after he returned from Helsinki, Romanov finally had a good reason to relax. Stalin died on March 3, 1953. After some initial bloodletting, the tide of poisonous paranoia that had saturated the Kremlin ebbed, and Romanov no longer needed to keep obsessively looking over his shoulder.

Stalin's death was also good news for TsSKA players. Their punishments were reversed, and the army team was resurrected. There were other changes that would affect the complexion of the team selected for the Melbourne Olympics. Beria's execution at the end of 1953 did not affect the fortunes of Dinamo, which continued to be a force in the national league. But soon Dinamo was challenged by Spartak, which no longer had to contend with Beria's persecution of its manager, Nikolai Starostin, who returned from the Gulag in 1954.

As 1956 approached, Romanov's next challenge was the Winter Olympics in Cortina d'Ampezzo (Italy). While those Games did not have the public profile of the Summer Olympics, he had good reason to be confident the Soviet Union would overtake the United States on the medal table. The United States was weak in many winter sports, with one exception: ice hockey. As the one sport in which the two superpowers would come head-to-head, Romanov believed a victory over the United States in ice hockey would be of enormous propaganda value.

CHAPTER 4

Sotto Voce

Thaw of Sorts

At the end of January 1956 fine weather welcomed visitors to the Winter Olympics in Cortina d'Ampezzo in the Italian Alps. The air was crisp, and there was not a cloud in the sky.

For the competitors, however, the weather could not have been much worse. In the days before the opening ceremony, a precious few flakes of snow fell. Unfortunately, little followed. And the last heavy downfall had occurred more than two weeks earlier, depositing 12 inches (30 cm) of snow. During the day the snow on some runs started to thaw, exposing bare ground and rocks, and by evening the slush froze, creating a malicious icy crust.

Even before the Games started, as skiers tried out the runs, the list of injuries began to mount. By the time competition began, more than thirty athletes had suffered bad falls. Russian skier Valentina Nabatenko broke her right leg. American alpine ski racer Katy Rodolph fractured a neck vertebra in a nasty spill and was flown to Salzburg for treatment. Others suffered strains, cuts, and abrasions.

The only athletes who welcomed the mild weather were the bobsledders, who worried that a heavy snowfall could slow their times down by as much as ten seconds. The track, though, was still too fast for Frenchman Serge Giacchini, who was injured when his two-man bobsled shot off the icy mile-long course at around 60 mph (100 kph).

As competitors looked to the heavens hoping to see snow clouds and checked the air temperature on their thermometers, Cold War warriors in Washington and Moscow were checking the political temperature. Much had changed since the Helsinki Olympics.

By 1956 Nikita Khrushchev had consolidated his power in the Kremlin and was dismantling some of the worst features of Stalin's regime. His foreign policies helped lower the global tension as he pursued détente with the West. The Soviet strategy was to peacefully extend its sphere of influence. By the mid–1950s, the Kremlin was particularly keen to win the hearts and minds of unaligned countries

Soviet athletes march into the main stadium during the opening ceremony at the winter Olympic Games in Cortina d'Ampezzo.

in Asia, Latin America, and Africa. Winter sports were, however, not popular in these areas. For that reason, Soviet Cold War warriors were subdued in Cortina, or were *sotto voce* as the Italians would say.

The United States had also seen a change of leadership, with President Eisenhower keen to ramp up his country's psychological warfare capability to counter the Soviet threat. Despite the near-miss at the Helsinki Games, when the Soviet Union almost beat the United States in the medal count, the Administration did not see the Olympics as a battleground for psychological warfare. It bought into the convention that sport was sport and politics should not intrude. This would change following the Cortina Games, in response to Soviet successes.

Winter sports were not popular in the United States, other than ice hockey and figure skating. While Americans did not expect to do well in most events, once the Games commenced, they were shocked by the Soviet's overwhelming dominance. Sixth on the medal table, the United States had two gold medals going into the ice hockey finals, in which it considered itself a chance. This compared with the Soviet tally of six gold medals, which put it easily at the top of the rankings.

To win gold in ice hockey the United States would have to overcome Canada and the USSR, the two favorites. A victory in this high-profile sport would help recover some of its sporting pride. As a direct East-West confrontation, it attracted intense interest from journalists.

The Red Icemen Cometh

Canada was the favorite, having been undefeated in every Winter Olympics except the 1936 Games in Garmisch-Partenkirchen (Germany). It was defeated by Great Britain, although it could take some comfort that almost all of the British players lived in Canada. The USSR and the United States were both confident that they could break Canada's dominance.

In the final round, the medals would be decided in a round-robin between six teams. Two points were awarded for a win and one point for a draw. At the end of the competition, in the case of a tie, the winner would be decided on the ratio of goals scored, for and against. Four critical matches in this round-robin would decide which team would win gold.

United States v. Canada

On January 31 the United States and Canada met on the ice. The Americans were not given much chance as they were mostly college boys who had only started playing together a few months earlier. Canada sent the Kitchener-Waterloo Dutchmen, a team from south-eastern Ontario, to represent their country. They were a cohesive team who had played as a unit for at least a year. On the downside, they could not send their best team to the Games because five of its players were professionals. They were replaced by Junior B players.

The U-shaped stadium was open at its southern end. Under the faint light of a crescent moon, the jagged peaks of the Dolomites provided a ghostly backdrop to the game. The night sky was clear and the ice hard, as the temperature dropped well below freezing. The capacity crowd of 12,000 was looking forward to a tight game.

The game was played at breakneck speed, and each side attacked and counterattacked. In the first period, the Americans took an early lead when John Mayasich scored two goals. The Canadians should have been ahead as they had fifteen shots on goal to six, but a heroic performance by the U.S. goalie, Willie Ikola, kept the Canadians scoreless.

In the second period, the Canadians scored one goal but could do no better as Ikola continued to defend brilliantly. The game ended in a rout after the Americans scored two more goals in the third period.

In what the Montreal *Gazette* described as "one of the greatest upsets in Olympic hockey,"[1] the United States beat Canada 4–1. The score line was unfair to the Canadians. They outplayed the Americans but could not convert their dominance into goals, thanks to the match-winning efforts of Ikola.

Rumors went around Cortina that the Canadians had gone out and partied the night before, perhaps thinking that they had the gold medal won.

Canada was now one game down, while the United States and USSR remained undefeated, as they easily beat the weaker sides in the round-robin.

Czechoslovakia v. the USSR

Two days later, the unbeaten USSR faced Czechoslovakia. This was a danger game for the Soviets. Czechoslovakia had won the silver medal at the previous Olympics and only missed out on gold on a countback, based on goals for and against. It did not do as well in 1952, as the team was in the process of rebuilding, having lost all the members from that golden period to Cold War politics.

After the communist takeover in February 1948, Czechoslovakia continued to send ice hockey teams into the West. At the end of the Spengler Cup competition, held in Switzerland in December 1950, team members were approached by pre-war star Josef Maleček, who had defected in 1948. He urged them to defect and form a Free Czechoslovakia team. After a heated discussion, the majority rejected his proposal. It was never a viable proposition as the new team would have had no financial backing and would not have been able to join a national league. All the players returned home except for Oldřich Zábrodský and Miroslav Sláma, who had been members of the 1948 Olympic team. These defections worried the communist government, which issued a statement that accused the defectors of carrying out "propaganda against our republic, and thus provoking hostility against the Czechoslovak Republic."[2]

Zábrodský defected because he knew he was a marked man if he remained in Czechoslovakia. In 1949 he had been summoned to the headquarters of the secret police, the StB, where he was asked to inform on teammates. He refused. Undoubtedly, this made him suspect in the eyes of the StB, and he feared he could be arrested on some trumped-up charge. He also found life under communism oppressive. "It was difficult to breathe there," he explained.[3]

Understandably, the communist regime became skittish about the possibility of further defections at the upcoming Ice Hockey World Championship, held in London in March 1950. And so, at the last minute, using the pretense that Britain had not issued visas to two Czechoslovak journalists accompanying the team, the government announced that in protest, the whole ice hockey team had refused to participate in the championship. This was news to the players, who first heard about it on the radio.

That evening four players met in U Herclíků, a tavern on Prague's Pštrossova Street, to lick their wounds. After a few drinks, the players became rowdy, loudly ridiculing, Václav Kopecký, who managed the State Office for Physical Education and Sport. More alcohol was consumed. And then, in a moment of foolish bravado, the players ran into the street screaming "Death to communism" and "We will not let you clip our wings; we want freedom!" Soon after, two policemen attending the disturbance were hospitalized. Next, twenty security officers arrived and dragged the players off to prison. Even players who were not at the tavern were picked up over the next two weeks.[4]

All the players were taken to Domeček, which had housed the Gestapo during the war, where they were brutally interrogated. This involved beatings: with truncheons and with a cat-o'-nine-tails with bullet casings knotted into the ropes, creating lacerating barbs. They were also starved, with the guards adding laxatives to their coffee to speed up the process. One of the players who was imprisoned was Tonda Španinger, who, after going without food for three days, announced, "If I could catch a bird sitting on the [goal window] ledge, I would eat it."[5]

At their trials, four players were convicted of espionage, treason, and desertion. They were sentenced to between 10 and 15 years of hard labor at the Jáchymov uranium mines, where they handled yellowcake without protective gear. Eight other players got off with lesser sentences for defaming the Communist Party. And so ended the golden age of Czechoslovak ice hockey.

Understandably the 1956 Czechoslovak ice hockey team was not well disposed towards the communist regime in their country nor its Soviet overlords. The game soon turned spiteful, and several Soviet players were left bruised and sore.

The Soviets dominated and won, 7–4.

Nevertheless, this game gave heart to the Americans and Canadians, who would meet the Soviets on the last two days of the competition. Up to this game, the Soviets had only conceded one goal. So by scoring four goals, Czechoslovakia showed that the Soviet defense was vulnerable.

On the last day of the competition, Czechoslovakia played the United States without conviction, losing 9–4. Journalists reporting the game suspected the Czechoslovak team did not want to win, a conclusion also reached by Soviet sports minister Nikolai Romanov. Fortunately for the players, they were not punished after returning to Prague.[6]

United States v. USSR

Two days later, the Americans faced a seasoned Soviet side, who were older and more experienced. They were called the Central Red Army team because all its players were in the military. *Sports Illustrated*'s Andre Laguerre accused the Russians of cheating because every athlete of "international promise has been taken out of his job and given year-round training which few in the West can equal and which, of course, is state paid."[7] This allegation was largely true.

The American media, however, turned a blind eye to how their own Olympic team also skirted around the rules, albeit nowhere near as egregiously as its Cold War rival. Goalie Willie Ikola was a prime example. In 1945 he won a sports scholarship from the University of Michigan, which paid his tuition fees and a living allowance. This gave him access to professional coaches and top-notch facilities. He then joined the air force as a navigator. He was not alone; over half the U.S. Olympic team were in military service at the time of the Winter Olympics and enjoyed the privileges that came with being in the armed services. "What happened was that USA Hockey, who ran the Olympic program, would contact the service and say, 'We'd like to have these players try out for the Olympic team.' So we got orders out of Special Services in Washington, DC, assigning us to USA Hockey for Olympic tryouts," recalled Ikola. "It was a pretty good deal for us because we were getting our military pay at the same time."[8]

The star of the Soviet side was its captain, Vsevolod Bobrov. He held the rare distinction of representing his country in two sports, the other being football, and is best remembered for almost beating the Yugoslavian team singlehandedly in the elimination match at the 1952 Helsinki Olympics. Now 33 years old, his very presence in Cortina was a tribute to his courage, the wizardry of Soviet doctors, and the liberal use of painkillers.

The game started at 9:30 p.m., with the Soviets wearing red jerseys with a white V stripe and the U.S. players in white.

Before the game, Western newspapers reported the Soviets played like "mechanical men" and the team resembled "a well-oiled machine."[9] Nothing was further from the truth. That evening, spectators saw a graceful team, verging on artistic in its movements, seemingly choreographed as players seamlessly moved around one another, shooting precise passes that confounded their opponents. Having been together for years, the Soviet players had an intuitive understanding of where to find a passing player. "We'd never seen anything like that before in North America. That Soviet game really took the wind out of us," recalled the United States forward, John Matchefts.[10]

From the start, both teams played defensively, making scoring difficult. The Soviets liked to keep possession, moving the puck around—passing, passing, passing—until they were in a good position to shoot. When the Americans were in possession, they relied on breakaways rather than offensive moves. But they found that the speedy Soviets mowed down the attacker before he could shoot. The United States countered with some tough body-checking.

The score was 0–0 at the end of the first period, with Ikola under much greater pressure than the Soviet goalie, Nikolai Puchkov.

The first goal was scored late in the second period by the Soviets when the Americans were one man down. Now ahead 1–0, the Soviets played conservatively, bottling up the Americans in their zone. Later in the period, when the Soviets were one man down, the Americans iced their number one power-play unit but failed to score owing to tight defense and the acrobatic efforts of Puchkov at the net.

Frustrated, the American coach Johnny Mariucci raged from the sidelines, kicking the bench and screaming out to his charges. This drew the attention of an Italian official, who bluntly told him, in broken English, that he would have to leave if he continued to be disruptive. The son of Italian immigrants, Mariucci blasted the poor official in fluent gutter-Italian. The red-faced official diplomatically withdrew, and Mariucci was once more able to focus on his players with language that had lost none of its color.

While Mariucci provided a distraction, on the ice neither team scored during the remainder of the second period.

In the third period the game continued to be played at a frantic pace. When an American player came off, he was panting, while the Soviets came to the bench breathing normally. This would be a telling factor in the last period. With just five minutes to play, Bobrov yelled "*dayte*" (give), and the puck was instantly delivered to him. Moving quickly around Ikola, he scored. In the next two minutes the Soviets scored another two times, winning the game 4–0.

Had it not been for the heroic efforts of Ikola, who made forty-three saves during the game, the loss could have been much worse. After the match, all Soviet players went up to the American goalie and applauded his heroic performance.

USSR v. Canada

On the final day of the ice hockey competition, the unbeaten Soviets faced the Canadians, who were one game down and had to win, and win by a decisive margin, to be a chance for the gold medal. The Canadians hoped that their loss to the Americans in an earlier game was an aberration, and they needed this win to demonstrate that they were still the best team in the world.

There was history between the two teams, and the game was always going to be fiery. The seeds of their enmity were sown two years earlier at the 1954 World Championship in Sweden. Before the tournament the Canadian newspapers patronized the newest kid on the block, referring to Soviet players as "green beginners."[11] A cartoon even showed Soviet champion Bobrov wearing short pants and sitting uncomfortably at a desk much too small for him, being instructed in ice hockey basics by a Canadian player. When the Soviets emerged victorious following a 7–2 rout, the Canadian newspapers excused the loss by claiming they had not sent their best team to Sweden.

The following year in West Germany, Canada sent a stronger team, and it regained the championship by beating the Soviets 5–0. The Canadian newspapers were quick to suggest the win the previous year was a flash in the pan.

After the game, sportswriter Jack Stepler framed the match in Cold War terms, as if Canada had just won World War III. He told his readers that the Canadians "broke the bubble of hockey prestige with all the subtlety of a hydrogen bomb." Building on his military theme, he added, "They left the highly trained Russian squad, drawn from the Central Red Army and airforce completely beaten, physically exhausted and mentally cowed and bewildered."[12] Referring to the same game, the *Southeast Missourian* explained that the "Reds are also trying to show that, thanks to Marx and Lenin, the Soviet Union has the best athletes in the world, and that they are good sports. Something went a bit wrong."[13]

Having overcome the United States, the Soviet Union was keen to beat the remaining surrogate from the capitalist West: Canada.

"There was an emotional factor," recalls Ernie Gorman, manager of the Canadian Olympic team. "We were receiving wires from home saying, 'You're the defenders of democracy' and 'You shouldn't set foot on Canadian soil unless you win.'"[14]

After both sides had glided onto the ice for the start of the game, the Soviet players noticed that the Canadians had black bars smeared on their faces, which they interpreted as Indian war paint. This was not another example of gamesmanship. Rather, the Canadians used eye black to cut down the glare off the ice, although their opponents did not know that.

From the very beginning the Canadians went onto the offensive. However, the Soviet goalie was able to repel each attack. The Soviets had fewer scoring opportunities because defender Art Hurst went hunting for their main striker, Bobrov. The Canadian hard man, 79 kilograms of brute muscle, upended the Russian champion three times in the first period with vicious hip checks. At the end of the first period neither side had troubled the scoreboard.

Bobrov had been hurt by the buffeting he received in the first period, and he was also nursing an iffy knee. So he did not return for the second period. With both defenses playing well, there were few opportunities to score. On one of the team's few forays forward, the Soviet Union scored its first goal at the seven-minute mark. There were no more goals for the period, which ended with the Soviets ahead 1–0.

At the end of the second period the Canadians insisted that the rink be re-iced. This led to an animated argument with Soviet officials. The Canadians got their way, and the ice was flooded, holding up play for 30 minutes. This may have just been gamesmanship to interrupt the Soviet team's momentum and to allow the Canadians to regroup.

At the start of the third period Bobrov returned but kept well clear of Hurst. The break did not seem to change the momentum of the game, which still favored the Soviets. Within the first minute Valentin Kuzin smacked the puck into the net, and now the Soviets were up 2–0.

Refusing to give up without a fight, for the remainder of the game the Canadians kept the play in the Soviet defensive end. The Soviet goalie was under siege but was able to repulse each attack, and the score remained unchanged for the rest of the period.

When the referee sounded his whistle to end the game, the Soviet players kissed one another, jumped into the air, and laughed, proving Western journalists were wrong to describe them as emotionless robots.

This loss marked the end of Canada's Olympic hockey dynasty. Future finals would be between the Central Red Army team and the United States.

Everyone Loves a Winner

The ice hockey gold medal added to the already impressive collection the USSR had gathered in Cortina. Overall, the Soviet Union ended up with seven gold, three silver, and six bronze medals, topping the medal ranking. Its athletes had excelled in both the men's and women's cross-country skiing and cleaned up in the men's speed skating.

On the other hand, the United States won just two gold, three silver, and two bronze medals. Its victories were in the men's and women's figure skating, and it came sixth on the medal table.

Using the points system devised by Romanov, the USSR scored 153 and the United States, 65. Unlike Helsinki, when Romanov claimed the USSR had drawn with the United States using some mathematical magic, in Cortina he could claim victory without fearing that his numbers would be challenged.

After the Games, columnist Frank R. Corkin, Jr., was alarmed at how the thumping Soviet victory would play out in the context of the Cold War.

One can almost hear the Communist laughter in the halls of the Kremlin; one can almost predict the words of the Communist controlled press. The losing athletes of United States will be symbolized as the weak product of a fat, rich capitalistic system. It is not impossible that there will be those who will conclude that if Russia can dominate the world in athletic tests of skill and endurance and strength, the Russia can conquer the world in a game of war.[15]

This theme was taken up by others. "Being strong believers in collectivism, the Soviets will make much out of national standings, especially since they have made a successful debut in the winter Olympics this year," wrote Austin Conover, a reporter for the *Hollywood Citizen News*. "It is grist for their propaganda mills."[16] And according to an editorial in the *Altoona Tribune*, "There is no question that Russian victories in the Olympics will boost Red stock around the world. Athletes are popular everywhere. Everybody likes a winner!"[17]

Looking ahead to the 1956 Summer Olympics, an editorial in the *San Francisco Examiner* warned that a "further Russian triumph at Melbourne would be a tremendous loss of international prestige to this country. There is a cold war going on in the athletic front, too."[18] While regretting the intrusion of politics, sports columnist Henry McLemore acknowledged that the Summer Olympics would be a contest of "America against Russia—and if Russia wins, it will tell the world of the supremacy of its way of life. Every country that it has under its iron rule will be told that its young men and young women were superior to the soft capitalist boys and girls."[19]

Sports officials did not agree that the Soviets were certain to come out on top in Melbourne. Dan Ferris from the U.S. Amateur Athletics Union was upbeat. "If Russia thinks it's going to repeat its winter games mastery at Melbourne I'm afraid they're in for a very disappointing night."[20]

With quiet confidence, Romanov predicted that "we're going to be way out in front at the Summer Olympics in Melbourne."[21]

The attacks directed toward the Soviet Union in Cortina about the inclusion of sham-amateurs in its team intensified as the Melbourne Olympics approached, as they would attract much more attention than the Winter Games.

CHAPTER 5

Stumbling Toward Melbourne

The Red Scare

Nikolai Romanov knew that after Helsinki, Brundage was under considerable pressure to investigate allegations that Soviet athletes were sham amateurs. If Brundage decided that these allegations were true, might he expel the Soviet Union from the Melbourne Games? Should that come to pass, Romanov knew that his plans to incontrovertibly beat the United States in the medal count would come to naught. More worrying, the Soviet Union would lose face with the international community, and a promising avenue for psychological warfare would be closed.

There might also be a personal cost. While the trains traveling to the Gulag were much less crowded since Stalin's death, they were not empty. Romanov was certain that he would be held responsible should the Soviet Union be thrown out of the Olympic movement. That would surely end his career.

The pressure was coming from the United States, stung by its near-defeat at Helsinki and driven by the fear that it would lose to the USSR in Melbourne.

Terry McGovern, a veteran U.S. Olympic official, grimly warned that "the Reds have launched a sports offensive designed to sweep us from the boards of the 1956 meet."[1] Don Canham wrote in *Sports Illustrated* that the Melbourne Olympics would "probably spell the end to the United States' long domination of the games."[2] Sports journalist Arthur Daley told Americans that they should be alarmed. "The Russians will knock the ears off the Americans.... It isn't a pretty fact but it's virtually an inescapable one." It was not just the loss on the sporting field that mattered, but that it would represent a loss in the Cold War. "The red brothers will scream to the world that this is merely one more proof of how decadent the capitalistic system is."[3]

These predictions were based on the growing prowess of Soviet sportspeople since Helsinki. In 1952, the United States held twenty-four world records in Olympic sporting events, although only one was held by a woman, indicative of the weakness of female athletics in America. In the same year the USSR had just seven world records, six by women. By 1956 the United States held twenty-three world records, none of which was held by a woman, while the USSR held twenty-one, almost equally divided between its male and female athletes. The USSR also showed that it had improved in team sports, with victories in basketball, water polo, and football against formidable opponents in international tournaments. And its gymnasts were world-beaters.

As news of Soviet sporting successes spread, U.S. politicians, journalists, and sports officials feared that their amateurs would be no match against Soviet athletes who were professionals in all but name.

First-hand evidence that they skirted around IOC rules on amateurism came in June 1955 when *Life* magazine published an exposé. The article was written by Yuri Rastvorov, who had been a lieutenant colonel in the Soviet intelligence service, the MVD, before defecting in January 1954.[4]

Rastvorov also happened to be a keen tennis player, although he was never good enough to be admitted into the top rank. Nevertheless, he witnessed first-hand the Soviet system that concealed "flagrant special privileges" given to athletes that, by any definition, made them professionals.[5]

Rastvorov explained that every elite athlete was a member of a sporting club, each of which was sponsored and generously funded by state institutions. For example, Dinamo was supported by the security police, TsSKA was the army's team, Torpedo was sponsored by the state-owned ZIL automotive plant, and Spartak by the food processors' union.

As a member of the intelligence service, Rastvorov played for Dinamo, where he saw how the security services recruited elite athletes, who became officers even though they seldom appeared in uniform. The army did the same for recruits to its sporting teams. While members of Torpedo were given the title of "senior automotive engineer" at the ZIL factory, they only made brief appearances at the factory to collect their paychecks or to pick up the latest model limousine.

Bonuses were handed to the best players. While a factory worker might take home 700 roubles a month, athletes usually earned 2,000 roubles or more. Cash bonuses of 5,000 roubles (US$10,500 in 2021) were added for winning a national or international championship or setting a world record. This allowed an elite athlete "to live as well as a top bureaucrat," explained Rastvorov.[6]

These rewards were hidden from the world. When athletes collected their monthly checks, they signed a declaration that threatened them with severe punishment should they disclose their real incomes.

From Russia with Love

To fend off the threat of expulsion, in 1954 Romanov invited IOC president Avery Brundage to see for himself how sport was organized in the USSR.

An independently wealthy man, Brundage covered all his expenses to not be beholden to his host.

Before Brundage arrived, Romanov must have wondered what sort of man held the fate of his country's Olympic ambitions in his hands. Brundage had a reputation for punishing transgressions against the IOC's amateur rules with Robespierrian ruthlessness. On the other hand, he was capable of bending to the demands of realpolitik, as a visit to Nazi Germany twenty years earlier had demonstrated.

As pressure grew in the United States to boycott the Berlin Olympic Games, in September 1934 Brundage undertook a six-day fact-finding mission to investigate whether the Nazis were discriminating against Jewish athletes. His report would determine whether or not the United States would participate in the Berlin Olympics.

Brundage met with some Jewish athletes at Kaiserhof Hotel in Berlin. He was accompanied by Arno Brietmeyer, the deputy Reichssportführer (sports chief), wearing his SS uniform, and Dr. Karl Ritter von Halt. Brundage knew von Halt well, having competed against him in the decathlon at the 1912 Olympics. They had become friends, even though von Halt was now a member of the National Socialist Party.[7] It would have been a brave athlete to tell Brundage the truth about how Jews were treated by the Nazis at this meeting. None did.

After Brundage returned home, he declared, "I was given positive assurance in writing ... that there will be no discrimination against Jews."[8] As a result of his report, the United States participated in the Berlin Olympics.

Had Brundage made some simple enquires, he would have discovered that to qualify for the German Olympic team an athlete had to be a member of an official sports club. In spring 1933 all Jews were thrown out of these clubs, automatically disqualifying them for Olympic selection. Instead, he willingly accepted assurances from von Halt that nothing was stopping Jews from competing in the Olympics.

The question was: would Brundage exhibit the same level of willful blindness as he had in Berlin when he examined whether Soviet athletes were true amateurs? And would he be as trusting of assurances given when he met sports officials that Olympic rules had not been broken?

When Brundage reached Moscow he met Romanov, confronting the Russian sports minister with allegations of Soviet cheating. He showed Romanov newspaper cuttings from Great Britain, Sweden, Switzerland, France, and the United States that accused the Soviet Union of breaking Olympic rules by passing off state-funded athletes as amateurs. Romanov brusquely dismissed the allegations, telling Brundage that the USSR "believe in, and respect Olympic Rules."[9] When questioned about state subsidies for its sportspeople, Romanov baldly told Brundage, "We have, and want, no professional athletes in the USSR, we operate no special training camps…. We give no special inducements, cash prizes, or other material rewards to our athletes."[10] Romanov conceded that in the past, cash prizes were given for outstanding performances. However, since the Soviet Union joined the Olympic movement this practice had ceased. He went on to say, "we believe champion athletes have moral and social responsibilities as well, that they should keep up with their work and studies first, and that they should set a good example for the youth of the country."[11]

Brundage was also worried the Soviet Union might corrupt the Olympics by using its victories for political propaganda. "Sport must not be misused for national aggrandizement," he lectured. "That is why there is no official scoring in the Olympic Games."[12] Brazenly, Romanov replied: "We do not believe in mixing sport and international politics."[13] Remarkably, Brundage accepted this assurance. Just two years earlier, during the Helsinki Games, Romanov had a board erected outside the Soviet Village that recorded the medals won by the USSR and served no other purpose than propaganda.

Just as in 1934, Brundage accepted his host's assurances without checking for himself whether they were true.

Big Red Machine

The highlight of Brundage's visit was the All-Union Parades of Fizkul'turniki, which he attended on July 18, 1954. There is no simple translation for *fizkul'turniki*. They are participants in physical culture activities (fizkul'tura) encompassing calisthenics, synchronized gymnastics, weightlifting, football, artistic performance, and everything in between.

In the VIP enclosure Brundage rubbed shoulders with Nikita Khrushchev. While the Soviet First Secretary was not particularly interested in sport, he saw its propaganda value and supported Romanov in strengthening Soviet sport on the world stage. Also present were other Politburo members, the deputy prime minister of East Germany, Walter Ulbricht, and sports leaders from Finland, Sweden, Switzerland, Italy, Austria, Egypt, France, and Lebanon.

The festival was in a state of transition. Originally it was mainly devoted to ordinary Soviet citizens who exercised "for improvement of their health and for training youth for labor and for the defense of the socialist Motherland."[14] This program, known as "Ready for Labour and Defence," was introduced in 1931 and was well suited to an inward-looking country fearful of invasions by its numerous capitalist enemies. After the Second World War the Kremlin placed greater emphasis on competitive sports, and so Olympic events were added to the program.

Romanov opened the festival, announcing that the Soviet Union looked forward to extending "our relations and competitions with athletes of foreign countries in the name of friendship and peace."[15]

Next, 30,000 *fizkul'turniki* from all the so-called autonomous republics—fifteen in total—marched into the Dinamo Stadium. It was a pageant that would have outshined a Roman Triumph in its magnificence. It also served much the same purpose. The only difference was that the people of subject nations came to entertain rather than being dragged into the stadium in chains. There were women from Moldavia in green and gold folk costumes, men from the Caucasus with falcons perching on their outstretched arms, and turbaned horsemen from the Tadzhik Soviet Socialist Republic.

Thousands of girls and boys, some as young as ten, performed mass demonstrations, tossing large red, gold, and blue balls into the air. In the stadium's main stand, under large portraits of Lenin and Stalin, thousands of children in red and blue uniforms created human banners. Unable to read the Cyrillic, Brundage was told by his hosts that they spelled "READY FOR LABOUR AND DEFENSE"; "GLORY TO THE FATHERLAND"; and "SUCCESS TO THE COMMUNIST PARTY." Here was evidence that sport and politics were inseparable, and it defies logic that Brundage continued to believe that Soviet Olympic athletes would leave the politics behind at home.

Later in the day weightlifters marched in, playfully juggling heavy weights. A hundred or so female fencers, in white tops and shorts, flashed their sabers in a synchronized display of fencing moves. In another performance, students from the Stalin Institute of Physical Culture rode a convoy of motorbikes. From each pillion, on which a two-meter stand was fixed, seven students in red head-to-toe outfits balanced. The display that most impressed Brundage was a human pyramid created by Byelorussian athletes. It consisted of a base of three layers of bare-chested men wearing white shorts, who held up four tiers of women, in red swimwear with thin gold sashes. A single woman stood at the apex of this human structure. It resembled "a living bouquet of beautiful flowers," wrote Brundage in an article describing his trip, which appeared in the *Saturday Evening Post*.[16]

The rest of the day was devoted to competitive sports, which were more familiar to Brundage. Many of them were Olympic events. This allowed Brundage to see how much progress Soviet athletes had made since Helsinki. Not only did he see remarkable sporting feats, but he noticed that Soviet athletes were no longer held back by poor technique and their equipment was the best money could buy, much of it imported from Western Europe.

During competitions, fans were vocal, reacting much as Brundage would have seen at home at a basketball or baseball game. Rather than hot dogs, they enjoyed *chebureki*, a greasy pastry stuffed with meat and cheese, washed down with Zhigulevskoye beer. Hopping from foot to foot in their excitement, children lined up, kopecks jingling in the hands, to buy an *Eskeemo*, a popular ice-cream on

Gymnastics performance by athletes from the Byelorussian Soviet Socialist Republic during the All-Union Parades of Fizkul'turniki, held on July 18, 1954, in the Dinamo Stadium (courtesy Sovfoto Archive, Maclaren Art Centre, Barrie, Ontario).

a stick, coated with chocolate. There were also hawkers selling programs, victory flowers, medallions stamped with peace doves, and postcards of Lenin and Stalin.

Afterward, Brundage gushed that the event "far surpassed in magnitude and beauty anything of its kind."[17]

That evening Brundage attended a sumptuous dinner where Romanov tried to ply him with vodka, perhaps hoping to get under his guard. Rather than accepting vodka toasts in a tumbler, Brundage pointedly asked for a shot glass and watched how much he consumed.

The next day Brundage embarked on a 3,000-mile (4,800-km) tour by plane and car. It took him north to Leningrad and then south to Kyiv, Odesa, and on to Uzbekistan, where he visited Tashkent, Samarkand, and Bukhara. He also visited small villages and collective farms. Wherever he went he saw numerous sporting fields and *fizkul'turniki* from all walks of life.

When he returned home, Brundage was fulsome with his praise.

> The lives of almost all of Russia's 200,000,000 are touched by the government's emphasis on sports and physical training. First, young boys and girls are encouraged to participate in activities on a general scale—light weightlifting, acrobatics and gymnastics. This is [*sic*] intended to build strength and condition. Later they are pushed into specialization, where they receive the finest instruction possible. Coaches and teachers are trained in institutes which deal scientifically with the mechanics and physiology of athletic competition, with biochemistry and psychology. There is a fierce drive to succeed, and, once successful, to go even higher.[18]

What Brundage witnessed was the "Big Red Machine," as it would come to be known in the West. It was lubricated by billions of roubles, which the government spent on sporting infrastructure and the clubs to provide elite athletes with the very best facilities.[19] Promising athletes also received calorie allowances—extra food. And success was rewarded with jobs and bonuses, but in ways that would not have been obvious to Brundage.

At the end of his trip Brundage concluded, "I saw nothing during my visit to cause me to question these statements [that Soviet athletes were strictly amateur] given to me by Nikolai Romanov."[20]

States of Confusion

Brundage's public admiration of the Soviet sporting system frustrated Cold War warriors in the United States, who were sure that the USSR was breaking the rules.

A vocal campaigner for banning the USSR from the Melbourne Olympics was Senator John Marshall Butler. On April 3, 1956, he explained that "the international Communist conspiracy, as an integral part of its worldwide cultural propaganda offensive, has an iron fist ominously pointed at Melbourne." He urged the United States to make every effort to keep Russia and "her barbaric goon squads" from the Olympics.[21]

Other politicians were alarmed at what a loss might mean for U.S. prestige. Republican congressman from Ohio, Frank Bow, warned that America's enemies might lose respect as "our physical prowess dwindles to nil, and they are tempted thereby to underestimate us in other fields and try to start trouble for us elsewhere."[22] Frank Thompson, Democrat congressman from New Jersey, stated, "the arms race is not the only event in which they're [the Soviets] competing with us. They have taken sports and culture and transformed them into arenas of the Cold War." He went on to argue that "the cause of freedom and winning world opinion to our side in the cold war will be dealt more good if the free nations win next year's Olympics."[23] Democrat Michael Feighan from Ohio pointed out "that the Russian Communists have the biggest propaganda machine in history and … they will pound away at all the people of the world—if they should win the 1956 Olympics, that our American democracy is decaying."[24]

There was little argument among politicians that the Soviet Union should be expelled from the Melbourne Olympics. But they also knew that the IOC would not entertain this course of action, particularly after Brundage's fact-finding tour had concluded that the USSR was not breaking IOC rules on amateurism.

Looking at how the United States could be more competitive, newspaper columnist Arthur Daley outlined the problem facing America. "If we don't get contributions in the million-plus brackets, we will start lopping off lesser sports teams and may have skeleton or token representation in some of the others." By contrast, "the comrades will be on the scene loaded to the gunwales with their very best. They have no intention of missing out on a propaganda vehicle as monumental as this one."[25]

There was a natural aversion, however, against government funding, as Senator Butler explained. American athletes "are not wards of the Government nor are they propagandists."[26] A partial solution was found, though, when Congress approved $900,000 for the training of athletes in the armed forces. This money was well targeted as 101 of the 338 athletes on the U.S. Olympic team who would go to Melbourne were in one of the services. While this was a disguised government grant, congressmen held their collective noses and approved the expenditure.

With the U.S. Olympic Committee struggling to raise funds to send a strong team to Melbourne, President Eisenhower proclaimed October 16, 1954, National Olympics Day. To make the day a success, there were TV advertisements during the *Game of the Week*, with Henry Luce's Time-Life company picking up the tab. Everyone pitched in. Boy scouts went door-to-door collecting contributions, and local Jaycees held fundraising dinners. At football games, volunteers handed around tins for loose change. And at Madison Square Garden weightlifters, gymnasts, wrestlers, and fencers put on exhibitions, with money raised going to the Olympic fund.

The campaign did not stop with the National Olympics Day. Advertisements appearing in *Sports Illustrated* continued to solicit donations. In one, Americans were told that unless they dug deep, Iron Curtain countries with "government subsidized teams" would have an unfair advantage. "Whether these nations are defeated depends in large part upon you," challenged the advertisement. It went on to appeal to "every American who would rather see the Stars and Stripes hoisted above the victor's stand" to send money to the Amateur Athletic Union.[27]

By the time the Melbourne Olympics came around, over a million dollars had been contributed to the Olympic cause.

False Starts

The United States Information Agency (USIA), part of the State Department, was created in 1953 to lead the Eisenhower Administration's psychological warfare campaigns. Its mission was to promote a positive image of America. And while not explicitly stated, it was also to cast communism as the enemy of freedom and democracy.

Before Abbott Washburn was appointed deputy director of the USIA, he actively shaped the Administration's psychological warfare policies. One area that attracted his attention was how adeptly the USSR had used its participation at the Helsinki Olympics for propaganda. He was particularly worried that the Soviet Union had every chance of overwhelming the United States in the medal ranking at the next Olympics, not because the United States had fewer talented athletes but because the U.S. Olympic Committee did not have the funds to send a strong team to Melbourne. If sport was to be deployed as a weapon in America's psychological warfare armory, not just for the Olympics but also to support goodwill tours, it needed to be adequately funded. He addressed this issue and how the United States could better exploit sport for propaganda in a report: "International Athletics—Cold War Battleground."[28]

Washburn saw how the well-funded Big Red Machine put the United States at a disadvantage. "Soviet victories, in virtually every form of sport, are creating the psychological effect the Soviets seek—impressing on the minds of youth everywhere that communist youth is the new symbol of athletic perfection and that the myth of American sports supremacy has been shattered."[29]

Washburn grudgingly admired the Soviets' strategy in which the "old vilification, name-calling and threats that mark the Stalin policy have gone into the discard," replaced by a subtle approach in which victories on the sporting field were proving "the most effective psychological weapons the Kremlin has yet unsheathed." Part of its success was because "the Soviets appear prepared to spend any amount of money to subsidize elaborate and comprehensive communist participation in international sporting events."[30]

Not only had the Soviets sent large teams to the Olympics, but the USSR also outgunned the United States when it came to sending sportspeople around the world as goodwill ambassadors. In 1955 the communist bloc sent out 493 missions involving 2,186 sportspeople. Athletes were mainly sent to Western European countries, with smaller numbers sent to Asia, Africa, and Latin America. By comparison, Washburn despaired that "we have done very little," other than sponsoring a few sporting clinics.[31] There were only nine U.S. goodwill tours in 1955 and fifteen the following year.

Funding problems had reduced America's presence in international sport in other ways. Every year the Amateur Athletic Union had to decline around fifteen invitations to international meets because it had insufficient funds. "Soviet athletes are winning their important psychological objectives largely through default on our part," wrote Washburn. He worried that communist propaganda would portray these absences as America running scared of being beaten by the Soviet Union.[32]

As Congress would not fund the U.S. Olympic team or goodwill tours, Washburn turned to the private sector for financial support. In 1955 and 1956, he approached corporate leaders and sporting leaders whom he believed would be willing to form a sports committee that would raise funds from the corporate sector.

To ensure the sports committee complemented the government's Cold War strategies, Washburn suggested that it work closely, though informally and entirely unofficially, with the USIA, the CIA, and the State Department.

Washburn first approached Bing Crosby to chair the committee. While he would have liked to be involved, he declined as he had television and film commitments that would not allow him to do justice to the job. Other public figures were approached, but they declined. Unable to find a suitable chairman, Washburn admitted defeat.

Had he gone ahead with his funding committee, Washburn may well have bought into a fight with Brundage. The IOC president opposed corporate funding of sport because companies might use athletes to promote their brands overseas. And Brundage was right. There is no commercial reason why a corporation would invest in an overseas tour of American athletes unless there was some payback.

As Washburn's hope of creating a private body floundered and with the Melbourne Olympics fast approaching, staff at the USIA turned their minds to other ways to counter the Soviet threat.

One suggestion was that the USIA plant stories with mainstream journalists that Soviet athletes were "soldiers of the state." To succeed, "the hand of the US Government must not appear publicly in operations, sponsorship, or management of American Olympic participation," argued Washburn.[33] This idea did not get off the ground after Brundage launched a concerted campaign to expose America's hypocrisy when it came to amateurism. "The fact that the complaints [against Russia] have come from a country that has been notorious internationally for gross irregularities in sport at educational institutions, of all places, has not added to their acceptance," he told the *Chicago Daily Tribune*.[34] He did not believe that generous athletic scholarships, access to expensive university facilities, and highly paid coaches conformed to the principle of amateur sport. Brundage also worried that the U.S. army had gone too far in supporting elite athletes in its ranks. "Special camps. Special training. Exactly what we're accusing the Russians of doing," he told *Sports Illustrated*.[35]

Perhaps more worrisome, Brundage exposed how the U.S. government was using athletes as agents for its propaganda. "The State Department sponsors tours of our athletes to other countries," he complained. "This sounds all right, on the surface. But what is it if it isn't using amateur athletes for political purposes? That is another thing we accuse the Russians of doing."[36]

Possibly intimidated by Brundage's attacks, the USIA prepared a modest package of propaganda to disseminate in Melbourne. Rather than criticizing Soviet athletes as sham amateurs, it published booklets that presented a seductive picture of American life and culture. The USIA hoped its information packages would be picked up as "unattributed" stories in the newspapers.

The USIA did still have one ace up its sleeve. It planned to sponsor an art exhibition, *Sport in Art*, which would be shown in Melbourne during the Olympic Games. It would provide an opportunity to create goodwill and showcase American culture.

Communist China, which hoped to compete in Melbourne, also had in mind using a tour of the Peking Opera, also known as the Classical Theater of China, to win hearts and minds during the Olympic Games.

CHAPTER 6

Sport, Art and Opera

Sport in Art

Prologue to a Debacle

The United States Information Agency (USIA) saw the Melbourne Olympic Games as an opportunity to showcase American art before an international audience, and so it sponsored the *Sport in Art* exhibition.

In 1955 the USIA asked the American Federation of Arts to curate an exhibition around the theme of sport, and it successfully borrowed 102 works from public and private collections. *Sports Illustrated* offered to sponsor a tour of the United States in which *Sport in Art* would be shown in seven regional galleries. After that, the USIA would take over and ship the paintings to Melbourne.

The USIA was keen to use this exhibition to deliver a major propaganda victory by showcasing American culture at its finest in a part of the world that was becoming strategically important. China had gone Red in 1949, and the Korean War, one of the first major proxy military conflicts of the Cold War, had just ended. The Indian and Indonesian governments were leaning towards the left. There were communist insurgencies in Laos, Vietnam, Burma (now Myanmar), and Malaya. The exhibition would help win the hearts and minds of Australians as well as of visitors who would be in Melbourne for the Olympics.

Ever since the early days of the Cold War, overseas tours of art exhibitions, authors, ballet groups, and orchestras were used as weapons, part of each bloc's psychological warfare armory. Successful tours allowed the sponsor to claim the superiority of its culture and, therefore, the political system that nurtured it.

In the cultural Cold War, each side worked to its strengths. For example, tours by the Bolshoi and Kirov ballets, violin virtuoso David Oistrakh, pianist Emil Gilels, and the Moiseyev Dance Company were winners for the Soviet Union. The United States successfully toured *Porgy and Bess*, jazz trumpeter Dizzy Gillespie, and the Boston Symphony Orchestra.

Since Stalin's death in 1953, the USSR had ramped up its cultural diplomacy while the United States lagged behind. When President Eisenhower arrived at the White House he was keen to close the gap. But he was often frustrated by Congress, which was miserly when it came to allocating funds to overseas tours.

Art was an obvious winner for the United States. Sophisticated elites, a prime target, appreciated the latest modernist art from America, which in some areas was overtaking Europe. In particular, Abstract Expressionism allowed America to present artworks that vibrated with creativity and energy. By contrast, the Socialist Realist paintings, favored by the Soviet Union, had few fans. They were little more than political lectures on canvas in which contented proletariat frolicked, muscular men and women cheerfully toiled to build a socialist paradise, and resolute soldiers bore the message that the Soviet Union was ready to defend world peace against capitalist warmongers.

USIA believed that it had an agreement from the National Gallery of Victoria to show its exhibition between October 4 and November 30, 1956, to coincide with the Olympic Games. That was news to the director of the National Gallery of Victoria, Eric Westbrook, who found out about the exhibition a couple of months before it was due to open. The arts committee of the Olympics had already booked the National Gallery of Victoria for an exhibition of Australian art. Its dates overlapped with those of the *Sport in Art* exhibition, and the gallery could not accommodate two major shows at the same time.

To solve this problem, Westbrook secured space for the *Sport in Art* exhibition in the Mural Hall. Located on the Myer emporium's top floor, it was designed like a grand European ballroom with soaring ceilings and Art Deco features. A versatile space, the Mural Hall was often used for art exhibitions, fashion shows, charity events, and could seat 1,000 people at a time. Westbrook hoped that the USIA would be happy with the new venue.

The cause of the mix-up was that the American Federation of Arts had written to James MacDonald and presumably believed he had given permission to show *Sport in Art* in the gallery. MacDonald's term as gallery director ended in 1941, and he had died in November 1952. It is possible (but difficult to understand) that someone at the gallery responded to this request, agreeing to the exhibition. Neither Eric Westbrook, who had become the director in January 1956, nor his predecessor, Sir Darryl Lindsay, were aware of this correspondence.

Before the exhibition was due to arrive in Australia, as it toured American galleries, it was caught in a political firestorm with Cold War overtones.

What Happens in Dallas...

After the exhibition had successfully toured the Museum of Fine Arts in Boston, Corcoran Gallery in Washington, D.C., and J.B. Speed Museum in Louisville, its next stop the Dallas Museum of Fine Art.

To generate interest, in December 1955, the gallery's director, Jerry Bywaters, released the list of artists who would be part of the *Sport in Art* show.

The Dallas County Patriotic Council compared the artists' names to a list of "subversive" artists prepared by George Dondero, a Michigan Republican congressman and ardent anti-communist campaigner. He was a close ally of Senator Joe McCarthy and used the same techniques to smear artists, accusing them of being communists, often with little or no evidence. Four artists were on Dondero's list: Ben Shahn, Yasuo Kuniyoshi, Leon Kroll, and William Zorach.

Among the members of the Dallas County Patriotic Council, Dondero was an infallible authority on the dangers posed by communist artists. He had gained national attention in 1947 when he condemned a touring exhibition, *Advancing American Art*, sponsored by the State Department. Dondero's campaign was supported by the Hearst newspapers, which attacked the works as being communistic. Faced with public outrage, the tour was suddenly canceled while it was touring Czechoslovakia. When the paintings returned to the United States, they were sold as surplus for knockdown prices.

Dondero tapped into widespread prejudices against abstract art. He was also able to exploit resentment by traditional painters, who were convinced that museums preferred modernist works to their conventional landscapes, portraits, and still-lifes.

"Modern art is Communistic," Dondero claimed, "because it is distorted and ugly, because it does not glorify our beautiful country and smiling people and our material progress." He also played on people's fear that left-wing artists were using their art to subvert America's will to resist communist aggression. "Art that does not glorify our country, in plain, simple terms, breeds dissatisfaction. It is therefore opposed to our government and those who create it and promote it are enemies."[1] On another occasion, Dondero told fellow Americans to be vigilant and "protect our cultural birthright from this horde of art saboteurs who would first destroy in order to control."[2]

After the *Advancing American Art* debacle, the State Department organized few exhibitions during the next few years, and those it sent overseas were conservative so as not to attract attention from the likes of Dondero.

When Dwight Eisenhower entered the White House in January 1953 he was keen to increase America's psychological warfare capabilities, including the use of touring art shows. Eisenhower argued that what was needed were American art exhibitions that would "capture the imagination of the people of the older, art-loving nations of the world."[3] Eisenhower was worried that the USSR was well ahead of the United States in cultural diplomacy (a euphemism for psychological warfare). He claimed that the Soviet Union was "making a deep impression, and with every Soviet success, American prestige ... suffers in proportion."[4]

The task of ramping up touring exhibitions was in the hands of USIA, which had a lot of catching up to do. An internal agency report estimated that in 1956 the Kremlin would spend $9 million (US$88 million in 2021) on traveling art exhibits. With its modest budget, the USIA could only afford to send two exhibitions overseas each year. In 1956, sending the *Sport in Art* to Australia was one of those shows. *Sports Illustrated* offered to organize the American leg of the exhibition.

Starting on October 31, 1955, the exhibition toured the United States without incident. However, its luck ran out in Dallas when the local patriotic league protested the inclusion of communist artists. This controversy divided Dallas, as liberals and conservatives saw this as a test of their vision for the city.

The liberals wanted to make Dallas "the Athens of the Alfalfa fields," the cultural capital of the South. Progressive businesspeople and civic groups saw high culture as one way to make Dallas "the best Northern city in the South,"[5] and securing the *Sport in Art* exhibition would help burnish the city's reputation.

Pulling Dallas in a different direction were conservatives, who were fiercely anti-communist and attached to traditional Texas values. When it came to art, they loathed modernist paintings. Lead by the Dallas County Patriotic Council, conservatives suspected that many artists used their art to propagate communist propaganda and diverted money from the sale of their paintings to fund subversive activities. The Council also attracted membership from local art clubs. Although most of their members were not as militant as the hardcore patriots, they were willing to support the campaign. They were motivated by resentment because the museum had refused to exhibit their wholesome artworks. Instead, it preferred to show art by politically suspect modernists, whose works they found incomprehensible and aesthetically unattractive.

These allies joined in attacking the Dallas Museum of Fine Arts for providing comfort and support to the communist cause by hosting the *Sport in Art* exhibition.

Divisions also existed among the members of the Dallas Art Association, who were trustees of the museum. On December 7, 1955, with a vote of 17 to 9, the liberal trustees reversed an earlier policy to not "acquire or exhibit work of a person known by them to be a Communist or of Communist-front affiliation." Instead, the museum would now "exhibit and acquire works of art only on the basis of their merit as works of art."[6] The *Sport in Art* exhibition became the first test for this new policy.

This decision infuriated the Patriotic Council, and it came out with all guns blazing. On January 12, 1956, the first volley was fired when Colonel John Mayo wrote to the trustees demanding that artworks by the four "communist" artists be removed from the *Sport in Art* show. They were Ben Shahn's *National Pastime*, Yasuo Kuniyoshi's *Skaters*, Leon Kroll's *The Park*, and William Zorach's *The Fisherman*.

Mayo's letter exposed divisions among the trustees. A conservative member,

Tom Suggs, argued he could not see the point of showing the works of a communist artist who "aligned himself with a cause that would destroy all freedoms, regardless of the merit of his art work."[7] However, the majority rejected the Patriotic Council's demand. Afterward, three liberal trustees—Jerome K. Crossman, Gerald C. Mann, and Waldo Stewart—wrote an open letter, which they sent to 2,000 Dallas business and professional leaders. They argued "that democracy cannot survive if subjected to book burning, thought control, condemnation without trial, proclamation or by association—the very techniques of the Communist and Fascist regimes."[8]

When its appeal to the trustees failed, the Patriotic Council held a public meeting to rally support. Around 150 of its members filled the Highland Park Town Hall auditorium, where they heard speeches brimming with bile, belligerence, and bombast. Colonel Alvin Owsley warned that the "Reds are moving in upon us."[9] The meeting was also addressed by Florence Rogers, who called on Dallas to be "a citadel of safety against these insidious threats."[10] William Ware from the American Legion suggested the trustees had been "very cleverly maneuvered into the position of serving as a Communist Front for the protection of pro–Communist artists."[11] Then Mrs. L.H. Hertz of the Delta Art Club put forward the issue that concerned local artists. "Different art clubs haven't been able to exhibit art out there in a long time. I know of local professional artists who can't show, and their works are good."[12]

In the past, Bywaters had not refused to show inferior works by local artists because they would harm the museum's reputation. Against his better judgment, he decided to appease local artists by offering to show their works at the same time as the *Sport in Art* exhibition. This concession won him no friends, and the local artists continued to support the Patriotic Council's campaign against the museum.

Fortunately for Bywaters, many were willing to defend the museum. One of its supporters was art critic for the *Dallas Morning News*, John Rosenfield. He argued that "no art should be censored, and that no Communist art would make a Communist out of any beholder who wouldn't be a Communist anyway." Appealing to civic pride, he said a ban would make the museum "the laughing stock of gallery circles."[13] Some in the business community were also willing to defend the museum. Eugene McElvaney, vice president of the First National Bank, made a well-received speech to the Dallas Rotary Club in which he mocked "certain patriotic groups, almost in desertion of the fundamental defenses of our freedoms from all forms of ideology encroachment, devote their major energies towards banning or censoring—and imagine they are fulfilling their highest devotion to home and country."[14]

The controversy attracted the attention of *New York Times* art critic Aline Saarinen. She accused the Patriotic Council of being "aesthetic vigilantes" at odds with "reason, decency and real Americanism."[15] Colonel Owsley, for the Patriotic Council, responded. "It is one of the basic premises of Communist doctrine that art can and should be used in the constant process of attempting to brainwash and create public attitudes that are soft towards communism."[16]

Some who were unhappy with the exhibition took direct action. Supporters of the Patriotic Council withdrew their children from art classes organized by the museum. Others canceled their memberships. A prominent liberal trustee, Stanley Marcus, suffered when shoppers boycotted his Neiman-Marcus department store. Bywaters also found himself at the sharp end of protests. On one occasion, some women barged into his office and demanded to see the "Red art."[17] Another time he found some protesters in his office, rifling through his desk looking for subversive material. Bywaters also received hate mail. One letter was addressed to "Dear Comrade" and urged him to go to Russia where "there is a real need for your type." Another accused him of being a "dupe for communist subversion by not knowing the truth."[18]

Years later, Bywaters struggled to make sense of what had triggered the firestorm that engulfed the museum. "It's like trying to make a piece of sculpture out of smoke," he told his biographer, Francine Carraro. "It isn't there, you can't pin it down."[19]

Gangly, with an angular face, a pert mustache, and thoughtful brown eyes, Bywaters had a burning ambition to make the Dallas Museum of Fine Arts the best in the southwest. He therefore could not afford to allow local patriots to censor the show. And while it came at a personal cost, he was determined that the exhibition would go ahead.

As the campaign against the exhibition became more vitriolic, there were real concerns the vigilantes might try to disrupt the show; some might even resort to violence. Such was the threat that just before the opening, Dallas Mayor "Uncle Bob" Thornton phoned members of the Patriotic Council seeking their assurances that they would not disturb the peace.

Red Alert

The day of the show's opening was very warm. It was a Sunday, and people were dressed to the nines. Some drove, while others strolled across Fair Park, past a small artificial lake called Leonhardt Lagoon and fragrant Bigtree plum trees. Spring had come early and blossoms pirouetted in a light breeze, their white petals spinning languidly to the ground.

Bywaters was understandably tense when the doors to the museum opened at 2 p.m. As Bywaters watched from the entrance, he was not surprised that so many people had come to view the show. The number attending was undoubtedly boosted by its association with the Melbourne Olympic Games, which was prominently advertised in the catalog. Its sports theme, Bywaters thought, might have attracted people who did not usually visit art galleries. He also knew that the show had attracted the curious, who came to see what all the fuss was about.

Most of the people filing into the museum headed for the *Sport in Art* exhibition, which was spread over five galleries.

A few visitors went down the corridor to Gallery A, where the local Klepper Art Club had a show of works by its members. Ladies served tea and cake to those who turned up. Their visitors saw wholesome work in pastels, oils, and watercolors that were thoroughly in line with the aesthetic tastes of members of the Dallas County Patriotic Council. Among the thirty-three paintings, there was a still life of satin-pink shells with milky highlights; another of white magnolia blossoms on a ground of glittering gold; in a third, a woman in a long gown was arranging irises. These works could not have been more different in quality from what was being shown in the galleries down the hall. A review of the Klepper show published in the *Dallas Morning News* was brutal. "The smattering of professional competence jumps out of the total mediocrity unavoidably."[20]

Back in the main galleries, it was not difficult to pick out the four controversial paintings. There was a small praetorian guard of patriotic ladies from Fort Worth standing around each of them. And they warned anyone who approached the paintings that they were produced by "Reds" and their inclusion in the exhibition was evidence that the museum was complicit with the communist conspiracy. They also handed out photostats of an editorial that had appeared in the communist newspaper, the *Daily Worker*, which praised the Dallas Museum of Fine Arts. This was a case of guilt by association. Watching the protesters were armed guards who had been employed to prevent violence and vandalism.

Visitors willing to brave the cordon of patriotic ladies were surprised by how small and innocuous the offending artworks were. One was a charcoal sketch of an old fisherman. Another was an ink drawing of a baseball batter in motion. People skated on a frozen pond in another, and the final painting was a winter-themed abstract painting. One patriot made a valiant attempt to explain how these incident scenes could drive someone into the arms of Marxism. "The more you try to find the subject in the paintings, the fuzzier you get in the head, and this is the way the communists want you to feel for when you are fuzzy in the head, you are ready for infiltration."[21]

Rual Askew, arts reviewer for the *Dallas Morning News*, wondered why the exhibition had attracted such venom. "Sport as a theme is as innocuous and noncontroversial as you can get and doesn't raise as much blood pressure as bluebonnets," he wrote. "There isn't a thing in it, least of all the works of the 'objectionable' artists, that smells of dirt and shovel, let alone hammer and sickle."[22] He concluded Dallas should be honored to be selected as one of the museums to show the exhibition before it went to the Olympic Games in Melbourne.

After the exhibition had left Dallas, it was shown in Denver, Los Angeles, San Francisco, and Dayton without incident, but it never reached Melbourne.

Gun-Shy

Unwilling to take any further pain, in late May the USIA quietly announced that it had canceled the Australian leg of the *Sport in Art* exhibition. By this time, the USIA was aware that arrangements to show the exhibition at the National Gallery of Victoria had fallen through, and the gallery's director, Westbrook, was scrambling to make alternative arrangements.

The cancellation came as a relief to Westbrook. However, it was tinged with regret as *Sport in Art* would have been a rare opportunity for Australians to see fine examples of American art.

Various reasons were given for canceling the exhibition, none credible. At first, USIA announced that it was for "budgetary considerations,"[23] even though the Australian leg was estimated to cost just $1,550. Another reason given, no more plausible, was that the USIA had already sent a photographic exhibition on sport to Australia and sending another show on the same theme was superfluous. If this were a genuine problem, it would have been picked up at the planning stage, not six months before *Sport in Art* was due to be shown in Melbourne.

Indeed, no one believed the reasons given by the USIA, and the agency came under attack. An editorial in the *New York Times* speculated that the real reason for the cancellation was opposition from the Dallas County Patriotic Council. "It may not be patriotic to point out that this sort of episode makes foreigners laugh at us," the editorial chided.[24] The USIA was also ridiculed by the editor of *Arts* magazine, Jonathan Marshall. By caving in, the USIA "saved our allies, the Australians, and others, from seeing communist-inspired pictures of ballgames, children playing, skaters, fishermen, boxers, horseracing, and other subversions."[25] Walter Lippmann wrote that the cancellation of the *Sport in Art* exhibition "provides proof to foreigners that we don't live up to our own principles of artistic and cultural freedom."[26]

Dondero was keen to take advantage of this victory. He credits the patriotic folk of Dallas with forcing the USIA to cancel the Australian leg of the exhibition. This was despite the pressure from "Red and left-wing publications," which presumably includes the *New York Times*. He went on to demand that the government should "put a stop once and for all to this device of including such flagrant Communist-frontiers in exhibitions."[27]

Evidently spooked by the anti-communist attacks on overseas tours of American art, neither Eisenhower, who was otherwise committed to employing psychological warfare, nor the USIA, defended this program. It was left to others to explain how important such tours were for winning hearts and minds.

Thomas Hess, the executive editor of *Art News*, pointed to the contradiction in the Eisenhower Administration's cultural Cold War policy. "The Government's position is that it wants to use culture in order to show the world a true aspect of America, but insists that culture conform to a governmental fashion of security clearance."[28]

After the *Sport in Art* fiasco, the USIA decided that future overseas exhibitions would only show artists who had died before 1917, the date of the Russian Revolution, so there would be no risk any of those artists could be accused of being communists. Not only was the policy short-sighted, but it ignored the historical fact that communism pre-dated the Russian Revolution.

This policy meant future USIA exhibitions did not include modern artists. What was sent overseas was dated, conservative, and often dull. This policy robbed American cultural diplomacy of the opportunity to show the world what a creative and vibrant country contemporary America was.

Not all was lost. Through a CIA front, the Congress for Cultural Freedom, funds were secretly funneled to support traveling shows of modern art. Tapping these funds, the New York–based Museum of Modern Art sent nineteen exhibits of contemporary American art overseas in the following years.

As for the Australian organizers of the Olympic Games, the cancellation was barely noticed. The exhibition had not been expected and had been imposed on them at the last minute.

Red Faces

Cultural Seduction

In a sublime irony, had the *Sport in Art* exhibition come to Melbourne it would have been shown in the Mural Hall of Myer emporium. It didn't come because of Cold War politics. On November 19, members of the Peking Opera Company[29] were due to attend a welcome reception at the same venue. This was postponed as its arrival in Melbourne was delayed because of Cold War politics.

Both cultural tours were psychological warfare operations designed to win hearts and minds. While the *Sport in Art* was an unmitigated failure, the Peking Opera Company's tour was a propaganda triumph, though not without drama.

Like art, dance was an effective weapon in psychological warfare. Its aim was to seduce the political and intellectual elites, who helped shape public opinion and public policy. Like art, dance was a useful medium for cultural diplomacy because it communicates directly to foreign audiences without the need for language.

In 1955, the *U.S. News & World Report* noted the upsurge of cultural tours.

"America and the Communist bloc are sending their finest talent—musicians, ballet dancers, actors—everywhere to build prestige among intellectuals." Putting this in a Cold War context, the newspaper concluded that the contest was lopsided. America had sent many fewer tours, particularly to developing countries, where they were particularly needed to counter anti–American feeling.[30]

As America's attention was drawn to communist threats in the Far East in the 1950s, the State Department looked to send more cultural tours to that region. A government memo argued that "Modern Dance"—in capital letters—was attractive because it is "the one art uniquely American."[31] This was presumably the State Department's thinking when it helped fund a tour by the Martha Graham Dance Company. It started in Japan in October 1955, and over the next four months traveled to Malaya, Burma, India, Pakistan, Ceylon (now Sri Lanka), Indonesia, the Philippines, and Thailand.

In October 1956, the USSR sent the Bolshoi Ballet to London for a four-week season at the Royal Opera House. The tour was a success but was cut short when the 150-member troupe was hurried back to Moscow following the invasion of Hungary by Soviet-led armed forces. Had they remained, the Kremlin feared that they could become targets for anti–Soviet protests.

Using culture to promote the superiority of its political system was mainly fought out between the ideological heavyweights: the United States and the USSR. This changed when, in 1950, the People's Republic of China quietly entered the fray. After establishing the Chinese People's Association for Cultural Relations with Foreign Countries, China started to invite overseas visitors to sample its rich culture. It was only by 1955 that China had the organizational capacity to arrange overseas tours, and it decided to start with the acclaimed Peking Opera Company, which combined dance, performance, and singing.

Peking Opera's tour started in Paris on June 4, 1955, at the *Festival international d'Art dramatique de la ville de Paris*, an international festival of the dramatic arts. After Paris, the company traveled to London. According to a review by the *Times of London*, its performances were "a sheer joy to behold, even without knowledge of the conventions which give significance to every movement."[32] It then went on to other European capitals. In August 1956 the Peking Opera traveled to Latin America where, starting in Argentina, it toured five countries on the continent. It then played in Japan, Burma, and other Asian countries before heading south to New Zealand. The final stop of the tour was Australia and was timed to coincide with the Olympic Games, where the company was to be one of the highlights of the cultural program.

On September 28, 1956, an advance party arrived at the Princess Theater, where the Melbourne performances would be held. The theater is a magnificent Victorian building, inspired by the great opera houses of Europe, with stained glass and a grand marble staircase. Among the delegation was the company's

A scene of the *Cowherd and the Village Girl*, performed by the Peking Opera during its tour of New Zealand and Australia (courtesy Marriner Theater Archive).

manager, who inspected the stage, meticulously measuring its proportions. As he explained through an interpreter, some performances included fight scenes with long curved swords—not made of metallic painted wood, but real swords, cut-throat sharp. If one of the performers miscalculated the dimensions of the stage, an actor could be hurt.

For those schooled in Western sensibilities of what opera is about—singing, splendid stage settings, lavish costumes—the Peking Opera integrates these elements with chanting, symbolic gestures, mime, dance, and even acrobatics. The performers wear gorgeous costumes, and their faces are painted with geometric patterns in a dazzling range of colors, which represents each performer's emotional state. Performances are accompanied by two-stringed violin, gongs, drums, and cymbals.

It was an odd choice by the communist regime to launch its psychological warfare operations with classical Chinese operas, which often glorify emperors, generals, mandarins, Buddhist monks, concubines, and aristocratic beauties. Its stories are based on classical literature, mythology, and philosophy, which owed more to China's feudal past than the tenets of Marxism or the maxims of Mao Zedong. Nevertheless, it was an astute choice because its classical roots made it more attractive to Western audiences than operas about noble peasants laboring in the fields or factory workers exceeding production quotas.

Banned

As the Peking Opera was coming to the end of its successful tour of New Zealand, it was hit by a bombshell. On October 17 the Australian government cabled the troupe, demanding it gives an undertaking that it would not perform in Melbourne during the Olympic Games. If it refused, its members would be denied visas to enter Australia. The Peking Opera had been due to open at the Princess Theater the day before the Olympic opening ceremony. It was booked for a nineteen-day season, which would end a few days after the closing ceremony.

The company's manager, Hsu Kuang-Hsiao, sent a telegram to the Australian promoter in which he said that "for the sake of our good relations and so that the tour may proceed in harmony, we agree to change the schedule and perform in Melbourne either before or after the Games."[33] By acting with good grace, the Chinese response made the government's action seem even more mean-spirited.

The ban required significant changes in the tour's itinerary. The Princess Theater replaced the Peking Opera with the musical *Kismet* for the duration of the Olympics. The Sydney season dates were changed, and the troupe then traveled to Brisbane, which was not on the original schedule, followed by Canberra and Adelaide, before opening in Melbourne.

The government was vague about the reasons for the ban. In Parliament, Prime Minister Robert Menzies explained that the presence of the opera company in Melbourne during the Games "was bound to be a matter of very considerable controversy" as some visitors would "have very strong views on some of the problems associated with these people."[34] What people? What problems? And what objections could they have to opera singers dressed in colorful costumes and garishly painted faces? They did come from a communist country, but in early November a large contingent of athletes from the People's Republic of China would be arriving in Melbourne to compete in the Olympics. Were communist opera singers that much more dangerously subversive than communist high jumpers or swimmers? This point was made by *The Age* in an editorial, when it pointedly asked, how can "a theatrical performance of the ancient Chinese opera ... cause a riot?"[35]

Hoping to strengthen its case, the day after it announced the ban, the government leaked that twelve members of the 86-member company held diplomatic and official passports, suggesting that they were government agents.[36] The implication was that they might be involved in espionage, possibly against athletes from Nationalist China, who would be competing in the Olympics. The real reason for the inclusion of government officials, some of whom would have certainly been secret police, had little to do with espionage. They would have been embedded in the company to ensure that no one defected. Nevertheless, the Australian government hoped that this would feed into Cold War paranoia and provide a more convincing reason for its decision than it had publicly offered.

The government also leaked that the ban was based on a request by unnamed Olympic officials, who feared "unpleasant incidents." Undermining the veracity of this leak, a number of Olympic officials denied that they had requested a ban.[37]

Significantly, no comment was provided by Wilfred Kent Hughes, who was the chairman of the Olympic organizing committee. He also happened to be a member of parliament, who had the ear of the Prime Minister. He had good reason to make trouble for the Peking Opera Company as he was a leading member of the "Formosa Lobby" in the government and a fervent anti-communist.

Kent Hughes showed his support of the Nationalist Chinese regime during a tour of war graves in early 1955, when he made a side visit to Taiwan. The government had not allowed ministers (as Kent Hughes was then) to make official visits to Taiwan. To get around this ban, he claimed he was on the island for a week's holiday. This was demonstratively false. He was welcomed with a seventeen-gun salute, usually the honor given to visiting government ministers. So the Taiwanese government certainly viewed his visit as an official one. Then he met with Vice Minister of Foreign Affairs, Shen Chang-huan, and dined with President Chiang Kai-shek. While in Taiwan, he endeared himself to his hosts by calling for steps to be taken "to halt communism from its predatory course in this part of the world." He also called for an investigation of "training and other practices among athletes in Red China." As sham amateurs, he was inferring that they were not qualified to participate in the Olympics.[38]

Possessing such a fine anti-communist pedigree and with access to the highest levels of government, it was probably Kent Hughes who lobbied to stop the Peking Opera from performing in Melbourne during the Games.

The government miscalculated if they thought that the ban would not attract controversy. An *Argus* editorial ridiculed the prime minister. "Wherever could he have got the idea that ALL the residents of Melbourne—and all our Olympic visitors—are morons, not to be trusted in cosmopolitan company?"[39] The editorial in the *Sydney Morning Herald* was also critical, asserting that Australians will be "embarrassed, even humiliated" by the ban, as it flew in the face of the Olympic spirit.[40] Columnist Peter Russo called the ban "juvenile." He went on to write that it was "embarrassing," as it "will appear abroad as such a little man's gesture."[41] And former Australian Olympian Judy Joy Davies explained that according to the Olympic ethos, "nobody cares what country a competitor, performer, or entertainer comes from, nor do they worry about their politics."[42] Letters to the editor were also hostile. For example, Clive Jackson complained that at "a time when friendship between nations is the keynote, the action of the Government in this matter can only be described as irresponsible."[43] Dr. Peter Wiener argued that the ban turned a gesture "to merely establish cultural relations with the new China ... into a political issue."[44] Leslie Hayden from the Fellowship of Australian writers called Prime Minister Menzies an "artistic hillbilly" for banning the company, an act, he wrote, was "too silly for words."[45]

Predictably, one of the few voices to support the ban was Dr. Chen Tai-Chu, chargé d'affaires at the Nationalist China consulate.

Just as the USIA had been mocked in the United States for stopping the *Sport in Art* exhibition traveling to Australia for the Olympics, the ban of the Peking Opera looked petty and churlish, if not nonsensical.

When the Peking Opera finally arrived in Australia, its performances were greeted enthusiastically. Reviewers praised the visual elements of the performance, which more than compensated for the discordant music and shrill voices of the singers, which were unfamiliar to Western ears. Australia's premier national magazine, the *Woman's Weekly*, devoted a two-page color spread to the Peking Opera, praising the "clever acting, miming, and dancing of the company," as well as "the barbaric splendor and brilliant color of the settings are enchanting all spectators."[46] The review in the *Canberra Times* praised the performances for their "precision, grace, sweetness, spectacle and colour," which made them "truly memorable."[47]

What the government was discovering, at some cost to its reputation, was how powerful psychological warfare was when it employed culture to win hearts and minds. While difficult to criticize, cultural tours during the Cold War were highly political, and the Peking Opera was no exception.

The political aims of China's cultural diplomacy were to reduce the country's political isolation and assert the new regime's legitimacy. In 1956, few non-communist countries had recognized the People's Republic of China.

The success of cultural diplomacy is that its political motives are denied. Not understanding this cardinal rule of cultural diplomacy, at a reception for the Peking Opera Company, Ron Mason of the New Zealand–China Friendly Society said what, until then, had been left unsaid. During the New Zealand leg of the tour, he claimed the "highly-talented and charming people" of the troupe had "won all hearts and delighted large audiences." He saw a political payoff after the tour. "Soon, we trust, through our door ... will walk the accredited ambassador of New China," he said.[48] Thomas MacDonald, New Zealand Minister of External Affairs, described the opera tour as one "for which the local communists had tried by every means to get some Governmental recognition."[49] And by generating goodwill, as the tour had done, it had countered anti-communist propaganda that portrayed China as a threat, which is precisely what its organizers intended.

CHAPTER 7

Long Journey from the Night

Dangerous Times

A week before he was to travel to Melbourne for the Olympic Games, Hungary's water polo captain, Dezső Gyarmati, did not have a care in the world. It was his very special day; a day to be celebrated.

In the course of this day and those that followed, his world was turned upside down. These events affected not only him but everyone on the Hungarian team, each reacting differently as they experienced traumatic events that would change their lives forever. For some, the coming week would be their last in Budapest as they would not return to their tortured homeland after the Olympics.

Yet, on the morning of October 23, there was not a cloud in the sky, and Gyarmati was looking forward to celebrating his birthday. He had turned 29 years old, and life was good. He was in prime physical condition, ready to compete in Melbourne, and had every reason to believe that the team he captained would repeat the success it found in Helsinki and win another gold medal. Success had made Gyarmati famous. Everywhere he went in Budapest he was recognized, and he just lapped up the adulation.

While life was good, Gyarmati had seen how people lived on the other side of the Iron Curtain when he participated in international competitions. For all the privileges, fame, and comforts he enjoyed in Hungary, they paled compared to the freedom he saw people enjoy in the West. He had seriously considered defecting on two occasions but never followed through.

After finishing a training session at the National Swimming Stadium (now the Hajós Alfréd Swimming Pool) on Margit Island, Gyarmati hopped into his newly-purchased car, his pride and joy. It was a light gray Volkswagen that he had imported from West Germany, and it still had its original number plates. There were only about 5,000 private motor vehicles in Budapest, so owning a car put Gyarmati into the elite, mainly populated by politicians and senior Party members, but also included top sportspeople.

From the pool, Gyarmati drove to the Margit Bridge to return to the Vörös

Csillag hotel in the nearby Svábhegy foothills, west of Budapest. This was where most of the Olympic team was billeted before leaving for Melbourne in a few days. However, as he approached the bridge he saw thousands of students joyfully singing and holding up placards attacking the communist regime. Some were in trucks waving the national flag with the communist emblem at its center cut out. They were coming from Bem Square, where a large demonstration had just ended.

The day was one of spontaneity; the simple demonstration by students had released a valve on a pressure cooker. Tens of thousands of people from all walks of life joined the students' protest against the Russian subjugation of their country and the hardships that came with communism. They hated Hungary's Stalinist regime, which stayed in power through the liberal use of terror and torture, dished out by the hated security police, the ÁVO.

After the speeches had ended, demonstrators in Bem Square moved on. Some headed to the Parliament building. They hoped that the former prime minister, Imre Nagy, might take over and reintroduce the reform program he had started in July 1953 before being removed by hardliners nine months later for going too far. Others went to the radio station, where students from the Technological University hoped their sixteen-point manifesto would be read. Their demands included the withdrawal of Soviet troops from Hungary and multi-party elections. Other protesters headed north-east towards Hősök Square, next to which stood Stalin's statue.

After Gyarmati parked his car, he joined marchers as they walked arm-in-arm, singing nationalist songs. "The day of liberty had arrived," Gyarmati joyfully announced. "We were united."[1] When Gyarmati reached Stalin Boulevard (now Andrássy Avenue), he joined some students who were scaling a three-story building and helped them pull down a large red star, a feature of many buildings in communist Budapest.

That evening, Gyarmati returned to the Vörös Csillag hotel. A few hours later, he heard gunfire coming from downtown Budapest. Although he did not know it at the time, the shots were coming from the radio station. This incident transformed a peaceful protest into an armed insurrection intent on overthrowing the communist regime.

Inside the radio station on Bródy Sándor Street was another sports personality, as well known as Gyarmati. He was György Szepesi, a radio reporter, and his voice was familiar to all sports-loving Hungarians. He had been at the Helsinki Olympics, and he expected to report on the Hungarians' achievements in Melbourne. Also inside the building were armed ÁVO agents, who were ready to stop the students from taking over the radio station.

To calm students milling around the building, Szepesi stepped onto the first-floor balcony to address the protesters. He got no further than saying "Dear

During the Hungarian uprising, Red Stars were removed by protesters from the tops of buildings (FORTEPAN/Robert Hofbauer).

comrades!" before he was shouted down and bricks were thrown at him, resulting in a hasty retreat.[2] One missile smashed the loudspeaker attached to the outside of the balcony, and Szepesi was lucky to escape uninjured.

Unable to help, Szepesi left for the headquarters of the ruling Hungarian Communist Party in Akadémia Street so he could touch base with government leaders. When he arrived, Szepesi was taken up to the first floor, where he waited outside the auditorium where the Central Committee was deciding how to respond to the demonstrations that were spreading around Budapest.

Back at the radio station, fearing that the building was about to be overrun, ÁVO agents opened fire on the demonstrators. Outraged by the slaughter, some policemen and soldiers standing outside the radio station handed over their guns to the protesters. And soon, Brody Sándor Street became a war zone. It was these shots that Gyarmati heard when he was back at the Vörös Csillag hotel.

At 5 a.m. the radio station stopped broadcasting after the building had been overrun by protesters.

The takeover of the radio station was a disaster for the government, which desperately needed to broadcast an appeal to protesters to lay down their arms.

After speaking to government officials, Szepesi left Party headquarters and went to the Buda side of the river, where he quickly commissioned an auxiliary antenna. Within hours Kossuth Rádió was back on the air. Szepesi then went to the Parliament Building, where he set up a makeshift studio on the first floor, which allowed the government to get its messages out to the public. The first announcement from the new locality reported: "Fascist and reactionary elements have launched an armed attack against our public buildings and against the forces of law and order."[3] Protesters were warned that the police would deal severely with "troublemakers."[4]

The next day Soviet tanks entered Budapest, turning protesters into freedom fighters, who were given or stole arms. On the same day, Nagy replaced the Stalinist prime minister, Ernő Gerő. Non-communist politicians were invited to join the government, and the hated secret police, the ÁVO, was dissolved. However, in the days that followed, it was clear that this directive was ignored by ÁVO agents.

While the streets were turning into a war zone, Szepesi was in his makeshift studio. There he played music, told after-school stories, read weather reports, and broadcast stern messages from the government, desperate to reassert its authority. Szepesi also decided to record a short speech. Claiming to be speaking on behalf of the Olympic athletes and Hungarian sportspeople, he argued that to restore "national honor and future success of our sportsmen," protesters needed to end all the "killing, looting, and destroying."[5] Believing that sports fans preferred football to revolution, he concluded his speech by calling for an end to protests so that an international football match between Sweden and Hungary, scheduled for the following Sunday, could go ahead.

Sports journalist György Szepesi alienated Olympic athletes when he urged them not to support the uprising (FORTEPAN/Sándor Bojár).

Gyarmati was furious when he heard Szepesi's speech, as were other Olympic athletes. Gyarmati joined with his teammates in denouncing Szepesi. They signed a statement that made it clear the sports broadcaster did not speak for them. Published in the newspaper *Népsport*, the statement declared that in Melbourne the athletes "will fight for the Olympic Games, for Hungarian national glory, for the victims of the revolution, and the Holy Spirit."[6] They also made clear that they would compete under the Kossuth coat of arms adopted by the freedom fighters. They would also wear black armbands in remembrance of patriots who had been killed by Soviet troops.

Szepesi quickly realized his blunder and apologized, but to no avail. When he approached boxer László Papp, Szepesi was told in no uncertain terms that he was persona non grata. The head of the Olympic delegation, Gyula Hegyi, added that some of the athletes were so angry that he should stay away from the team if he valued his personal safety. Szepesi decided to give the athletes time to cool off, but he still intended to go to Melbourne and report on the Games.

On the day of Szepesi's broadcast, Gyarmati was back in central Budapest doing errands for his friend, the police chief Sándor Kopácsi. Gyarmati was asked to get the word out to police stations not to resist requests from freedom fighters for weapons from their armories. Gyarmati was a good choice because he could travel around Budapest in relative safety as he was recognized wherever he went. Kopácsi could not use his people because there was a rumor circulating among freedom fighters that ÁVO agents were disguising themselves as police officers. Kopácsi worried that if he sent his officers on this errand they risked being shot or lynched. Not only was Gyarmati well known, but he was driving a Volkswagen with West German number plates, and he had attached two Olympic flags to its bonnet so that there would be no mistaking who he was. Moreover, everyone knew that no self-respecting ÁVO agent would drive a Volkswagen.

Out of curiosity, Kopácsi decided to look at contingency plans prepared by the government to deal with an uprising. The front of a large red envelope was marked, "PLAN M. Top secret! Open only in case of ABSOLUTE NECESSITY." Inside were five large and fourteen small envelopes with an exhaustive list of weapons and ammunition stored in police headquarters to handle widespread unrest. Kopácsi knew that the police did not have any of the munitions listed. Also itemized were "fresh underwear and uniforms, tinned foods, cigarettes, etc. for 1,000 people," which was expected to last for six days of fighting. "We had none of these except for a few uniforms and a few crates of apples," recalled Kopácsi. "The famous Plan M was a fantasy and a fraud."[7] Kopácsi should not have been surprised. The government did not trust the police force and expected ÁVO, which was well resourced, to put down any rebellion.

Gyarmati visited police stations and passed on Kopácsi's message.

Afterward, Gyarmati visited Corvin Passage and nearby Üllői Street, which was littered with burnt-out Soviet tanks and armored cars. This locale had several natural advantages for freedom fighters. Overlooking Üllői Street, snipers had a good vantage point to pick off Soviet soldiers, while the narrow passageway off the main street provided an escape route for hit-and-run attacks on Soviet tanks. Inside the passage was a 1920s cinema that had a petrol storage reservoir behind it. Pairs of children, some as young as 13 years old, carried laundry baskets door to door where they collected bottles and rags. They took their haul back to the petrol bowser where they helped make Molotov cocktails. These missiles were then stored in the bathrooms of rebel-occupied apartments. When a tank was seen coming along Üllői Street, the petrol-soaked rag was lit and lobbed at the tank, frying soldiers inside.

Gyarmati did not see any fighting, but he did arrive soon after a fierce battle and he ferried the injured to nearby hospitals in his car. The euphoria Gyarmati had felt on the first day of the revolution was quickly ebbing as he saw its appalling human cost.

In Széna Square, Gyarmati helped build barricades from overturned wrecked train carriages and trams. He also met Lóránt Somóczy, a legendary water polo player who had represented Hungary nine times between 1935 and 1942. Somóczy was no friend of the communist regime, having spent three years in Recsk prison camp. He was starved, forced to sleep under bright lights, and given the "treatment," which involved brutal beatings with rubber pipes and other vile tortures. At night he slept in a cell strewn with excrement. During the day Somóczy worked in the granite pit, where he reduced rocks into fine gravel. If he did not meet his daily quota of two wheelbarrows of gravel he was severely punished. Somóczy never spoke about his experiences at Recsk. He didn't have to, as his body, once erect and sturdy, was now bent over. And he limped from a poorly healed fractured femur, which had been broken when he was thrown into a 60-foot (20-meter) pit. "You have to stop this and go to Melbourne," Somóczy insisted.[8] Gyarmati knew that Somoczy was right. Representing a free Hungary at the Olympic Games before the world would better serve the revolution than getting killed at the barricades.

Every athlete experienced the uprising in different ways.

Gymnast Erzsébet Köteles had two sons, 10-year-old Gyurika and 8-year-old Lacika. After lunch, she heard the roar of tank cannons. Worried that her sons could both be killed if they were in the same place, she quickly dressed the children. She took the youngest to her father's house in Zugliget on the outskirts of the capital, while her husband took their other son to his parents' home in Pest.

When she heard shooting, 16-year-old swimmer Zsuzsa Ördögh was at the Vörös Csillag hotel. Her family lived in the XII district, near Moszkva Square (now Széll Kálmán Square). The news was both good and bad. A Russian tank, returning to base after fighting in Széna Square, still had two shells left. It decided to fire them into an apartment building where Zsuzsa's parents lived. Shrapnel strafed the ground-floor kitchen where her mother had been preparing the midday meal. Minutes earlier, her mother had left the kitchen to attend the call of nature and was thankfully unharmed.

Water polo player Ervin Zádor walked home from the hotel to check that his family was safe. When his mother opened the door she slapped him across the face, angry that he risked getting killed in the crossfire.

Pentathlete Géza Ferdinandy received a desperate phone call from his mother. She, his two brothers, and his grandmother lived on Üllői Street, which was opposite Kilián Barracks, a center of resistance. Three Soviet T-34 tanks had arrived and were firing down the street. To reach the family apartment from the Vörös Csillag hotel, Ferdinandy had to cross the Danube River. He decided to cross at Petőfi Bridge. Unfortunately, like all the other crossings, it was under siege by Soviet tanks. The Russians were firing at anything that moved on the bridge. He crawled along the bridge, dodging bullets, and almost made it to the other side before turning back. He never got to see his family before he left for Melbourne.

Some athletes were simply curious and walked the streets to see what was happening.

Pentathlete Gâbor Benedek walked around Budapest on the first day of the revolution. At Petőfi Statue he listened to actor Imre Sinkovits recite the poem written for the 1848 revolution, thrilling to the words, "Stand up, Hungarians, the homeland calls!" As evening fell, Benedek noticed that even though some shop windows were broken, there was no looting. Arriving on Dózsa György Avenue, 500 yards from Hősök Square, he watched workmen with blow torches cut into the 24-foot (eight-meter) bronze statue of Stalin, just above his boots. Around the dictator's neck hung a sign that read: "Russians, if you are rushing off, don't leave me here!" Nearby, a communist bookshop was emptied of stock. And the collected works of Marx, Lenin, and Stalin were fueling a magnificent bonfire. At around 9:30 p.m. steel cables were attached around the statue's neck, and a lorry pulled it over. All that was left on the plinth were Stalin's boots. Once the statue was down, it was dragged through the streets of Budapest like a trophy. People took to the statue with hammers, breaking it apart. Someone had painted "WC" on the side of Stalin's dismembered head, an invitation to piss on it.

Other athletes soon discovered just how dangerous the streets of Budapest could be. Long-distance runners László Tábori and Sândor Rozsnyôi were walking down Lenin Boulevard (now Erzsébet Boulevard) where they were stopped by freedom fighters, who backed them against a brick wall, menacing them with their guns. The two athletes were wearing leather coats, which also happened to be the fashion choice of many plainclothes ÁVO agents. Such was the hostility towards the ÁVO that they risked being shot on the spot. They tried to explain that they were Olympic athletes. The freedom fighters were not convinced until

Stalin's statue was pulled down on October 23, 1956. It was then dragged around Budapest by protesters (FORTEPAN/Róbert Hofbauer).

a passerby, an old man, shouted at them, "Are you kids idiots or what? Can't you see you've got Tábori and Rozsnyôi?"[9] When they realized their mistake, the freedom fighters put away their guns and hugged the much-relieved athletes.

Less well known than Tábori and Rozsnyôi was fencer Jenő Hámori. He too was stopped at a checkpoint. As freedom fighters asked him for his papers, they noticed that he had a military ID card. He had to work hard to persuade them that he was really an Olympic athlete and not an ÁVO agent. Opening up his equipment bag, he showed them it contained his fencing saber, not the weapon used by the security police.

Some athletes actively supported the uprising. Pentathlete Antal Moldrich had quietly slipped out of the Vörös Csillag hotel one night. He made his way to the Lampart Paint and Enamel Factory, which he knew was a front for arms production. He passed on muntions he stole to the freedom fighters. Some of the Olympic shooters also left the hotel and went to downtown Budapest to target Soviet troops.

These were just a few of the incidents that athletes experienced over the course of the first phase of the revolution, which ended after five days when a ceasefire was declared. To everyone's relief, Soviet troops started to withdraw from Budapest.

By this time, many of the athletes were thoroughly traumatized and uncertain whether they wanted to leave for Melbourne. However, with the ceasefire in place, reformist prime minister Imre Nagy urged the athletes to continue to Melbourne, where they would be the first to represent free Hungary overseas.

Once the decision had been made to compete in the Olympics, athletes were directed to meet at the Grand Hotel on Margit Island, where transport would be waiting. The problem was that they were widely scattered. Some were living with their families. Others were still arriving from the Tata training camp. And the rest were at the Vörös Csillag hotel. As most public transport had been knocked out during the revolution, athletes who could not get a lift had to walk. Remarkably, they all arrived.

The hasty departure caught several athletes unprepared. Members of the modern pentathlon team, for example, did not have time to collect their saddles or boots. And over half the team had not been issued with their official uniforms.

Uncertain Times

While the athletes were arriving at the Grand Hotel, the team head, Gyula Hegyi, was informed the two French planes chartered to take them to Australia could not land at Budapest's Ferihegy Airport, which was still under Soviet control. Instead, the planes would wait for the team in Prague.

Freedom fighters in Teleki László Square.

Improvising, Hegyi hired five buses, and the team left at noon on October 29. Large Olympic flags were attached to the sides of the buses to ensure that no one fired at them.

After crossing into Czechoslovakia, a train took the Hungarian team to Nymburk, 28 miles (45 km) from Prague. They were billeted in the Secondary Technical College, where security guards patrolled the perimeter, presumably to ensure that the Hungarian athletes

Graffiti scrawled on the Szechenyi Chain Bridge. Translated, it reads: "Russians go home" (FORTEPAN/Pál Berkó).

did not contaminate the contented Czechoslovak populace with their dangerous counterrevolutionary ideas.

The morning after they arrived, the athletes held a meeting. The revolution had changed everything, and they were no longer willing to accept the authority of the communist officials. The meeting was convened in a large classroom; there were not enough chairs, and many stood, leaning against the walls.

At the start of the meeting, a three-member committee was elected: Gyarmati, running coach Mihály Iglói and discus thrower Ferenc Klics. The election of a revolutionary committee was a slap in the face for Gyula Hegyi and the other Olympic officials. Already overwhelmed by events back home, Hegyi was unsure about his future under the new regime in Budapest and was adrift. His mood darkened even further when he came under attack from a few athletes who accused him of being a communist apparatchik. Coming to his defense was fencing coach György Jekelfalussy-Piller, who was universally respected. Considered a class enemy because he had been part of the National Guard for the previous non-communist regime, he was rehabilitated largely because Hegyi supported him. Piller praised Hegyi's commitment to the Olympic campaign's success and downplayed his membership in the Communist Party. This ended attacks on Hegyi.

After their election, the members of the revolutionary committee showed little interest in running the team's affairs. Their election was symbolic, and Hegyi and his subordinates continued to administer the team, although their authority was much diminished.

A vote was then taken on whether the team should continue onto Melbourne. Most athletes were pragmatic. Having trained for years, they did not want to give up the opportunity of a lifetime. Moreover, it looked like the revolution had succeeded and that the Russians were about to leave Hungary. Others were not as confident that the Russians had given up but were too timid to speak up.

Next, the meeting decided the team would compete under the Hungarian tricolor with the Kossuth coat of arms at its center. This flag had been adopted by the revolutionaries. While not selected for the Olympic team, two well-known athletes had died during the fighting—István Hegedüs and József Nagy. The meeting decided to drape the flag with black ribbons to honor their heroic sacrifices.

Hegedüs's good friend, fellow pentathlete Gábor Benedek, called on team members to have no contact with Soviet athletes during the Games. They should not shake their hands during the competition. And should ignore them in the Olympic Village and at other Olympic venues. "The Soviet Union oppressed our little country and they murdered my friend," he told the meeting.[10] Hegyi's next in command, László Nádori, mocked the idea, arguing that the Soviet athletes were not aware of what happened in Hungary. Their only sin was to wear the communist insignia on their tracksuits.[11] Canoeist Ferenc Mohâcsi also disagreed with Benedek. "I do not believe that the Olympic Games should be an outlet for political animosity," he argued.[12] Finally, a compromise was found. They would not shake hands with Soviet athletes during competitions.

Those athletes who were close to the communist regime kept quiet. One of those was gymnastics referee István Sárkány, who confided in his diary that he was "shocked at the ingratitude, hate, and envy expressed by those at the meeting." He went on to remark that the Olympic athletes who criticized the communist regime had forgotten the privileges it provided them.[13]

Ágnes Keleti, who had won four gold medals in the Helsinki Games, had been stridently pro-communist before the revolution. Rather than keep quiet, she stood up at the meeting and, weeping, told her teammates: "I was fooled by the regime and used."[14] Many felt her outburst melodramatic and embarrassing. "We were one team all sitting on the same boat," responded Gyarmati, "and there was no need to go back over old history of who had supported the communists and who hadn't."[15]

The original plan was for the team to be taken to Melbourne on board two planes chartered from TAI, a French company. However, TAI demanded a $150,000 surety before the planes would take off.

As Hegyi only spoke Hungarian, he asked multilingual fencer Béla Rerrich to approach embassies of Western countries that might be sympathetic to their plight and provide the surety. Rerrich was accompanied by Nádori and fencing coach György Rozgonyi. Some embassies invited them in for a coffee but declined to help. Sometimes they didn't get past the front gate. At the Belgian Embassy, Rerrich was told that they were wasting their time. No Western government wanted to antagonize the Kremlin, which might interpret assistance to the Hungarian athletes as a hostile act. For Rerrich, this was a hard lesson in the brutalities of realpolitik and made him realize how alone Hungary was in the world.

In desperation, they approached members of the Czechoslovak Olympic Committee, who convinced their government to provide the surety. Rather than an act of generosity, it was probably motivated by the Czechoslovak government's desire to rid themselves of the troublesome Hungarians, who might act as a rallying point for local discontents.

The day before the team was to leave, a rumor circulated that heavy fighting had broken out once more in Budapest. Later that day Nádori saw a Czechoslovak newspaper with the headline "Hungarian counterrevolutionaries defeated. Bodies everywhere."[16] In Nymburk, athletes could only receive Czechoslovak radio stations, which provided them with scant details.

Few athletes trained. Some sat around, engaged in whispered conversations. Others played cards. Many wondered whether they had made the right decision to go to Melbourne.

With most of the phone lines down, Hegyi was the only one who could get through to Budapest, and he spoke to Béla Kalen, the only person left at the sports ministry. He was told that prime minister Imre Nagy had fled to the safety of the Yugoslavian embassy after the Soviet forces had entered Budapest early in the morning of November 4. The Kremlin had replaced him with János Kádár. "If it's János, then everything will be all right," he told his athletes.[17] Kádár had every reason to hate the Stalinist regime. In 1951 he had been arrested and brutally interrogated by ÁVO torturers. They had torn out his fingernails, shattered his teeth during beatings, and humiliated him by pissing into his mouth. In July 1954, after three years in solitary confinement, he was released. On October 25, 1956, Nagy had appointed Kádár General Secretary of the Party, giving the impression that he supported the new government's reformist program. Time would show that Hegyi was wrong, and over the next few weeks it became clear that Kádár had abandoned the revolution. Instead, he acted as the Kremlin's puppet and was determined to crush "counterrevolutionary elements in a reign of terror."[18]

There was no way, however, for athletes to know anymore what was happening at home. They could only speculate, based on poor and incomplete information they gleaned from foreign newspapers.

On the morning of November 5, still uncertain about whether they had made the right decision, the athletes gathered at Prague Ruzyně International Airport, where the first of two TAI planes awaited them. The other plane would leave the next day.

In the terminal, Hegyi read out the final list of athletes who would be traveling to Melbourne. When water polo player Árpád Domjan's name was not read out, his fiancée, swimmer Kato Szôke, was distraught. Not able to speak French, she asked multilingual Béla Rerrich to approach the TAI captain to see whether he would allow Domjan to stow away on board. The captain refused, explaining that he needed to consider issues such as insurance. Rerrich then told the captain that if he did not let Domjan on board the two lovers would "never meet in this life."[19] What Frenchman could resist such an appeal? The captain said that Domjan could go onboard and hide in the toilet until Istanbul, after which it would be too late to send him back. But there was still a problem. Hegyi was standing near the plane's stairs, making it impossible for Domjan to get past him unseen. So Rerrich enlisted the help of Hegyi's good friend Piller to distract him. While the two men played cards on the tarmac, Domjan sneaked on board.

No Way Back

The first plane, an Armagnac, took off with ninety-two passengers and one stowaway. Domjan emerged from the toilet when the plane landed in Istanbul. With no spare seats available, he sat on a wooden box for the rest of the journey. The second plane, smaller than the first, left the next day with sixty-three passengers.

The journey would take almost six days. The reason was that the chartered flights had no change of staff, and therefore the pilots and air hostesses needed rest during stopovers.

At every stopover, the athletes tried to obtain news on the situation in Hungary. People were being hung from the bridges. Budapest was in flames. Corpses littered Budapest. Looting was widespread. Refugees were streaming out of Hungary. Were these news reports exaggerated? Or could it be worse? "I wondered whether there would be a home to go home to," István Hevesi wrote in his diary.[20] Many athletes now doubted that they had made the right decision to go to Melbourne.

The two planes next met in Karachi. The weather was hot and dry, the city chaotic, and there were street demonstrations against the invasion of the Suez Canal. Vultures roosted on buildings.

After dropping off her luggage at the airport hotel, Éva Székely returned to the airstrip later that morning. There she approached a U.S. pilot who had just landed his fighter jet. She tearfully explained to him in fractured English that she was a Hungarian swimmer and had a two-year-old daughter at home. She begged him to take her back to Europe. "I'm military," he patiently explained. "I can't take civilians on the plane."[21] This answer only upset her further. To put an end to what was becoming an uncomfortable scene for the pilot, he told her to come back at midnight and he would take her to Italy. Székely returned to the airport at 11 p.m., but there were no American planes on the tarmac. The pilot never intended to take Székely anywhere. The local Pakistanis at the airport laughed at the petite white woman, wearing shorts and a sleeveless blouse, who sat on the tarmac crying as she finally realized there was no way back.

For Gyarmati, the euphoria he felt on the first day of the revolution was replaced by despair.

Arrival in Australia

When the first plane landed in Darwin on November 9, around fifty Hungarian-Australians stood at the quarantine barrier singing nationalist songs. The athletes were wearing the revolutionary Kossuth emblem on their coats and black armbands. Hugs and tears flowed freely.

The Hungarians then continued onto Melbourne. On their arrival they were greeted by several hundred Hungarian-Australians, some dressed in folk costumes, chanting, *"Huj! Huj! Hujra!"* (Go! Go! Hungary!).

After singing the Hungarian national anthem, locals mingled with the athletes, urging them to stay. They promised them good jobs, handed out business cards, and even gave them cash.

Once the athletes had settled into the dormitories in the Olympic Village, they sought out the communications room, where they hoped to speak to family members. Were they alive and well? Had Soviet tanks damaged their homes? For those who had joined the flood of refugees, had they reached Austria safely? With most of the phone lines down in Budapest, few messages were getting through, which further unsettled and depressed the athletes. They were desperate for information.

Unfortunately, getting information out of Hungary was almost impossible because the country's phone system was down. Until it was repaired, family members had to find an undamaged post office to send cables to Melbourne. In the first week or so after the athletes arrived, there was a trickle of telegrams. And even those were suspect. For example, István Sárkány, a referee in the gymnastics competition, received a cable that read "THE FAMILY IS FINE AND WE THINK ABOUT YOU. TAKE CARE AND PERFORM WELL IN THE COMPETITION. GABIKA [their son] HAS A GOOD APPETITE. YOU'RE WELCOME HOME."[22] Did this mean all was well at home? Had the cable been doctored? Or had the family prudently omitted news that could result in a visit from the ÁVO, who in all likelihood were intercepting telegrams?

Others were more fortunate and were able to be candid in what they wrote.

Distance runner László Tábori's older sister Erzsébet had a friend in the post office, so she was able to tell him the unvarnished truth. "WE ARE WELL. THE APARTMENT IS OK. IF YOU CAN STAY THERE, THEN STAY. THE SITUATION IS BAD. DO AS YOU THINK IS RIGHT." Like many of the athletes, Tábori worried about what might happen to his family if he did not return. He sent back a telegraph to his sister: "YOU COME TOO IF YOU CAN."[23] Erzsébet started to make arrangements to flee Hungary. On November 29 Tábori heard disturbing news from visiting journalist László Lukács. There was a dangerous rumor going around that the Soviets believed some Olympic athletes had fought their way through a ring of Russian tanks to escape Budapest. Lukács advised Tábori to lie low, which made sense as he did not want to jeopardize Erzsébet's chances of getting out. The story has a happy ending as Erzsébet escaped to Yugoslavia. After six months in a refugee camp, she was reunited with her brother in New York, with the help of *Sports Illustrated*.

For weeks, athletes' sole source of news about their families was from telegrams. They were relieved when, on November 23, phone calls started to come through. Once they could hear the voices of loved ones they could get a much better feel for what was really going on at home. However, making a call was anything but easy, with connections having to thread their way through at least five international exchanges. This frustrated callers and ate up time when they should have been training. To save time, athletes took turns waiting for incoming calls. Those who received good news were kissed and hugged, but the prevailing mood was somber as only a trickle of phone calls was getting through.

Valéria Gyenge, a gold medalist in Helsinki in the 400-meter freestyle swimming, received both cables and phone calls, but they did nothing to help her decide whether to return home or not. On the eve of the Games she received a telegram from her fiancé, Janos Garay, who had escaped Budapest and was in Vienna. He planned to immigrate to Canada and wanted Gyenge to meet him in Toronto, where they would marry. Totally in love, she said yes. Then, the night before the preliminary rounds of the 400 meters freestyle swimming competition, her mother rang. Unable to withstand her mother's tearful pleas, Gyenge promised to come home. Then another call came from her fiancé, who warned that if she returned to Hungary she would never get out again, and they would never be together. Again Gyenge promised him she would meet him in Canada. Emotionally a mess, Gyenge knew she would have to break her promise to one of the two people she most loved in the world. On the day of the final, Gyenge was in a daze as she stood on the starting block. And as she dived into the pool, her arms felt like they had weights attached to them. Not surprisingly, she came last. As Gyenge was about to get out of the pool, the timekeeper bent down to tell her she had an urgent phone call from Budapest. Her mother had relented and gave Valéria her blessing to go to Toronto.

When swimmer Éva Székely spoke to their daughter, Andrea, the two-year old pleaded, "Mummy, mummy come home quickly by airplane."[24]

In an act of kindness, Soviet sports minister Nikolai Romanov invited the Hungarians to the Soviet ship *Gruzia* where he arranged a radio linkup, using a Melbourne–London–Moscow–Budapest channel. Many Hungarian Olympic athletes were able to contact their families to make sure they were alive and well. However, they kept quiet about the help the Soviets had rendered.

Those athletes whose calls got through were relieved to hear that their families were safe.

For the first time since they left home, the Hungarians were able to obtain reliable news. After five days of fighting, the Soviets had staged a tactical withdrawal to Czechoslovakia and Romania, giving the impression that the freedom fighters had won. On November 4 they re-entered Budapest. This time they arrived with tanks that would not be vulnerable to Molotov cocktails and better-trained troops. They had learned from their experiences and would not be caught unprepared again. Over the next seven days the revolution was brutally crushed. An estimated 2,500 Hungarians were killed and another 20,000 wounded. By the time the borders were sealed, 200,000 refugees had poured into Austria and Yugoslavia.

As Soviet troops took control of the country, prime minister Nagy issued an appeal to Western countries for military intervention. Dwight Eisenhower, who had just won the U.S. election, ignored this appeal. Instead, he offered a few empty words of sympathy. Other Western countries also refused his appeal. Direct military confrontation with the Soviet Union was unthinkable. Even providing arms to freedom fighters would escalate Cold War tensions in ways that were unpredictable and dangerous.

Instead, Western countries looked at other ways to express their displeasure with the invasion of Hungary. Ten days before the opening ceremony, Melbourne's daily newspaper, *The Argus*, reported that seven countries were considering not sending their athletes to the Olympics.[25] Most were protesting the invasion of Hungary. For others, it was the invasion of Suez by Israeli, British, and French forces, which had occurred two weeks earlier.

These threats demonstrated that the Melbourne Olympics had been drawn into Cold War politics even before the opening ceremony.

CHAPTER 8

Should the Show Go On?

Sacrificial Lambs

In the Netherlands, the reaction to the Soviet invasion of Hungary ranged from bewilderment to outrage. In horror, Dutch listeners tuned into NCRV radio, where they heard a graphic account from foreign correspondent Alfred van Sprang, who reported from central Budapest.

Early on November 4, 1956, a cold Sunday morning, van Sprang was woken by gunfire, the roar of tank cannons, and MiG fighters strafing the streets. Like everyone else in the city, he was shocked to discover Russian tanks were once again in the streets wreaking havoc. The Red Army had re-entered Budapest from Romania after an absence of four days, determined to crush the revolution.

Starting at 8 a.m., van Sprang reported the drama as it unfolded. "This morning before dawn, the Hungarian capital had been rocked by the thunder of tank guns." By mid-morning, fighting had intensified around his hotel, and tanks were indiscriminately shelling buildings. Soon after, van Sprang ended his live broadcast and fled to the relative safety of the Dutch Legation, located on the outskirts of Budapest, where he continued to report. "Budapest is completely surrounded by the Russian army, and in many places in the city there is heavy fighting." He finished by saying that Prime Minister Imre Nagy's final appeal to the world was "not to abandon Hungary."[1]

Van Sprang's broadcast had an immediate impact. That same morning, churches were full as people prayed for the safety of Hungarians. Many took to the streets, some singing, others holding silent vigils, and there were large, noisy demonstrations in Rotterdam, Arnhem, Eindhoven, and Utrecht.

There were also protests, some violent, outside the Soviet Embassy and offices of the Dutch Communist Party in Rotterdam, Heemraadssingel, Utrecht, and The Hague, with the police doing little to prevent the destruction of property.

If there was a single dominant message to the government from protesters, it was that Holland should sever relations with the Soviet Union. The Dutch government had no appetite for taking concrete measures such as trade sanctions or

Dutch protesting the invasion of Hungary. The protest took place on the evening of November 5, 1956, in Eindhoven (Wim van Rossem, National Archives of the Netherlands/Anefo).

withdrawing its ambassador from Moscow. Instead, it preferred empty gestures to signal its disapproval, such as lowering flags on public buildings to half-mast. The government also decided to suspend all cultural and sporting exchanges with the Soviet Union. Parliamentarian Jan Peters went further and called on the Dutch Olympic team to be withdrawn if the Soviet Union was not banned from participating in the Games.

Neither the IOC nor the Australian Olympic organizing committee would entertain withdrawing its invitation to the USSR. So the only choice was a boycott of the Games.

The president of the Dutch National Olympic Committee (NOC), Hans Linthorst Homan, did not need to be pressured to act. That same Sunday, Linthorst Homan hit the phones to rally support. "We cannot compete against the Russians with their blood-stained flag," he raged. Linthorst Homan, understood that a boycott would not be popular among athletes. "It's hard, but we have to be hard in this harsh world," he argued.[2]

At 8 a.m. the next day, Linthorst Homan saw momentum for a boycott grow when he received a telegram jointly signed by the Dutch Christian Sports Union and the Dutch Catholic Sports Association. "DUTCH HONOUR WOULD BE DISGRACED AND HUMANITY BETRAYED IF AT THE NEXT OLYM-PIAD THE BLOOD DRENCHED RUSSIAN FLAG FLEW NEXT TO THE DUTCH FLAG."[3] They wanted the Russians to be banned, and Holland should withdraw from the Games if this did not happen. Cables of support for a boycott were also received from the Dutch Power Sports Association, the Royal Dutch Cycling Union, the Gymnastics Federation, the Dutch Federation, the Catholic Youth Council, and the Dutch Cultural Sports Association.

Alarmed at the growing support for a boycott, the IOC cabled Linthorst Homan reminding him that the "OLYMPIC IDEAL MUST PREVAIL OVER POLITICS." In response, Linthorst Homan asked the IOC: "HOW CAN SPORT PREVAIL OVER WHAT HAPPENED IN HUNGARY?"[4]

At 5 p.m. the next day, Linthorst Homan summoned the NOC board to a special meeting at Kasteel de Wittenburg, a hotel in The Hague. He told its members that the Dutch government would "welcome a decision by the NOC not to go."[5] The board agreed to a boycott, as did an extraordinary meeting attended by thirty-eight sporting federations, Linthorst Homan then officially announced that the Netherlands would boycott the Melbourne Olympics. "We have now seen the real face of Russia," he thundered. "It is a face that is not worthy of being met in sport, and it would be contemptible if we were to engage with them."[6] He argued that it was naïve to believe that sport and politics did not mix. "We believe in sportsmanship, but we are not stupid."[7]

After the meeting, NOC member Kees Kerdel said, "It is precisely the sacrifice made by the athletes that gives meaning to this decision."[8] As it turned out, not many athletes were all that thrilled with the sacrifice being imposed on them.

The NOC received objections from several yachtsmen, cyclists, and hockey players calling on it to abandon its boycott. They had no success. Others kept quiet, knowing the depth of feeling in the Netherlands against the Soviets.

The impact on individuals was severe, such as 18-year-old Cornelia "Cockie" Gastelaars. She was one of the fastest swimmers in the world, having broken the world record twice in early 1956. She fancied her chances for two gold medals in Melbourne in the 100-meter freestyle and 400-meter medley. When she found out she would not be competing in Melbourne she burst into tears. "I felt like there was no longer a floor under my feet," she recalled.[9]

She had been treated appallingly by the NOC. It callously intended to use her sacrifice and that of her fellow teammates to give weight to their political protest. Having trained six hours a day and gone to night school to not affect her Olympic preparation, Cockie's sacrifices were considerable.

No one from the NOC ever bothered to speak to Cockie about its decision. The only communication she received was weeks later when a letter arrived asking her to return her plane ticket.

Cockie was lucky enough to compete in Rome four years later, but she had passed her peak and was unplaced.

Once the decision to boycott had been taken, the NOC faced a difficult problem. An advance party of athletes had arrived early in Melbourne to complete their preparation. As winter was fast approaching at home, making outdoors training difficult, this was a practical plan.

Having recovered from their long flight, the Dutch team members sat down to a hearty breakfast in a dining room in the Olympic Village. They were decathlete Evert "Eef" Kamerbeek, high jumper Dini Hobers, sprinter Puck van Duyne-Brouwer and long jumper Henk Visser. They were joined by coach Jo Grootewal and team leader Dr. Wim van Zijll.

During the meal they were serenaded by the cooks, who enthusiastically, although not very tunefully, belted out *Hup Holland Hup!* (Go Holland Go!). They had borrowed the chorus from a popular football song, and they hoped it would become the unofficial anthem to cheer Dutch athletes to victory. The cooks were Dutch émigrés who had taken time off work to help. Like the rest of Melbourne's Dutch community, they were thrilled that Holland would be competing in Melbourne and wanted to do whatever they could to help the athletes settle in.

Over breakfast, while the athletes burbled away about what they had seen and done in the Village, van Zijll was unusually subdued, lost in his thoughts. After they had finished eating, van Zijll suggested they go outside. Sitting on a scant cover of lawn under a gray sky, he grimly read aloud a telegram that he had just received from the NOC. While plane tickets back home were being arranged, "EVERYONE MUST LEAVE THE OLYMPIC VILLAGE AND SEEK ACCOMMODATION ELSEWHERE. WEAR CIVILIAN CLOTHES AND IF POSSIBLE REMOVE YOUR BADGE … SORRY COURAGE."[10]

The athletes did not know how to take this announcement. "The man's going crazy," thought van Duyne-Brouwer. "Surely, he's making a joke."[11] When she realized he was deadly serious, she burst into tears.

The telegram felled the athletes as if they had been struck by a blunt instrument. Years of training wasted, and, having reached their peak for the Olympics, they wondered whether the opportunity would come again.

While unhappy with the decision, two days later, van Zijll dutifully carried through NOC's instructions. He moved everyone out of the Olympic Village and into the Victoria Coffee Palace Hotel, where they would stay until he arranged the flight back home.

Not all the athletes accepted the decision. Kamerbeek was so furious that he decided to defy the NOC and remain in Australia, even if it had to be as a spectator. Moreover, he had fallen in love with an Italian athlete, Paola Paternoster, and was keen to pursue the romance.

Back in Holland, news of Kamerbeek's intransigence was undermining the boycott, and Linthorst Homan was determined to force the decathlete to leave Australia immediately. But his task proved difficult as Kamerbeek's character had been forged by overcoming obstacles, and he was determined to stay.

Kamerbeek's road to the Olympic Games had been a difficult one, unlike his opponents. His main rivals were the Americans Milt Campbell and Rafer Johnson. They enjoyed university scholarships, the best facilities in which to train, and professional coaches. The other contender was the Russian Vasili Kuznetsov, who enjoyed first-class facilities at the Burevestnik Moskva sporting club and a cushy position as a lecturer at the Lomonosov Moskva State University, which allowed him time off to train. On the other hand, Kamerbeek was a real amateur or "*superamateuristisch*," as he described himself.[12]

Kamerbeek usually trained by himself in Utrechtse Heuvelrug, a forested area of oaks and beech trees near his home in Doorn. He worked out his own routines, many unorthodox. For example, he used ballet exercises to help with his flexibility and weightlifting to help with strength. And because his tracksuit pants hung too low to properly jump over hurdles, Kamerbeek took to wearing women's tights during training.

Getting time to train was another problem he faced. He worked a 48-hour week at the Philips factory as a fitter, and by the time he finished work it was getting dark. Without access to sporting facilities with outside lighting, he was restricted to indoor workouts, often in a makeshift gym at home.

Dutch decathlete Eef Kamerbeek remained in Melbourne when the rest of the team were recalled home to protest the invasion of Hungary (Eric Koch, National Archives of the Netherlands/Anefo).

His paltry salary left little money to buy training equipment. To save money, his mother darned the sleeves of his training jersey when they frayed. His aunt and uncle also helped, occasionally giving him 25 guilders so he could buy himself a steak.

After winning the Dutch Championship in 1954, Kamerbeek was considered one of the best decathletes the Netherlands had produced, and he had been looking forward to testing himself against the world's best in Melbourne.

Kamerbeek obstinately

resisted pressure from the NOC, even when it threatened to cancel his return flight home. He would rather wash dishes than surrender.

Three days before the Games commenced, the Dutch team flew out, leaving Kamerbeek alone in Melbourne.

Kamerbeek's resolve was finally broken when he received a telegram from his brother letting him know that their mother was sick. Thinking the worst, he quickly booked his flight home.

The first flight he could secure out of Melbourne was the day of the opening ceremony. As his plane flew over the main stadium, Kamerbeek could see the athletes gathered outside, ready to enter.

After arriving back in Holland, Kamerbeek rushed home to see his mother. She was quite well and had redecorated the house in anticipation of his return home. Only then did Kamerbeek realize he had been duped.

To Boycott or Not

Switzerland

In Switzerland, like in Holland, the news of the Soviet invasion of Hungary brought people into the streets to protest, particularly those living in German-speaking parts of the country.

There was no pressure, however, from the Comité Olympique Suisse (COS) to boycott. The decision was left to the athletes.

On November 7, at an extraordinary meeting of athletes in Lausanne, gymnast Josef Stalder held up over thirty telegrams he had received that demanded Switzerland boycott the Olympics. After a heated debate lasting over four hours, the vote was 15–5, with three abstentions, in favor of sending a team to Melbourne. Stalder was supported by gymnasts, rowers, and shooters. There was, however, a critical rider to the boycott motion: all athletes would have to agree to go to Melbourne, or none would go. With a minority of athletes, led by Stalder, adamant that they would boycott the Games, it was decided not to send the team to Melbourne.

A second meeting was held the next day. Stalder refused to change his mind and, as the decision to go was still not unanimous, the COS canceled the Swissair plane it had chartered.

IOC chancellor Otto Mayer tried to pressure the COS to abandon the boycott. "It is a disgrace that Switzerland, a neutral nation and the very country where the IOC has its headquarters, should set such a shameful example of political interference with the Olympic ideal."[13] IOC President Avery Brundage also cabled COS members, appealing to them to revisit their decision, pointing out the Hungarians were already in Melbourne and intended to compete.

Just like the athletes, the Swiss public was divided between French-speakers who, in the main, opposed the boycott, and German-speakers, who supported the boycott.

The German-language newspaper *Der Bund* criticized athletes for failing to understand how "deeply upset" many Swiss were over events in Hungary.[14] French newspapers took the opposite view. André Rodari described it as a "farce" in the *Journal de Geneve*.[15] In the *Gazette de Lausanne*, Colette Muret complained that "by surrendering to the temptation to make a virtuous gesture, the gymnasts have deprived our country of a magnificent opportunity of celebrating the Olympic ideal."[16]

Many athletes were upset with the decision to not compete. "We have made sacrifices, bought fresh clothes, suitcases, suffered wounds ... no, really I cannot find the right word which can describe this stupid and unjust decision," said fencer Werner Walter. "This is a heavy blow, and I'll take a while to get over it!" explained gymnast Roger Fehlbaum.[17] Some athletes who spoke out in public received hate mail. Pentathlete Werner Vetterli received an anonymous letter that warned, "If you compete against the Russians.... I'll torch your house."[18]

On November 11 the COS convened a third meeting, this time in Bern, to settle the matter once and for all. Although the vote was 13–5, with seven abstentions, those supporting the boycott stated that they would not stand in the way of those athletes who wanted to go to Melbourne. However, Stalder and nine others declared they would not go to Melbourne with the rest of the team.

But getting the Swiss team to Melbourne at this late stage was no simple task. The original Swissair plane was no longer available. All long-distance Swissair planes had been diverted to help with airlifting UN peacekeepers to supervise the withdrawal of Israeli, French, and British forces from the Suez Canal. Avery Brundage appealed to President Eisenhower to make a U.S. plane available, but this came to naught. Having exhausted its options, on November 16, the COS told the athletes that they would not be going to Melbourne.

The story does not quite end there. The vice-consul at the Melbourne Legation, Hans Steinacher, who also happened to be a Swiss fencing champion, announced that he was willing to represent Switzerland. The next day he arrived at the Olympic Village. In front of around twenty Swiss-Australians, he kissed the national flag. It was then raised, officially announcing the arrival of Switzerland's one-man team.

Back home, Steinacher's participation was mocked by Colette Muret, who wrote in the *Gazette de Lausanne* that "this solution may not be distinguished in itself ... its greatness frankly lies in its cheapness."[19]

A shy man and unhappy at being embroiled in a public controversy, Steinacher left the Olympic Village the next day. Moreover, he did not march in the opening ceremony and did not compete in the fencing competition.

With no one from Switzerland participating in the official proceedings, historians have wrongly claimed that Switzerland boycotted the Olympic Games. In fact, the majority of athletes voted three times in favor of sending a team to Melbourne.

Spain

On November 6, the Spanish government announced it would "suspend sending Spanish athletes to Melbourne for the XVI Olympiad" to protest against the "bloody horrors" of the invasion of Hungary.[20]

Its sincerity, however, was immediately questioned. "I'm only guessing," said IOC President Avery Brundage, "but I believe Spain's problem is one of finance."[21] There is an element of truth in Brundage's allegation. Looking back at earlier announcements shows that Spain was ambivalent about sending a team to the Olympics.

A year earlier, the Comité Olímpico Español announced that it would not send a team to Melbourne. It argued that holding the Games so late in the year would interfere with the studies of athletes, many of whom were students. Besides, it wanted Spanish athletes to concentrate on local and regional competitions.[22]

This decision was partially reversed on October 3, 1956, when the Comité Olímpico Español decided to send just four athletes, who they believed had a good chance of a medal. President Francisco Franco was not particularly interested in sport. Still, he reluctantly agreed as it offered Spain the best chance of winning medals for the least cost. The invasion of Hungary allowed Franco to reverse his decision, and on November 6, the Spanish government announced its Olympic team would not compete in Melbourne.

Olympic committees are meant to be independent of governments. But the decision to boycott was not made by the Comité Olímpico Español, although it meekly endorsed the government's decision afterward. This decision provided Franco with the opportunity to burnish his anti-communist credentials. It had the added benefit of avoiding the considerable expense of sending athletes to Melbourne.

Troubled Waters

The *Encyclopaedia of the Modern Olympic Movement* lists three other countries—Egypt, Iraq, and Lebanon—as boycotting the Olympics over Israel's invasion of the Sinai Peninsula and occupation of the Suez Canal by Israel, Great Britain, and France.[23]

A closer examination of the circumstances behind these so-called boycotts shows that there may have been other reasons why these countries did not send athletes to Melbourne.

No one was surprised when on October 12, 1956, Egypt announced to the IOC it was boycotting the Olympic Games as a protest over Israeli belligerence over its nationalization of the Suez Canal.

After the invasion, Egypt called on the IOC to have "nations guilty of cowardly aggression against Egypt" banned.[24] This would mean excluding France, Great Britain, and Israel.

However, an earlier newspaper report reveals Egypt that withdrew from the Olympics on August 13, 1956, well before it announced its boycott.[25] The reason, according to the Egyptian Superior Council of Youth and Sport, was "Egypt would not participate in the Melbourne games because no [sporting] federation can currently ensure an honorable representation of Egypt abroad."[26] The withdrawal, therefore, had nothing to do with politics and was motivated by the fear that the country would not win any medals. So Egypt's announcement, months later, was opportunistic, using the Olympic Games as a way to draw attention to Israeli aggression.

The positions of Iraq and Lebanon are less clear.

Iraq was no friend of Egypt, being its main rival to lead the Arab world, and hoped the Suez Crisis could be used to its advantage. When its ruler, King Faisal II, dined with the British prime minister on the day after the Suez Canal was nationalized, the Iraqi monarch advised Sir Anthony Eden to "hit Nasser hard, hit him soon, and hit him by yourself."[27] He was therefore privately pleased when, four months later, France and Great Britain occupied Suez. The involvement of Israel, however, made the war unpopular among ordinary Iraqis, and the king was compelled to show solidarity with other Arab countries by publicly condemning the invasion.

So why did Iraq announce that it would not be attending the Games? Its statement did not explicitly mention the invasion but gave as its reason the "grave situation in the Middle East."[28] This decision was most likely prompted by the country's inability to find a long-distance plane to take the Iraqi team to Melbourne, as the region was still a war zone.

Lebanon withdrew from the Olympic Games on November 10, claiming that it had done so "in solidarity with Egypt."[29] Despite being close to the West, the Lebanese government had little choice but to condemn the occupation of Suez, knowing that if it did not do so it would face street protests. But the Lebanese government did not cut diplomatic ties with France and Great Britain, as other Arab countries had done, so its outrage was probably confected.

So, like Iraq, Lebanon might have withdrawn from the Olympics in protest, but it is more likely it could not find a plane to fly its athletes to Melbourne.[30]

Who Blinks First?

At the same time as the IOC and Australian organizers were fending off boycotts, they faced an impossible situation when the two Chinas—the People's Republic of China (or Communist China) and the Republic of China (or Taiwan)—insisted the other should be banned from the Games.

This situation arose after the IOC, at its Athens meeting in 1954, narrowly voted to allow Communist China to join the Olympic movement. Taiwan was already a member. Later, Chancellor Mayer regretted the decision. "The quarrel of the 'two Chinas' has been, from 1954 on, the main burden of Olympism."[31]

The problem was that both Chinas claimed they were the only legitimate representative of the Chinese people, and the other was a pretender that should be thrown out of the Olympic Games.

Once Australia invited both Chinas to compete in Melbourne, each government engaged in Cold War games as each tried to provoke the other to blink and withdraw.

Even before the Athens meeting, Taiwan tried to intimidate the IOC, threatening to pull out of the Olympic movement if Communist China was admitted. This would have suited Communist China nicely. In the end, Taiwan decided not to blink, and on June 9, 1954, announced it would participate in the Melbourne Olympics. On December 20, 1954, Communist China announced it would also attend.

Four days later, Taiwan insisted the Melbourne organizers revoke their invitation to Communist China. On February 19, 1955, Communist China insisted Taiwan be banned from the Games because "the Chinese people and athletes will never recognize the so-called sports organization of the traitorous Chiang Kai-shek." The Melbourne organizing committee dismissed both demands. "If they both come to Melbourne next year, there will be no special privileges and they will have to rub shoulders with one another in the Olympic Village," announced the head of Melbourne's organizing committee, Wilfrid Kent Hughes.[32]

Communist China came up with another way to exclude Taiwan. It planned to send an advanced delegation to Melbourne and arrange to have its flag flying over the Olympics Village before the Taiwanese arrived. "This preemptory action was important because at the time we surmised that if we went, Taiwan would not go," wrote Liang Lijuan, senior journalist for the *People's Daily*.[33] As the wife of He Zhenliang, the honorary president of the Chinese Olympic Committee, she had inside knowledge of Communist China's tactics. However, traveling to Melbourne proved difficult, as few countries on the route recognized the People's Republic of China. Taiwan had the same idea and arrived first.

On October 20, 1956, a four-member advance party of Taiwanese officials arrived in Melbourne. They immediately rushed from Essendon Airport to the Olympic Village, arriving 20 minutes before the official opening of the Village, when the flags of countries already in Melbourne would be raised.

Once the Australian flag was raised, the flags of Malaya, Hungary, and Ceylon, whose teams had arrived before the Chinese officials, were raised next. After an impatient wait, the Taiwanese officials were happy when the Republic of China's flag was ready to be unfurled. Much to their horror, it was the wrong flag; it was that of the People's Republic of China. The head of the Taiwanese delegation, Hao Gengshen, cried, "Take it down; it's a mistake."[34] Kent Hughes fully understood the political significance of the blunder and ordered the communist flag be immediately lowered "even if I have to pull it down myself." Kent Hughes had another reason to be upset. He had colluded with Hao Gengshen to allow the Republic of China flag to be raised ahead of the People's Republic of China.[35] Politically sophisticated in the intricacies of the Cold War, he knew such a gesture would probably lead to Communist China withdrawing. This would not have overly concerned Kent Hughes, who was a fierce anti-communist.

The mix-up arose when Corporal Brian Agnew went to the Flag Locker to find the flag. He was told to hurry. In the locker he saw two flags labeled "China," but was uncertain which one to select. Taking a chance, Agnew picked one. As he was about to return to the ceremony, he was stopped by a correspondent for the *People's Daily*, Chao-Ling Zhang, who told him that he had the wrong flag. Agnew gratefully accepted the helpful Chinese journalist's advice and collected the other flag in the locker. After the incident, Agnew commented: "I didn't know the difference between the Red and Nationalist Chinese flags, so I didn't notice the mistake. I know the difference now."[36]

Once the wrong flag was lowered, Geoffrey Ballard, Deputy Commandant at the Village, returned it to the Flag Locker and picked up the correct flag. There he was met by Chao-Ling Zhang. "Why have you taken down my country's flag?" he asked. Angry at having been tricked, Ballard barked, "We will put up your flag when your team comes to the Village."[37]

Five minutes later, the correct flag was unfurled. While Taiwanese officials were still furious, they decided not to blink. They knew that Communist China's 92-member team was in Guangzhou waiting to fly to Melbourne should Taiwan pull out. Instead, they demanded an explanation and an apology, which Kent Hughes provided on the spot. He followed up with a written apology.

On November 4 the advanced party of three officials from Communist China finally arrived in Melbourne. Two days later the leader of the delegation, Jung Kao-t'ang, wrote an angry letter to Kent Hughes, objecting to hoisting the "flag of the Kuomintang clique [Taiwan's government] which has long been renounced by the 600 million people of China." He went on to complain that the Chinese Olympic Committee could not "tolerate this scheme of artificially splitting China."

Airily dismissing this petition, Kent Hughes informed Jung Kao-t'ang that the People's Republic of China would be identified as "Peking-China" while Taiwan would be known as "Formosa-China." This was the last straw. Jung Kao-t'ang attacked this decision as "unwarranted interference in the internal affairs of the Chinese people, quite unscrupuously [sic] changing the name of our country."[38]

With just over two weeks until the opening ceremony, Communist China withdrew from the Melbourne Olympics. There was no apology or effort by Kent Hughes to placate Jung Kao-t'ang. Instead, he shot back a patronizing reply. "I am sure you had no desire to give offense as guests to your hosts, and, therefore, I believe that someone has given you bad counsel." He obliquely blamed Communist China for the flag mix-up. "I was accosted by someone, who said he represented the Peking press, and who tried to tell me how to run the Village." Ingeniously, he added: "I am sure he was not your representative as he was rude."[39]

Both sides had played a ruthless game to provoke the other to blink. Finally, it was Communist China that blinked, unwilling to compete against what it considered its rebellious province.

On Uncertain Seas

Australians and IOC officials were extremely worried about these well-publicized boycotts. Still, they were thankful that none involved a major sporting power, or so they thought.

On October 31, 1956, sports minister Nikolai Romanov issued an instruction to Soviet athletes who were about to start their journey to Melbourne to stay where they were. No explanation was given.

This directive applied to athletes training in camps in Moscow and Tashkent. The unexpected and unexplained delay depressed the athletes. "Guys, we're never going to be allowed to fly," pole vaulter Vladimir Bulatov gloomily told athletes at the Tashkent training camp.[40] The plan was then to fly to Rangoon on board an Aeroflot plane and connect with a chartered Pan Am plane, which would take them to Melbourne. In Rangoon, Pan Am officials were in the dark when the athletes did not arrive.

This directive also applied to the *Gruzia,* a passenger ship, which was carrying to Melbourne most of the Soviet team and a few Eastern Europeans. A day before the ship was due to dock in Melbourne, its captain was ordered to maintain radio silence and cut the ship's engines until he received further instructions. Understandably, port officials became anxious when the ship failed to respond to radio requests to confirm its position and estimated time of arrival.

At the same time, a telegram from Moscow advised Orbit Travel Services in Australia to cancel accommodation booked for a group of sixty-seven Russian tourists. Again, no explanation was given.

The decision had been made by Khrushchev two days after Israel had invaded Sinai, triggering the Suez Crisis. "In Egypt, there is war," he told Soviet Premier Nikolai Bulganin in a phone conversation. "Australia is an ally of England, and our athletes will get arrested if they go there."[41] Soon after, Romanov arrived at the Kremlin and he was able to assure Khrushchev Soviet athletes would not be thrown into Australian jails.

After a hiatus of five days, Romanov ordered the captain of the *Gruzia* to resume the journey to Melbourne. Aeroflot aircraft left Moscow and Tashkent for Rangoon, connecting with Pan Am flights to Darwin, then Melbourne.

The first plane carrying Soviet athletes from Rangoon finally arrived at Melbourne's Essendon Airport at 1:35 p.m. on November 6, and any fears the Soviet team would be shunned were quickly dispelled. Waiting in the terminal were Australian Olympic officials, led by Sir William Bridgeford, who had gone through several packets of cigarettes anxiously waiting for the Soviets to arrive. First off the plane was basketballer Jānis Krūmiņš, keen to stretch his 7'2" (2.18 meter) frame after the tight confines of the plane, followed by the rest of the team. As well as the official party, they were greeted by a large crowd of supporters from the Communist Party of Australia and peace groups, who handed bouquets to the athletes.

The next day, the *Gruzia* berthed at Appleton Dock at around 7:30 a.m. The athletes were warmly welcomed by Australian officials and a handful of well-wishers. In the crowd there was also a photograph recording the moment for the Australian Intelligence and Security Organization (ASIO), the national counter-intelligence agency. ASIO was certain that Soviet agents were embedded in the Soviet team, and it wanted photographs of them, so they could identify foreign agents.

CHAPTER 9

Operation Griffin

Fans are Enemies

The following cable was received by the New York office of Time-Life Inc. on November 23, 1956: "ESTIMATES OF LIKELY AUSSIE FOOTBALL PLAYERS AVAILABLE AFTER GAMES VARY BETWEEN 20 AND 50 PERCENT OF TEAM."[1]

This cable was the first of many that passed between Coach Greg Turnbull in Melbourne and Charles Johnson of the Merion Cricket Club during November and December 1956. Taken at face value, they were about exhibition matches of Aussie Rules football in the United States, with the authors dwelling on which players would be joining the tour. Curiously, the numbers fluctuated from day to day, suggesting the Australian footballers were a flighty lot, uncertain about whether they wanted to go to the United States or not.

As it turned out, the cables had nothing to do with football but were coded to disguise their real purpose. They concerned Operation Griffin, which aimed to encourage Hungarian athletes to seek asylum. They would then be invited to join the Freedom Tour of the United States. And the names were changed to protect the real identities of those considering not returning home.

For Cold War warriors engaged in psychological warfare, high-profile defectors like Olympic athletes were high-caliber ammunition. After the Games, the authors of Operation Griffin intended to parade them around the United States, giving defectors an opportunity to speak to the media, giving voice to the horrors of communism. Their personal stories would be powerful and provide opportunities for anti–Soviet propaganda.

Encouraging Hungarian athletes to defect during the Games, though, was opposed by the Australian government, which feared that teams from the Iron Curtain could walk out. For this reason, the government banned the CIA from Melbourne, concerned that its agents might run an anti–Soviet operation. Instead, Operation Griffin was a private venture by Cold War warriors outside the ambit of the U.S. government.

Operation Griffin had been launched by Count Anthony Szapáry, who, in 1949, founded the Hungarian National Sports Federation. Based in the United States, the Federation encouraged athletes to defect and helped exiles continue their sporting careers in the West. Following the Hungarian Revolution, Szapáry wanted to extend the scope of his operations to the Olympic Games. Needing someone on the ground, he sent a senior member of the Federation, George Telegdy, to Australia.

Szapáry quickly realized that Telegdy needed assistance, so he approached *Sports Illustrated*. Part of the Time-Life company, the magazine was owned by Henry Luce, a fervent anti-communist who had publicly denounced the Soviet invasion of Hungary. Journalists from *Sports Illustrated* could help Telegdy by approaching athletes without drawing attention to the covert operation. Szapáry also wanted to tap Luce's deep pockets as he lacked the funds to house, feed, and fly the athletes to the United States. The pay-off for Luce would be that *Sports Illustrated* would get free publicity during the Freedom Tour and exclusive copy.

Szapáry's proposal landed on the desk of Charles Douglas Jackson, Luce's vice president, known as CD. Four years earlier, Luce had loaned his deputy to Eisenhower as his speechwriter during the 1952 campaign. After the election he stayed on to advise the new president on how to make best use of psychological warfare in the Cold War. CD immediately saw the propaganda potential of defecting athletes and committed to helping.

CD had another reason for wanting to support Operation Griffin. Following the Soviet suppression of the Hungarian uprising, he had urged Eisenhower to intervene. In response, the president told CD, "I know that your whole being cries out for 'action.' ... I can assure you that the measures taken there by the Soviets are just as distressing to me as they are to you." Eisenhower believed, though, that escalating the conflict would result in a dangerous confrontation with Khrushchev, and so he concluded, "But to annihilate Hungary ... is in no way to help her."[2] Frustrated, CD believed that Operation Griffin was a small way to embarrass the Soviet Union for its aggression.

Even though CD was no longer in the Administration, he still had extensive networks within the private sector, State Department, and possibly the CIA, who he could call to make the operation a success.

The code telegrams kept CD abreast of the progress of Operation Griffin. The code was not particularly sophisticated. Each of the Hungarian athletes was given the name of an Australian Rules footballer. The water polo captain Dezső Gyarmati became David Gregory, and his wife, the swimmer Éva Székely, was Edward Shawn. Had the KGB intercepted these cables its agents would have only needed a basic knowledge of Australian Rules football to know something was afoot. A quick check of the Australian newspapers would have shown these names did not correspond to any current or past players. Another flaw in the code was that male athletes were footballers from Victoria and women footballers from NSW. The problem was that, at the time, Australian Rules was not played in NSW, where rugby was its ruling passion. So the proposition that NSW had an Aussie Rules team worthy of touring the United States was risible.

CD became Charles Johnson, who was organizing the exhibition Aussie Rules football matches, which was code for the Freedom Tour. The Football Federation stood for the State Department. Coach Turnbull was George Telegdy.

By November 23 Telegdy had made some progress, as described in a cable sent to New York. It reported that up to half the team was thinking of defecting. This cable also warned: "AUSSIE FOOTBALLERS REPORTEDLY CLOSELY WATCHED BY FANS AND FOLLOWERS AND IT'S NOT EASY TO TALK TO THEM AT THE MOMENT." Decoding the cable, the "fans and followers" were the secret police.[3]

Home or Away

The Hungarian athletes were fully aware they were being watched by the secret police: ÁVO and possibly by the KGB. They also suspected that there were informers in their ranks. Consequently, those thinking of defecting put out their feelers discreetly.

Every athlete's circumstance was unique, and each struggled to decide whether to stay or return home. For some, their task was made a little bit easier when, on November 29, the new Hungarian government issued an amnesty, provided athletes and officials return by March 31, 1957. Telegdy used this announcement to tell athletes they could go on the Freedom Tour, which would allow them to see whether they liked the U.S., and to return home afterward should they wish.

For water polo player László Jeney the amnesty was a godsend. "It was a big decision to go to the US, and although I could not contact anyone at home to see what they thought, I decided to go and see what happens."[4]

However, not everyone took the amnesty at face value. Gymnast Erzsébet Köteles, for example, would have loved to have toured but did not believe the government would honor the amnesty and was "afraid of the consequences."[5]

The fear of consequences was real. A year before the Olympics, Ferenc Keleti, from the sports ministry, let athletes know "that their relatives would be subject to retaliation if they absconded."[6] This warning undoubtedly worried many athletes.

Responsibility for the team was squarely on the shoulders of Gyula Hegyi. As head of the Hungarian Olympic delegation, he knew the new regime could reprimand him, or worse if he failed to bring the team home intact.

His main consolation was that he was held in good stead by the athletes. While they accepted that Hegyi was a good comrade, they also suspected he loved sports more than he loved communism. He was a tall, stout man with a light dusting of snow-white hair and eyebrows that were defiantly black. Most of the athletes liked Hegyi and called him "*bácsi*" (uncle).

Hegyi may not know about Operation Griffin, but he did know many of his athletes were giving serious consideration to seeking asylum. In the vain hope of stemming the flow, Hegyi appealed to the athletes at a meeting held soon after the Games commenced. "Everyone can serve their country better at home," he argued.[7]

In the final week of the Games a stream of athletes knocked on Hegyi's door to tell him they would not return home. They were emotional meetings, and many athletes left Hegyi's room in tears.

The fencer Béla Rerrich told Hegyi, "I'm not a Communist, but you've treated me so well that I thought I'd let you know my intentions." He announced he was going to Sweden where his wife and two daughters were waiting for him. Hegyi replied, "I used to be a refugee [he had fled Hungary when Germany invaded], so I understand what you're going through." He then handed him a pack of unfiltered cigarettes, a pungent blend from home that only a Hungarian could love, and a garlicky Csabai salami, saying with a twinkle in his eye, "You never know when you might need it."[8]

Radio broadcaster György Szepesi believed he was out of favor with the new regime and turned to Hegyi for advice. "You have a younger sister here," said Hegyi. "If I were you I'd spend time with her." He went on to point out that Szepesi's Olympic visa did not expire until February 1957, so he could delay his return. Hegyi then quoted an old Hungarian saying, "He who manages to win time, wins life."[9] As Szepesi left, Hegyi handed him a bottle of Hungarian wine and one of his seemingly endless supplies of salamis. Szepesi took Hegyi's advice. To support his asylum application, he informed the Australian Security Intelligence Organization (ASIO) he wouldn't return home because he would be subject "to pressure to disseminate propaganda, which would be repugnant."[10] He then moved to Sydney and worked in his brother-in-law's café. In early 1957 the Hungarian government told him it would welcome him home. This should have been no surprise as Szepesi had, since 1950, been an informer for the Political Investigation Department, with the codename "Galambos."[11] So, forgetting his repugnance for being a conduit for communist propaganda, he returned to Hungary and resumed his career as a radio sports broadcaster and presumably continued his career as an informer.

Water polo player Miklós Martin also knocked on Hegyi's door. "Gyula bácsi, I've decided not to go back to Hungary." Practiced by now, Hegyi replied, "Good luck, but if you change your mind you'll always be accepted back home with open arms."[12]

As the final week of competition approached, Hegyi became increasingly worried the Hungarian team was unraveling. Out of touch with what was happening, he asked Éva Székely how many she thought would not return home. Unwilling to add to his anxiety, she equivocated, "Bácsi, I don't know." Pressed, she said, "Perhaps ten or even a few more."[13] She knew the number was many more, but seeing how fragile Hegyi was, she downplayed the situation. She was right to be worried, as Hegyi was teetering on the verge of a nervous breakdown and had turned to the bottle for solace.

Late one night, after an evening of meeting athletes who intended to defect, Hegyi went on an epic bender. In the early hours of the morning some athletes watched him stagger out into the forecourt of the Hungarian compound wearing his pajamas. Standing unsteadily before the flagpole, he solemnly saluted. He would not have been human if he was not worried about his future. And he had much to be worried about. In Nymburk, en route to Australia, he had not prevented the revolutionary committee from usurping his authority. With many athletes not returning to Hungary, the new government could accuse him of being weak and even incompetent. He had also made conciliatory comments to Australian newspapers that the new regime could see as giving athletes permission to defect. "There is no compulsion on anyone to return," he had told *The Argus*. "It is up to each individual to make up his own mind."[14] And here he was saluting the Kossuth flag in the middle of the night, the same flag that the freedom fighters had adopted.

The very fact Hegyi was meeting a stream of athletes contemplating defecting showed that Operation Griffin was making headway. But not all was well within the *Sports Illustrated* camp, as can be seen from a telegram that arrived in New York on December 6. It reported that the athletes' "CONFIDENCE IN COACH TURNBULL SEEMS BY NO MEANS UNANIMOUS."[15] Certainly, Telegdy (codename Coach Turnbull) was a difficult character. He also had an inflated opinion of his importance and promoted himself to the aristocracy, calling himself "Count Telekdi" and had even designed his own coat-of-arms. Athletes became upset when he tried to use Operation Griffin to promote the royalist cause. During a meeting with water polo players Telegdy tried to hand them badges of the Kossuth coat-of-arms capped with the royal crown, which was used during the war by the Arrow Cross dictator Miklós Horthy, who acted as regent for the exiled Charles IV. Telegdy soon found that the athletes were not royalists, which they associated with Horthy's fascist regime, and they dismissed Telegdy as a "fool" and a "joker."[16]

Another reason athletes did not take Telegdy seriously was that he couldn't answer their questions. When would the Australian government process their asylum applications? If they agreed to join the Freedom Tour, when would the State Department process the athletes' entry visas? When would the plane be available? What support would they have when the athletes arrived in the United States? After the tour, would they be offered jobs or university scholarships to support themselves? Unless they had answers to these questions, the athletes were reluctant to commit and then find that they had been left stranded.

Telegdy felt that unless he obtained satisfactory answers to his questions, the athletes might look elsewhere for help. On December 9 a cable arrived in New York, for once not in code, reporting that Telegdy had discovered "HUNGARIANS BEING TOLD BY RIVAL GROUP THEY SHOULD NOT WAIT FOR US. THAT THIS GROUP WILL TAKE CARE OF THEM BETTER AND GET THEM TO THE US QUICKER."[17]

The "rival" group was the International Rescue Committee (IRC), which was run out of New York. It is unclear, however, why it diverted scarce resources to Australia at a time it was being overwhelmed helping Hungarians fleeing over the border into Austria. One explanation was that it saw an opportunity for extracting propaganda, as had the authors of Operation Griffin, and the IRC may have been urged to get involved by the CIA. According to historian Eric Chester, during the Cold War the IRC was part of a covert network "helping the US intelligence community to implement a variety of clandestine operations designed to destabilize the Soviet Union and its dependent allies."[18]

IRC's agent was Harry Roskolenko, a writer who was in Melbourne on assignment for several American magazines, or so he claimed. Roskolenko was an odd choice. A GI who spent time in Australia during the war. A modernist poet. A writer of high-minded novels and trashy pulp fiction. A former Trotskyite, who, in the late 1930s, had become an anti-communist. He claimed to be in Melbourne on an assignment for *Sports Illustrated*. Yet he remained unpublished in that magazine. A flabby shambles of a man, he claimed that as a teenager he had raced against the Finnish Olympic multiple gold medalist Paavo Nurmi in Madison Square Garden. And he was a fraud, claiming to be a Ukrainian refugee when he had been born in New York to Polish-Jewish parents. Lastly, his name was not Harry Roskolenko but Robert Rosen.

Roskolenko spent time in the Olympic Village speaking to Hungarian athletes. But he does not appear to have had much impact, other than putting a few dollars in the pockets of some of the athletes who had eventually decided not to return home.

The IRC operation did not appear to be well thought through, and its authors seem to have no knowledge of Operation Griffin. Once CD became aware of the activities of the IRC, he probably spoke to Leo Cherne, IRC's chairman, who he had known for three years. In any case, the "rival" operation went no further, and Roskolenko returned to the United States.

As the end of the Games approached, the athletes were in a bind. The Hungarian team was due to fly out on December 7, a day before the closing ceremony, so they would need to commit themselves before that date. The Australian government was unhelpful. Up until the closing ceremony, "the Australian authorities would have nothing to do with us," complained Miklós Martin.[19] As one of the few Hungarian athletes who spoke English, he often interpreted for those in the team who wanted to defect. Understandably, athletes did not want to burn their bridges by declaring they were not going home until they were confident they would be granted asylum. With unintended cruelly, the Australian government denied them that luxury. And so they had to take a calculated risk that their status would be quickly resolved once the Games ended.

The Americans were more welcoming. Two days before the Olympics ended U.S. Consul-General Gerald Warner told the *New York Times*, "The United States would look with favor on any pleas for political asylum from any Olympic Games athletes—Hungarian or otherwise."[20] This was good news but did not resolve the question of asylum. Also, many athletes had entered Australia on Olympic entry papers and would need exit visas to travel to the United States.

Departures

After the closing ceremony, one part of the Hungarian team returned home, but not without drama, while the remainder hoped to have the asylum applications process and begin their adventure in the United States as part of the Freedom Tour.

Returning Home

Behind the scenes, as the departure date approached, officials within the Hungarian team had their own dramas. On December 6 Hegyi was told that French airline TAI wanted a £46,000 deposit by 6 p.m. that day before it would fly the team back to Europe. Getting so much money in such a short time from Budapest was impossible. But within three hours he was able to raise the funds: the USSR provided £44,000, and several Eastern European countries made up the balance. It was all in hard currency. Why this generosity? Had the Hungarian team been stranded in Australia for any longer, more athletes might decide to defect.

Special Olympic Attaché for the Hungarian team József Molnár took a suitcase with the money to a suburban branch of the National Bank of Australasia, located near the Olympic Village, to transfer it to the airline's account. He arrived ten minutes before closing. When the teller opened the suitcase he panicked. Alarms went off, and police quickly surrounded the building. It is not entirely clear why the teller became frightened. Thieves are not known to arrive with suitcases full of cash; instead, they come with empty suitcases which they hope to fill with money from a bank's safe. Nevertheless, he was a foreign gentleman, and the teller felt something suspicious was afoot, even if he could not quite work out the angle. Once Molnár was allowed to explain the transaction, the teller transferred the money to the TAI account before the deadline.

There is one more twist to the story. When the team met for the last time at the Olympic Village, Hegyi shocked everyone when he announced he would not be going home immediately. He claimed he needed to go to Sydney to have a cancerous lump behind his ear treated by a certain Australian specialist. It is evident to all this was a ploy to stay behind. Worried about his fate, he was just taking the advice he had been providing to the athletes: delay returning to Hungary until the political situation became clearer. After the meeting, senior officials loyal to the government confronted Hegyi and insisted he returns home. It was a heated exchange, and eventually Hegyi backed down.

Home, Defection, and Re-Defection

One prominent athlete who was on the plane to Budapest was the water polo captain Dezső Gyarmati. Returning home was risky as he was a member of the revolutionary committee, and in Melbourne he had been photographed arriving at the airport, wearing sunglasses and carrying the Kossuth flag.[21] He had also made anti–Soviet statements to the press. His wife, swimmer Éva Székely, also returned to Budapest, where their two-year-old daughter Andrea was being cared for by his mother. However, she was worried about what would happen to her husband. "At home you'll get into trouble," she told him. "The regime will hold you to account."[22] Like Éva, he was desperate to see Andrea, so they both returned with Hegyi and the remainder of the team.

In Budapest, there was a large crowd to welcome the team at Nyugati train station, and, ever the provocateur, Gyarmati wore the Kossuth badge on his overcoat for his homecoming.

Gyarmati had won a gold medal in Melbourne, which offered a modicum of protection against retribution by the government. For a while, life returned to normal. However, he was ostracized by the other members of the Honvéd Sport Club after security police warned them not to fraternize with him.

One afternoon after training Gyarmati was driving north along Margit Island towards Árpád Bridge when he noticed that a car was tailing him. Then a second car pulled in front of him, forcing him off the road. Four men emerged and forced Gyarmati to get into one of their cars. They then drove him to an empty house on the outskirts of Budapest. Once inside, they gave him a thorough beating, viciously punching and kicking him. The beating lasted 15 minutes, and the men left without a word of explanation.

Gyarmati was left on the floor, his shirt soaked in blood, and it was some time before he could get up. After being examined at the hospital, where they found no broken bones, he went home. It was now late at night, and as soon as his wife saw him she said, "Let's pack."[23] They woke up Andrea and collected his mother, and then left for the border. They all had valid passports so they were allowed into Austria. The Austrian newspapers ran a story about his escape, which included photos of his bruised back. At home, the newspaper *Nepsport* had a different story: it accused Gyarmati of fleeing his creditors, claiming they had beaten him up.

The only clue as to who beat up Gyarmati was that they spoke Russian. They may have been Soviet soldiers who had wanted revenge the hiding Soviet water polo players had received in Melbourne. It is highly unlikely they would be KGB, who would have arrested Gyarmati and taken him back to their barracks for a professional going over.

Once in Vienna, Gyarmati approached Gerald Smith, who was attached to the U.S. Embassy. Within a few days, Smith provided his family with all the papers they needed to enter the United States and arranged places on a plane to take them to New York, where Éva had relatives. However, when they showed their tickets and passports at Vienna airport they were pulled aside. As the plane took off they were left on the tarmac with no clue why they had been knocked back.

It took a few days to get hold of Smith, who explained that U.S. officials had received information that Gyarmati was a member of the Hungarian Communist Party, and it would take time for them to check this out. American officials eventually established the allegation was baseless, and Gyarmati and his family were allowed to board a plane to New York. Gyarmati later discovered that a number of his teammates, who had gone to the United States after the Olympics, had denounced him. It is possible they took this action in the belief he had sold out by returning to Hungary.

As soon as Gyarmati arrived in New York he stirred the pot. Quoted in *Sports Illustrated,* he said, "Uprooted and exiled as we are, we are free. We must cherish this freedom, not for any ulterior or personal sake, but for the sake of those who look to us for encouragement and support."[24]

It did not take long before Gyarmati decided he had made a mistake. "I felt lost in the darkness of the New York skyscrapers," he complained.[25] After two months, Gyarmati returned to Europe, hoping to get a coaching job. While he had attracted interest from clubs in West Germany and Sicily, no firm offers materialized.

With debts mounting, Gyarmati started to negotiate with the Hungarian government for his return. First, he was told he and his family could not return under any circumstances. After a second approach, he was told Éva, Andrea, and his mother could return without being punished, but he would be arrested and jailed. After some more negotiation, the government said they would be allowed home, but Gyarmati would be suspended from domestic competition for two years and banned from international competition. Realizing this was the best deal he could expect, he and his family returned to Budapest after 18 months away.

While he was suspended from playing water polo, Gyarmati worked as a bartender outside the entrance gates of the Csepel ironworks factory, serving thirsty workers thousands of pints of beer from a small booth. But as the 1960 Rome Olympics approached, and with many of its best water polo players now living in California, the government relented and allowed Gyarmati to participate in his third Olympics, in which the Hungarian team won a bronze medal.

United States Bound

While Hegyi and the team were winging their way back to Hungary, the Australian authorities decided that the athletes seeking asylum were in danger of being kidnapped by the KGB and held aboard the Soviet ship, the *Gruzia*. They were staying with Hungarian families and could easily be abducted.

The ship was due to leave on Monday, December 9, but the captain claimed there was a superstition that a ship should not sail on a Monday. This suspicious excuse only added to the anxiety of Australian officials and police.

At 2 a.m. Sándor Hetyei, head of Council of Hungarian Associations in Australia, was woken up by Wilfrid Kent Hughes, chairman of the Olympic organizing committee, and two police officers. Fearing for the safety of the Hungarian athletes, they asked him to locate those athletes billeted with local Hungarians. Over the next few hours Hetyei, accompanied by police, knocked on doors around Melbourne. Even when they tracked down an athlete, they had to convince him or her they were Australian officials intent on protecting them, not KGB agents in disguise determined to force them on board the *Gruzia*.

Most of the athletes returned to the Olympic Village, where they were placed in protective custody in the U.S. compound on the aptly named Liberty Parade. All cars arriving and leaving the Village were checked by gatekeepers; armed guards circled the compound, and security guards slept in the dormitories. Even the wives of security staff were enlisted to stay with the female athletes. The protective cordon remained in place until after the *Gruzia* sailed.

On December 10 the athletes were interviewed at the Village by Australian immigration officials, who promised, now the Olympics were over, to quickly process their asylum applications. But if they wanted to go on to the United States to participate in the Freedom Tour, they would require visas from the State Department, which could take considerable time.

Lengthy delays might jeopardize the whole operation as athletes might decide to drop the idea of participating in the Freedom Tour. This would have robbed CD of the propaganda dividend he hoped the United States would pocket from Operation Griffin. Working through his contacts in the State Department, CD tried to cut through the red tape. Tracy Voorhees, who was handling the matter from the State Department, resented the pressure being put on him by CD. There were genuine refugees in the queue "who have had their horses shot out from under them," Voorhees explained, and he did not believe the athletes' situation was "anywhere near the desperate or urgent as the plight of refugees in Austria."[26] CD was a very persuasive man with powerful friends in the Eisenhower Administration, and he eventually pressured Voorhees to allow the Olympic athletes to jump the queue.

Once the formalities were out of the way, a total of thirty-four Hungarian athletes and officials, four Romanian water polo players, and one Czechoslovakian were ready to depart for the United States.

A Pan Am plane had been waiting in San Francisco for the immigration formalities to be completed before it flew to Melbourne to pick up the athletes.

Who paid for the charter flight out of Australia, however, is a mystery. A document from *Sports Illustrated* disclosed that CD "scrounged" a plane, suggesting the head of the airline company, Juan Trippe, had agreed to carry the cost.[27] Trippe was involved in several private anti-communist groups, and it would not be surprising if he was willing to support Operation Griffin. The problem with this explanation is that the U.S. Civil Aviation Authority rules made it illegal for Pan Am to offer free flights. When questioned, its director in the Central Pacific region denied Pan Am was covering the costs. "Someone must be paying for them," he responded without naming who had picked up the bill.[28] So who was the anonymous benefactor able to cover the cost of the chartered plane, which must have been several thousand dollars? While there is no evidence, the tantalizing possibility is that CD used his excellent contacts within the CIA to secure funds for the charter from the pools of black money it did not have to account for. Or a CIA front picked up the bill.

The plane departed at 2:30 p.m. on December 23 from Melbourne.

Operation Griffin was not the only instance of psychological warfare being waged in Melbourne, and the KGB and Eastern European spy agencies were kept busy, as was ASIO.

CHAPTER 10

Games Within the Games

Spy v. Spy

Over the course of the Olympic Games, the Australian Security Intelligence Organization (ASIO) would face off against communist intelligence agencies. So one set of games was played on the fields, in swimming pools, and sporting arenas, between athletes who were all striving to win. There was another set of games played in the shadows, away from the public gaze, between the KGB,[1] Eastern European security agencies, and ASIO.

Before the Olympics, ASIO was alarmed at the number of auxiliary staff that the Soviet Union intended to accompany its athletes. Supporting 314 competitors were 206 coaches, judges, physicians, masseurs, and interpreters. Also, Soviet journalists and tourists would be in Melbourne for the Games. How many of them were KGB agents? And of the athletes, how many were informers? Officials with Eastern European teams would also have been intelligence agents.

During the Olympics, ASIO ramped up its counterintelligence efforts by launching Operation Robin Redbreast.

What would have come as a surprise to each side, had they known the objectives of the other, was that they both hoped for similar outcomes.

In Melbourne, the KGB's main focus was defensive—to discourage Soviet athletes from defecting. Security agencies from other Iron Curtain countries had the same objective. Even had the KGB wanted to, it was too short a period, and too many eyes were fixed on Melbourne for it to undertake offensive espionage operations. Defections, the KGB knew, would be exploited by the USSR's enemies, and it was willing to deploy significant assets in Melbourne to manage this threat.

By perverse logic, ASIO probably hoped that the KGB would succeed. Otherwise, defections could become a political minefield and tarnish the reputation of the "friendly" Games, as Australians hoped they would be remembered.

A month before the Olympics opened, Prime Minister Robert Menzies approved a proposal put to him by ASIO Director-General Colonel Charles Spry.

It would be tragic, indeed, if the premature acceptance of an applicant for political asylum before the Games had begun, or indeed before they had ended, were to result in the withdrawal of a whole team in protest. I am thinking, in particular, of the Soviet team. To avoid this contingency, I would recommend that where such a course is practicable an applicant for political asylum should be encouraged to defer his final break until the competitive events are over.[2]

His proposal was accepted. Nevertheless, the government realized it could not turn its back should a defector come forward before the Games ended, so safe houses were made ready for just such a contingency.

Although ASIO had good reason to believe KGB agents would be occupied keeping tabs on their own athletes, it still wanted to know exactly what they were up, which became the prime preoccupation of Operation Robin Redbreast. After all, you can't have foreign agents on your turf without keeping an eye on them. The operation was headed by Michael Thwaites, director of ASIO's counter-espionage branch, known as B2.

In the run-up to the Olympics, Thwaites asked Vladimir and Evdokia Petrov to help identify agents who might enter Australia as part of the Soviet contingent. Before they defected in April 1954, Vladimir was a lieutenant colonel in the KGB, and Evdokia, a captain. So they were well placed to identify intelligence agents, having worked in Moscow as well as overseas.

Thwaites had got to know the Petrovs when he spent 18 months holed up in a safe house in Palm Beach, a Sydney suburb, debriefing them and ghosting their book *The Empire of Fear*.[3] It was published in early 1956 and was designed to evoke sympathy for the Petrovs while painting a dark picture of the communist system they had fled. The Australian government's involvement in helping produce this book shows that it was willing to engage in psychological warfare when given the opportunity.

While Thwaites admired the Petrovs, others found him easy to dislike. Dr. Michael Bialoguski, who he had helped engineer their defection, detested Vladimir. "No sign of expression or emotion passed across Petrov's large face. When he laughed, he sounded hearty, but laughter never showed in his eyes. He looked at the world suspiciously, and talked little." He also discovered that the ex–KGB agent was an obnoxious drunk and a womanizer, with a taste for prostitutes.[4]

To execute Operation Robin Redbreast, photos of Soviet athletes, officials, and journalists were sent to the Petrovs so that they could identify intelligence agents. ASIO was particularly interested in those who were part of the First Main Directorate. This KGB unit conducted surveillance over the "soviet colony" (SK—Sovetskaya koloniya), which included any Soviet citizen who lived overseas, either temporarily or permanently. ASIO feared that the KGB could target anti-communist émigrés.

The Petrovs were not the only source that ASIO tapped for information. It used its own blacklist of intelligence operatives, a CIA directory of Soviet officials abroad, a list provided by MI5 of foreign agents who had served in the UK, and the 1955 compendium *Soviet Political Leaders: Biographic Directory*. In addition, ASIO had been handed reports written by Yuri Rastvorov, who had defected to the United States in January 1954. He had been both a MVD agent and a tennis player, so he understood how Soviet security agencies exerted control over sporting teams competing overseas. These reports helped ASIO plan its counter-espionage operations.

In the case of the Petrovs and Rastvorov, their information was at least two years out of date. Moreover, it would have been surprising if they could remember the faces of the hundreds of KGB agents they had come across during their careers. As for the Petrovs, they may have exaggerated the number of agents they recognized to convince ASIO they were still useful. The other problem with the Petrovs was their reliability. Derek Hamblen, MI5's security liaison officer stationed with ASIO, reported that Vladimir was "inaccurate, vague, and erratic." He judged that Evdokia was a little more reliable.[5]

From information collected from various sources, ASIO believed that there were forty-six confirmed agents in Melbourne. Another thirty were suspected to be part of the Soviet intelligence community. A further sixty-two individuals had once been intelligence operatives and might still be active. ASIO also identified ten agents in the delegations from other Iron Curtain countries and twenty-two suspected agents.[6] As for the number of informers, this was unknown. The high proportion of intelligence officers was not unusual and reflected the paranoia of communist officials.

With the benefit of hindsight it is possible to see that the quality of the information provided to ASIO was not always reliable. For example, Alexei Adjoubei was identified as a journalist from *Komsomol Pravda*, and Khrushchev's bastard son, conceived during an affair he had in Kyiv in the early 1920s.[7] Had ASIO looked at the public record it would have discovered that Adjoubei was born in the Ukraine in 1924 and married Nikita Khrushchev's youngest daughter Rada in 1949. By 1956, he was a prominent figure in Moscow society. Another KGB agent in Melbourne was Major Vasili Mitrokhin, whose name was on the passenger manifest for the *Gruzia* but not on any ASIO list. He had been a foreign intelligence officer since 1948.

Scandal in Paradise

Even if the information the Petrovs provided was, at times, out-of-date and inaccurate, they were assets that ASIO had an obligation to protect. With the

Soviet officials photographed by ASIO as they arrived in Melbourne at Essedon Airport (courtesy National Archives of Australia. NAA: A9626, 827).

arrival of enemy agents into Australia, ASIO worried that there was "the possibility of such specialists [KGB hit men] being included in the Soviet party, who would be able to make surveys and plans for later assassination," of the Petrovs.[8]

Vladimir Petrov was certain that the risk of assassination was more immediate. He particularly feared KGB's 13th Department tasked with *Mokrie Dela* (liquid affairs): abductions and assassinations. His fear was well-founded. According to a CIA document describing the 13th Department, "The Soviets have gone to great lengths in the past to silence their intelligence officers who have defected."[9] Petrov knew that it was normal for defectors to be charged with treason and tried in absentia. The sentence was always death.

In *Empire of Fear*, written before the Olympic Games, Petrov alerted his readers to the activities of the "assassination department," presumably referring to the 13th Department. He wrote that should he or Evdokia die suddenly, "the whole world will know that our death was deliberately planned by a Government which regards political murder as a normal way of dealing with those who differ from it."[10]

ASIO understood the need to protect the Petrovs, as well as to be realistic about the risks. "An occasion like the Games would seem most unsuitable, from the point of view of the Soviet Government, for an attempted assassination in

Vladimir Petrov and Evdokia Petrov inside the safe house. During the Olympic Games they identified KGB agents for ASIO (courtesy National Archives of Australia. NAA: A6285, 11).

view of the publicity it would arouse." However, ASIO believed "that a special appeal might be made to Mrs. Petrov to make contact with the Soviet authorities for news of her family."[11] She was homesick, and ASIO worried that the KGB might try to entice or even blackmail her into returning to Moscow. Just as the defections of the Petrovs had been a major Cold War win for Australia's fledgling spy agency, her re-defection would be humiliating for ASIO. It would also provide the KGB with an opportunity to debrief Evdokia and find out what secrets she and her husband had divulged.

As a precautionary measure, ASIO relocated the Petrovs away from Melbourne to Southport in Queensland for the duration of the Games.

One evening, the Petrovs were in the kitchen arguing. This was not unusual, as both were haunted by guilt. Vladimir never wanted to defect. He was a loyal servant of the Motherland but defected because he believed he would be purged should he return home. Petrov felt bad about betraying the Soviet Union and allowing himself to be used for anti-communist propaganda, but that was the price of finding a safe haven. As a result, he drank heavily (although admittedly he had been an alcoholic beforehand). Evdokia regretted defecting, which she believed may have endangered the lives of her mother and younger sister.

On this particular occasion, it is not clear what the row was about, but it ended when Vladimir stormed out of the apartment. There are two versions of what happened next.

According to Vladimir, he went to a local pub, had a couple of beers, and was attacked as he returned home. He was then picked up by police, who released him at 5 a.m. This story was a concoction, a habit that came as second nature to the ex–KGB agent.

ASIO pieced together the true story from witnesses. After leaving the house, Petrov went to the Surfers Paradise Hotel, where he had quite a few more than a couple of drinks. Returning to the safe house, he passed an apartment where he heard music, and he may have assumed that a party was in progress. To him, that meant free booze and women. There was no party, just a record player on loud. The apartment's occupier, Sergeant Bill Thompson, a serviceman, asked Petrov to leave. When he wouldn't, Thompson tried to eject him by force. Soon two neighbors joined the fray, with Petrov putting up a game fight against the odds. After a wild swing, Petrov fell on his face. Then the three men jumped him and held him down. The only injuries Petrov sustained were a lacerated lip, abrasions to his ribs and back, and a bloody nose.

When the police arrived they found a portly man, agitated, wearing just his underpants and shirt. They handcuffed him and threw him into the back of the police van. At the police station he was charged with being drunk and disorderly. In his statement, Petrov gave his name as "Jack Olson" and told police that he believed he was entering his apartment. But he refused to provide them with his address. After spending the night in a cell to sober up, the police released Petrov early the next morning on 10 shillings bail.

It did not take long for journalists to realize that "Jack Olson" was none other than Petrov, and the next day the incident was sensationalized by the newspapers, leaving ASIO red-faced.

The day after the newspaper stories appeared, ASIO's director-general Colonel Spry wrote a groveling letter that started, "My dear Mr. Prime Minister. No doubt you have seen in the newspapers a report to the effect that a person, who gave his name as V. PETROV, was charged with drunkenness in the Southport police court on November 28, 1956. I regret to say that the person concerned was our Vladimir PETROV."[12] The letter went on to accuse Petrov of being "psychopathic." Covering his own backside, Spry assiduously stepped around taking responsibility for the fiasco.

Spry understood the politics and knew that the government was most unhappy with ASIO over this incident. In May 1954 the Menzies government had won the election, helped along by the anti-communist scare campaign it unleashed in the wake of the Petrovs' very public defection. Should this incident reveal Petrov was an alcoholic then his value would be questioned.

On the same day, Spry wrote a ferocious letter to Petrov. "I personally am fast reaching the end of my tolerance and sympathy for your predicament. You have received a great deal from our country: safety, protection, subsistence, and many kindnesses. Any further acts such as this will utterly destroy my little remaining patience." Spry ended his letter by warning that if there was "another scandalous act, I intend to reconsider your position in relation to my Service."[13] Petrov was being threatened to be turned out into the cold, a possibility that terrified him.

Following this incident, the Petrovs were discreetly transferred to a new safe house nearby, and there were no further incidents.

The Tedious Business of Spying

Back in Melbourne, with the help of the information provided by the Petrovs, ASIO set about the tedious, time-consuming, and labor-intensive business of surveillance.

In the reports collected by ASIO during the Olympics, there were a few gems buried in the dross of inconsequential overheard conversations and drab reports by informers. Much of what ASIO agents recorded was little more than gossip and snippets of irrelevant banalities. For example, there was an interview report with a Russian-speaking chauffeur who drove sports minister Nikolai Romanov and other senior officials between Olympic venues. She reported that Romanov was courteous and even cracked a joke with her. However, she was unable to hear any conversations because they were whispered, and they were drowned out by the car radio, which was on all the time. Another informant reported a conversation in which rowers complained to their coach Konstantin Kroupine about their per diems. And an ASIO agent overheard a conversation in which a Soviet official said that Hungarian discontents would be punished on their return home. Most ASIO reports were like these: unreliable and of little practical use.

Over the five weeks that the Soviet team was in Australia, ASIO devoted its limited resources to collect thousands of pages of intelligence but undertook little analysis, undermining the effectiveness of Operation Robin Redbreast. For example, by the end of the Games, ASIO did not even know who headed the KGB's operation in Australia, although it suspected Yuri Filimonov, who accompanied the Soviet Union's temporary envoy Dimitri Zaikin. Filimonov spoke English, dealt with politically sensitive matters, and received reports from the heads of other Iron Curtain countries on security matters.

As ASIO kept watch on KGB agents, so KGB agents kept watch on Soviet athletes. However, they had to be discrete as athletes were also fodder for the Soviet propaganda machine, which wanted its athletes to embrace the Olympic ethos of international peace and friendship. And that meant mixing with athletes from other countries. These encounters, however, were confined to carefully selected athletes and were carefully choreographed. For example, even before the Games started, sixty Soviet athletes trooped over to the Australian section of the Olympic Village and handed them gifts and badges. An hour later, Soviet officials entertained U.S. officials in their dining room, where vodka flowed freely. Welcoming his American guests, Soviet athletics coach Leonid Khomencov told them, "We are preparing sportsmen, and hope to advance the honor of the Soviet [*sic*] by winning at the Games, but it is more important that friendship be the first winner."[14] The Recreation Hall also saw dances in which Soviet athletes were taught to jive by Americans. On another occasion there was a friendly game of table tennis, with an Australian and Russian at one end and an Italian and Romanian at the other.

Other than such staged events, Soviet athletes did not mix freely with competitors from Western countries. According to one ASIO source, "there were severe restrictions in regard to the Soviet athletes 'fraternization with other competitors, spectators, and even official interpreters and officials.'"[15]

Defections were a constant worry for KGB agents, as they knew that anti-communist émigrés were actively trying to encourage athletes to stay in Australia. However, by carefully weeding out athletes who might be susceptible, these attempts to engage with athletes failed.

For example, in downtown Melbourne, émigrés approached Latvian basketballers Valdis Muižnieks, Maigonis Valdmanis, and Jānis Krūmiņš, who were standing outside Myer emporium admiring the Christmas display. The athletes were told they would have a better life if they stayed. The basketballers quickly ended the conversation. An hour later, they were stopped by another Latvian-Australian, but again they cut the conversation short and moved on.

In another encounter, weightlifter Vasili Stepanov stepped out of the Olympic Village to buy some cigarettes. He did not speak English and asked whether anyone in the store spoke Russian. Two men offered to help. After he had bought his cigarettes, one of them asked whether he had anything that obliged him to return home. He explained he had a wife and children. "It doesn't matter," he was told. "Stay here and you'll live happily ever after." One of the men then reached into his pocket and pulled out a large wad of money. "You bastard!" Stepanov screamed at him. "I'll make cat mince out of you, and no surgeon will be able to put their pieces together."[16]

ASIO was also worried by the activities of anti-communist émigrés because they may "embarrass the [Australian] government as the host at the Games."[17] Protests, in particular, were a worry. The KGB was also concerned about protests but could do little other than complain about "provocateurs."

The first protest occurred after the *Gruzia* arrived, when anti-communists stood on the dock, chanting and harassing anyone boarding or leaving the ship.

Another demonstration occurred at the entrance of the Olympic Village, where the Hungarian flag was vandalized. Hungarian émigrés had climbed up the flagpole and cut out the communist symbol at its center.

Then, a day before the closing ceremony, long-distance runner Vladimir Kuts attended a function in his honor, organized by the Australian Soviet Friendship Society. A table had been set up where those attending could leave presents for Kuts. Gifts included a boomerang and a stuffed koala. There was also a small box on the table, nicely wrapped and tied with a red ribbon. It was unclear who had placed it on the table. When Kuts opened the box, it contained a dead rat covered in yellow paint.

There is a postscript to this episode. When the Soviet team returned home, this incident became useful fodder for the propaganda machine. In an article published in *Literaturnaya Gazeta*, this incident was described, with some embellishments. The CIA was accused of being behind the incident. Rather than a single rat, the number had increased to eight, and they were smeared with red, not yellow, paint. And the rats were scampering around, not immobilized by rigor mortis. "This savage, hooligan prank stirred all persons at this banquet with loathing towards the provocateurs," reported the magazine.[18]

The article also made other sweeping accusations. It claimed a "team of American professional spies and provocateurs headed by their captain—the chief of the CIA in the USA, Allen Dulles—was flown there [Melbourne]."[19] This was untrue as ASIO had explicitly banned the CIA from being in Melbourne for the Games, and Allen Dulles never visited Australia. Then there were allegations that "American agents tried to plant on our young men and women secret documents and photos of military installations in order to accuse them of spying."[20] Evidently, they did not do a particularly good job because no Soviet athletes were caught in possession of Australian military secrets. The CIA was also accused of spreading anti–Soviet literature around the Olympic Village. This charge has an element of truth to it. Anti-communist literature *was* circulated around the Village, but it was likely to have been planted by local anti-communist émigrés rather than the CIA.

Operation Wren

ASIO was anxious about the welfare of the Hungarian athletes. So it launched Operation Wren, which involved monitoring the activities of ÁVO and the KGB to ensure that no Hungarian seeking asylum was being intimidated.

The situation within the Hungarian camp was chaotic. The manager of the Olympic team, Gyula Hegyi was unwilling to assert his authority over athletes and was often drunk. While other senior officials tried to step into the breach, they had little success.

ASIO did not know that when the revolution broke out in Hungary, seven

ÁVO agents, due to go to Melbourne, were recalled to Budapest to help combat freedom fighters. Athletes were substituted in their places on the understanding they would act as informers. One of those informers was a fencer, whose code name was "Somogyvári." His controller notated Somogyvári's report, "It contains little useful intelligence and resembled a travel log."[21] This may have been deliberate as Somogyvári was probably unwilling to inform on his teammates.

Unlike Operation Robin Redbreast, ASIO was flooded with information from Hungarian athletes, keen to denounce possible ÁVO agents in their midst. Initially, this must have seemed like a gift to ASIO; intelligence laid out on a silver platter. But soon, ASIO was swamped by contradictory reports—some accurate, but most just gossip or motivated by malice, as a way of settling old scores.

From its informants, ASIO was handed the names of seventeen officials and coaches who were allegedly ÁVO agents or informers. Most of these officials were not ÁVO agents but just trying to do their job of restoring discipline within the team. Others were loyal communists or patriots just trying to protect the honor of their country.

There was probably just one confirmed ÁVO agent in Australia, Zoltan Taródi. His official position was head of Magyar Úszó Szövetség, the federation that managed swimming and water polo. Each morning, Taródi reported to correspondent Daniil Kraminov. According to an ASIO report, "Kraminov appears to be a Russian Intelligence Service worker who is exercising indirect control over the Hungarian Olympic Delegation."[22] Taródi was not popular within the Hungarian team. It was common knowledge that he had been commander of the Kistarcsa labor camp between 1947 and 1951. Taródi was often in the company of Bela Fehérvári, an official of the sports ministry, and he may also have been an ÁVO agent.

While most of ASIO's attention was on the Hungarian team, it also discovered all was not well within the Polish contingent. An informant had told them that, "originally three members of the Polish Security Service were to accompany the team to the Olympic Games, but because of the pressure of public opinion following the disturbances in Poland in June 1956 only one such official made the trip, this person being [Jan] Gorzelanczyk."[23] The "disturbance" was an uprising in Poznań, which was put down by the army. Months later, this anti–Soviet protest inspired the Hungarian students to protest in Budapest, which in turn triggered the Hungarian Revolution.

In Melbourne, Polish authorities were keen to avoid any incidents. And so the Polish attaché asked the Australian organizers not to accommodate his team next to the Russians. As a result, the Polish team was given a building one street away from the USSR compound.

Had the Australian officials known a little more of recent Polish history, they would have understood why many Poles hated the Russians.

In the winter of 1945 the Red Army swept through Poland, pillaging crops and looting houses as they went. Rather than protecting the civilian population, they created a famine in which many perished.

Anna Wojtaszek, a javelin thrower, was just nine years old at the end of the war but she vividly remembered that winter. She lived in the small town of Krzanowice, a mile from the Czechoslovak border, with her mother, two sisters, and baby brother. Her father had been conscripted into the German army.

When the Red Army entered Krzanowice, Wojtaszek remembered gangs of soldiers roaming the streets. They were very young, many barely 18, but they were dangerously drunk and searching for loot and women. And girls. Young girls. With food in such short supply, Anna's sisters had to leave their cellar's relative safety to forage for food. On one such expedition, Russian soldiers caught and raped them. They were just 15 and 16 years old. Another day, soldiers tried to drag her mother and two aunts out of the cellar, where they were hiding, to rape them. The women screamed so loudly that the soldiers left.

These were not isolated incidents; thousands of women and girls were raped by the advancing Red Army. The incidence of rape in Germany, Poland, and Hungary was particularly high.[24] Significantly, the first large-scale protests against the USSR were in East Berlin in June 1953, followed by Poland and then Budapest.

Wojtaszek was not the only athlete from Eastern Europe whose family had suffered at the hands of the Red Army or who had sisters and mothers raped. Most of the athletes were children when the war ended and witnessed atrocities that gave them no reason to love the Russians.

By the end of the Games, Wojtaszek was the only Pole to defect.

There was also unrest among the Romanians. The head of its delegation, Manole Bodnăraș, was worried the Hungarian disease might spread to his athletes. They may wish to defect, particularly several Romanian water polo players, who were ethnic Hungarians.

Bodnăraș's problem was that the plane taking his athletes to Bucharest would not depart until six days after the closing ceremony. This would provide ample opportunity for them to seek asylum in Australia. He asked comrades in the Communist Party of Australia to arrange a trip to Tasmania or find accommodation for the whole team at a secluded location outside Melbourne so that they had no opportunity to defect before their flight home.

This operation came to naught, and four Romanian water polo players, pentathlete Cornel Vena, journalist Raul Bart, and the team's head coach, Ion Nicoara, defected.

A total of sixty-one athletes, officials, and journalists from Iron Curtain countries sought asylum. Some stayed in Australia, many moved to the United States, and a small number went to Sweden, Israel, West Germany, and Canada.

The list does not include Nina Paranyuk, who was the only person from the Soviet Union to stay in Australia.

CHAPTER 11

Nina Vanishes

Gone Missing

While no Soviet athletes defected during the Games, there was a major hunt on for 33-year-old Nina Paranyuk, with Australian police, Soviet agents, and presumably ASIO, trying to find where she was hiding. Nina was a Ukrainian stewardess on board the *Gruzia*.

On the Sunday before the opening ceremony, a party of thirty-four crew members, including Nina, went on a sightseeing tour of Melbourne. The highlight was a visit to Melbourne Zoo, an opportunity to see kangaroos and other Australian animals.

As the party left the zoo at 1:30 p.m., the tour leader realized Nina was missing. When the bus returned to the *Gruzia*, the ship's captain, Elizbar Gogitidze, phoned Dmitri Zaikin with the bad news. Zaikin was Envoy Extraordinary and Plenipotentiary for the duration of the Olympic Games, responsible for handling diplomatic relations with the Australian government.

Summoning his car and driver, Zaikin picked up Captain Gogitidze, and they drove to police headquarters. They reported Nina missing and supplied the police with her passport photograph. The Soviet envoy insisted she be found quickly. Later that evening Gogitidze phoned through her description.

Anything to do with the Olympic Games was sensitive, and a defector fleeing the Soviet ship could be politically explosive.

For the KGB agents in Melbourne, Nina's escape was a catastrophe as their primary task was to prevent such defections.

This could not have come at a worse time, five days before the Olympic Games was to open. Nina's file was immediately handed to the Special Branch of the Victorian Police, whose remit was to investigate political crimes. In this case, it worked closely with ASIO.

That evening, a missing person's bulletin was sent to all metropolitan police stations. "PARANYUK, NINA, steamship S.S. 'Gruzia.'—18.11.56—Description: 28 years, 5 ft 8–9 in, dark-brown to black hair, medium solid build; wore short brown coat, blue dress, black heel shoes." Interstate police were also alerted, as was the stationmaster at Spencer Street Station, where trains left for Adelaide and Sydney. Victoria Dock police also kept a watch out to ensure she had not stowed away on ships leaving Australia.

Crime reporters from main newspapers were based at police headquarters and listened to chatter from police radios. Smelling a big story, they besieged the police for details.

Later that evening, Charles Spry, director-general of ASIO, and Arthur Tange, secretary in the Department of External Affairs, met with Prime Minister Robert Menzies in Canberra. The meeting discussed the impossible position Nina's disappearance had placed the government in. Handing a defector back to the Soviets was politically untenable, as she would surely be severely punished. But Menzies worried that the Soviet Union could walk out of the Olympics in protest if she was found and not handed back. This possibility "must be avoided," said Menzies.[1] While unstated at this meeting (or at least not recorded in its minutes), it would be best that she not be found before the Games were over.

Detective Sergeant Jim Rosengrin from Special Branch headed the investigation, and the next day he interviewed Captain Gogitidze and looked around the ship. He found none of Nina's clothes missing.

The next day Zaikin and his assistant and possible KGB agent, Yuri Filimonov, met with Francis Stuart, chief of protocol with the Department of External Affairs. With the Russians present, Stuart phoned the police, who told him there was no progress. Zaikin was most unhappy with this news and warned that the incident could "affect relations between Australia and the Soviet Union."[2] He made no specific threat that the USSR might withdraw from the Olympics, but Stuart was left with the impression it might.

Soviet officials were worried that this incident might be used by Western imperialists to discredit the Soviet Union. Might not the stewardess's disappearance be just another Cold War trick to embarrass the Soviet Union in front of a world audience during the Olympic Games? Was it possible the Australian government had hidden Nina in a safe house?

This last accusation was not at all far-fetched. Before the Olympic Games, ASIO established several safe houses to protect defectors. Moreover, ASIO set up a desk that operated 24 hours a day to respond to asylum requests. However, officers were warned not to "take any provocative action," meaning soliciting defections that might "interfere with its [the Olympic Games] success."[3]

As a result of Nina's disappearance, Captain Gogitidze ordered extra security around the *Gruzia,* and guards on the ship were armed with automatic pistols.

After Nina's disappearance, crew members found it extremely difficult to get shore leave because "one had to get 10 signatures on a permit before being allowed to go ashore," one sailor complained.[4] And while excursions continued, they were limited to parties of two or three, with everyone asked to keep an eye on the others.

With Nina's photo splashed on the front pages of Australian newspapers, the police should have been able to wrap up the case within 24 hours. But to everyone's surprise, she continued to evade all efforts to apprehend her.

One problem with finding Nina was that the description police circulated was inaccurate. Nina was just 4 feet 11 inches, almost a foot shorter than stated in the police description, and she was wearing a full-length black coat, not a short brown coat. Her shoes were gray, not black. Evidently, Captain Gogitidze relied on the women who worked with Nina for her description. The other steward-esses were also Ukrainians, with no love for the Soviet Union, and may have given this false description in the hope of helping Nina avoid getting caught.

Over the next few days Zaikin pestered Stuart, demanding Nina be found. By the time the Games started, Zaikin's conversations with Stuart no longer contained threats. Nevertheless, the Australian government was keen to do what it could to placate the Soviets (other than finding Nina), such as clearing the dock where the *Gruzia* was moored of anti–Soviet demonstrators. It also studiously avoided publicly commenting on her disappearance.

Captain Gogitidze's public statements to the press were also designed to downplay the importance of her disappearance. "She may have become lost and as she does not speak English she may have a lot of trouble getting directions back to the ship."[5] He added that Nina had a husband in Odesa who would be anxious. In fact, she was not married.

Despite his outward calm, Gogitidze must have been worried. As captain, Nina was his responsibility. He knew from personal experience how easily careers, even that of a war hero, could be damaged in a country where paranoia was a national pastime among its apparatchiks.

During the war, Captain Gogitidze had been part of transport convoys that had run military materiel and supplies between the USSR and the United States across the North Atlantic. This theatre of war became a watery hell as ships were attacked and many sunk by German U-boats and fighter planes.

After the war, rather than being treated as a hero, Captain Gogitidze had his passport canceled and was demoted to a cargo run for the Black Sea Shipping Company, sailing between Odesa and Batumi. His "mistake" had been to fraternize with British and American naval officers. It was only in 1956, as Khrushchev's de–Stalinization policies started to take effect, that Gogitidze was given another chance to command an ocean-going liner.

Having been rehabilitated once, he knew another "mistake," like Nina's defection, might make the *Gruzia* his last command.

Nina's Backstory

Certainly, Nina was determined not to be found, a determination born of her bitter experience growing up in Ukraine.

A devout Christian, Nina lived in the small town of Hrushka, 60 miles (100 km) north of the Black Sea. "Ever since Stalin ordered the destruction of our tiny stone church I have prayed for somebody or something to take me away from the USSR," explained Nina. "The priest was taken away and not seen again."[6]

Her father had owned a small farm, but by the time Nina was born it had been taken over by an agricultural collective. When Nina was nine years old, her father died during the Great Famine of 1932, leaving her mother to care for Nina, her two older brothers, and her baby sister.

Then the war started. First, Germans occupied her village, then the Red Army took it back. "I was only 13 when I was sent to work in the fields," she explained. "I worked from sunrise to sunset." She had no choice as her two brothers were conscripted into the Red Army, leaving Nina and her mother to eke out enough to survive those hungry years. There was another famine in the winter of 1946–47 when Nina almost starved to death. It was a hard life in the countryside. "Peasants who stole food were deported to Siberia," she explained.[7]

In 1951 Nina was lucky enough to land a job in Odesa, first in a sugar factory. Then, a year later, she worked as a receptionist in an exclusive sanatorium. Even though she worked for high Party officials, Nina's pay was barely enough to survive on, and she often went hungry towards the end of the month.

While she was fed propaganda that the Soviet Union was a workers' paradise compared to capitalist countries, she came to doubt this when she met sailors who painted an attractive picture of life on the other side of the Iron Curtain.

Having applied for several jobs that might take her overseas, in late September 1956 she received a letter telling her to report to the *Gruzia*, where she would work as a stewardess. Most of the crew were Ukrainian, the captain Georgian, and the officers Russian.

Soon after she boarded, she found out the ship's destination. "When you go to Melbourne, you will meet strange people," an official told the crew. "You might meet a few of your people living in Melbourne. But don't talk to them or tell them anything." Although Nina did not have a clear idea of where Australia was, she was sure it was in the West. And during the journey south, all Nina could think of was "that the escape to freedom I had hoped for, for so many years, was getting closer."[8]

Nina was on duty when the ship landed and could not leave her post. On the deck, other crew members stood at the ship's rail, overlooking the dock, where they were showered with flowers and thrown presents. Australians welcoming them sang "Waltzing Matilda" while the crew sang folk songs.

Afterward, an angry Captain Gogitidze called the crew together. "You were running up and down the gangplanks like monkeys to get presents from the capitalists."[9] This was hardly the message of goodwill and friendship pumped out by Soviet propaganda during the Olympics. Moreover, it was ironic as most of the people on the dock were comrades, members of the Communist Party of Australia, or communist front groups.

While unhappy with the crew's behavior, Captain Gogitidze told them they would all have an opportunity to go ashore for sightseeing, but they were not to speak to anyone or accept gifts, not even flowers.

On her day off, Nina was thrilled when her name was called over the loudspeaker; she had been selected to go on a tour of Melbourne.

The moment had finally arrived, and while her determination to defect remained undiminished, she had no specific plans as to what she would do after she left the tour.

Nina Escapes

It was mid-morning when Nina and other members of the crew boarded a bus for their tour. The weather was overcast, and there were occasional showers. It was also cool, and Nina wore a threadbare woolen coat to keep warm.

Her first opportunity to escape was when the party visited Captain Cook's Cottage. But when she saw the minder with the party keeping an eye on her, she decided to wait until later. As the bus drove through the inner suburbs not much was open as it was a Sunday. Also, there was little traffic, although no less than she would have found in Odesa on a busy weekday.

When the bus pulled up at the zoo, Nina knew it would be her last chance to escape.

On arrival, they were told they had an hour to look around. As soon as the Soviet party was through the main gate, Nina lagged behind. When she thought no one was watching, she headed for the exit but quickly turned around when she saw the bus driver, who was Russian, coming towards her, as he joined the tour. Now back with her party, Nina stopped at an aviary near the entrance and watched exotic-colored birds fly around. As the party moved on, disappearing behind a hedge, Nina once again headed towards the exit and walked onto Elliott Avenue. She needed to move fast before the officials realized she was missing. "I knew I wouldn't get another chance," she recalled.[10]

After leaving the zoo, she headed towards Royal Parade and made several unsuccessful attempts to hail down cars. Eventually, two men, one in his fifties and the other a little younger, stopped and picked her up. This was not unusual; during the Olympics locals bent over backward to help foreign visitors. The men tried to question her, but without a word of English, she could not even tell them where she wanted to go. All she could do was wave her hands around, hoping they understood she wanted to get away from the zoo and as quickly as possible.

They wanted to drop her off one mile north of the zoo, near a tram stop, but she refused to get out. "I knew I hadn't got far enough away from the Zoo,"[11] she recalled. The men relented and continued their journey due north. Worried the police might already be looking for her, Nina hid her face.

They finally left her on the side of the road, next to Broadmeadows train station, nine miles (15 km) from the zoo. After thanking them in Russian—"*spasibo*"—she offered to pay the men for their trouble. They refused and drove off, wishing her good luck.

Broadmeadows was on the edge of Melbourne. The suburb was a mixture of prefabricated concrete and timber houses, and paddocks where cows and sheep grazed. Along the train line was a row of pine trees, providing a windbreak across its flat expanse. Nina had been dropped at Camp Road, a bitumen and dirt road, and the fields were muddy from recent rain.

What were her chances of finding someone who spoke Russian or Ukrainian and who would be willing to harbor her from the police? More worrisome were KGB agents, who she was sure would soon be looking for her.

After wandering around, she built up enough courage to ask a woman walking through a field whether she spoke Ukrainian. Incredibly, the woman was German but spoke a few words of Ukrainian.

Nina did not know how lucky she was to end up in Broadmeadows. It was one of the few places in Melbourne where there was a Ukrainian community. Many arrived as migrants after the war and were accommodated in a migrant camp, which happened to be less than a mile from where Nina had been dropped off. After leaving the camp, many settled in Broadmeadows, where rentals were cheap and land was inexpensive.

The German woman pointed to some nearby houses. As Nina approached, she heard children playing and, more importantly, burbling away in Ukrainian. She asked a young girl where her mother was. A few minutes later Nina was being assured, "Don't be afraid, you are among friends now."[12] The woman had heard of Nina's escape on the radio and assured the fugitive she would be protected.

Later that evening a man came to the door. He had been told about Nina by the German woman. Speaking Russian, he warned the woman who first gave Nina refuge, "you should hand her over to the authorities. If you don't they will hang the captain when he gets back to Russia."[13] He was told there were no strangers in the house.

It was now clear Nina needed to move to a more secure location. That evening a taxi arrived and took her to the first in a series of safe houses, where she lived with Ukrainian families.[14]

Nina had a good idea of what would happen to her if she was apprehended. "I would be treated as a deserter and returned to the Gruzia," Nina said.[15] Back on board, she would undoubtedly be imprisoned. And when she reached Odesa, she could only imagine the worst, having embarrassed the government before the world.

With the police after her and her photo splashed all over the newspapers, she had to undergo a makeover if she was to avoid capture. One evening a hairdresser arrived and cut and waved her hair, and she was supplied with new clothes. She wore sunglasses when outdoors.

Two days after Nina escaped, Police Commissioner Selwyn Porter issued a statement to the press. "It would be amazing for a woman who cannot speak English to remain lost in a big city for so long." Knowing the Russians had threatened to pull out of the Olympics, he added, "It isn't true that Nina has been given political asylum and is being held by Commonwealth authorities to save embarrassment until after the Games."[16] By now, it was evident to the police that members of the Ukrainian community were hiding Nina. This statement was directed at Soviet officials who suspected a conspiracy by Australian authorities.

On November 23, Detective Sergeant Rosengren followed up a tip that Nina was in Broadmeadows. With the support of six detectives, Rosengren undertook a house-to-house search but did not find Nina. The delay is odd as there had been four earlier sightings reported to the police. And in Broadmeadows, she had been seen by at least two people before she entered the first safe house, including the Russian who had suggested she hand herself in.

The next day, Rosengren issued a warning to those harboring Nina: "People may have innocently concealed Nina out of pity but they should know that it is a serious offense to harbor an illegal immigrant."[17]

Threats and the use of informers were familiar to Nina. In Ukraine, becoming an informer was a reliable career for the morally compromised, and there were plenty who happily took the State's silver to report on neighbors, friends, and even family. Might it be the same in Australia? "I was always expecting someone to turn me in," Nina said. "I didn't realize then that Australia was such a free country."[18]

After Nina had been missing for fifteen days, journalists started to question the competence of the authorities. Even if she was being hidden by locals, "surely the Security Intelligence Organization knows where to look for the plotters," complained *The Argus*.[19]

Nina was continually on the move, staying no longer than a day or two in one place. There was the constant fear of being discovered. Even the children in the places where she hid kept a lookout for suspicious strangers. During the day Nina would learn English. Occasionally she went out at night to the homes of local Ukrainian families for dinner. If one of their friends dropped in unexpectedly, Nina would hide in a bedroom until they left.

On one occasion she was taken to a farm in Geelong, 45 miles (75 km) from Melbourne. For Nina, having been raised on a collective farm, this was an eye-opener. "We could have small gardens at the back of our living quarters but were unable to keep many animals. The Government allowed us to keep only cows, pigs, and hens."[20] One cow would be shared between ten families, few could afford a pig, and the better off might have as many as ten hens. She marveled that there were no such limits on Australian farmers, whose fields were full of all sorts of animals.

On the eve of the *Gruzia*'s departure, Captain Gogitidze made a final appeal. "She will suffer no harm for her escapade," he promised. "She is just a silly young woman who has made a rash decision." Rather than coming on heavy-handed, he said if she decided to stay, "I wish her luck in Australia. We do not want ill-feeling with Australians over her disappearance."[21] By being magnanimous, Gogitidze hoped to undermine the negative propaganda that defectors always drew.

Nina's original plan was to hand herself over to police when the *Gruzia* had sailed. However, Nina decided to remain in hiding after reading a news report that the ship may return in January to take on a cargo of Australian wool.

After the *Gruzia* sailed, an immigration official told *The Argus*, "Nina will be allowed to stay here and will have exactly the same privileges and safeguards as the ordinary European migrant in Australia."[22] Now the Olympic Games were over, there was no need to appease Soviet officials, and talk of her being a "prohibited immigrant" was forgotten.

It was not until January 18, 1957, that Special Branch finally tracked down Nina in Brunswick, an inner northern suburb of Melbourne. Her English was rudimentary, and she did not understand what they were saying. But they were smiling, and she did not feel threatened. "Instead of the bullying types I saw in the police force in Ukraine, they treated me like a lady," she said. While she felt safe, she was uncertain whether the Soviet government would take action against her family. "I don't know what's going to happen to my elderly mother, and my brothers and sister who are still in the Ukraine."[23]

After dealing with immigration formalities, Nina disappeared once more, still fearing the long reach of the KGB. It took several more years before Nina finally felt safe in Australia.

Looking back, it seems extraordinary that the combined efforts of the Victorian police, Special Branch, and ASIO could not locate Nina for two months. The KGB and journalists were also after her. Eric Nave, who was seconded to help counter-espionage operations during the Olympic Games, answered this conundrum. In his unpublished memoir, he revealed: "The Russians demanded we hand her over, but although the police knew where she was, I opposed handing her back as it was clear that now the woman's life was at stake."[24] Had the USSR discovered that the police had found Nina, the Australian government would have faced a dilemma: return her to the *Gruzia* or face a major international incident by granting her asylum. Pretending they had not found her was a sensible solution under the circumstances.

The story of Nina's defection was front-page news, which for the Soviet Union was bad news. However, there was a much better story in the main stadium, where Soviet athletes were winning races, as well as the hearts and minds of spectators.

CHAPTER 12

The Making of an Olympic Hero

The Cold War's Sporting Heroes

Every Olympic Games craves heroes. Heroes tower above mere champions, whose fame is fleeting. They are champions because they break records and win gold medals. But their achievements are soon overshadowed by new Olympic champions, who will create new records and win more medals. Olympic heroes, however, are eternal, honored in the pantheon located on the summit of Mount Olympus.

There is no simple formula for how such heroes are chosen. It is more than the number of gold medals they win or world records they smash. They are athletes whose feats excite the imagination, inspire, and personify the Olympic spirit.

Paavo Nurmi, nicknamed the "flying Finn," dominated the Olympic Games between 1920 and 1928. He won nine gold medals, set twenty-two world records, and was described as athletics' equivalent of "Napoleon Bonaparte."[1] In 1936, Jesse Owens amazed the sporting world on the track, winning four gold medals. He is remembered because, as an African American, he challenged Nazi racist theories that blond, blue-eyed Aryan athletes would always beat those from "inferior" races. In character, Jesse Owens stood out. He was dignified when faced with racism, humble in victory, and had an endearing personality. And then in Helsinki, Czechoslovak long-distance runner Emil Zátopek won three gold medals with an unorthodox running style described as like "a man wrestling with an octopus on a conveyor belt."[2] What made him stand out was his sunny disposition and, above all, his nobility. In July 1966 Ron Clarke visited Zátopek in Prague. Although the Australian had broken several long-distance world records, Olympic gold had eluded him. He was now thirty-one years old and past his peak. On parting at Prague airport, Zátopek handed Clarke a small parcel and told him to only open it once he was in the air. It was Zátopek's 10,000-meter gold medal from the 1952 Olympics, now engraved with Clarke's name. It is gestures like this that transform talented athletes into heroes.

The Cold War gave new importance to Olympic heroes, and each side saw the value of having one of its athletes assume that mantle. While neither the U.S. nor USSR were able to manufacture heroes, they were keen to promote the credentials of their outstanding athletes. Winning the medal count was still important but putting a face to claims of ideological superiority had immeasurable propaganda value.

There was no lack of candidates in Melbourne—some from the major superpowers and some from other countries. Hungary's László Papp became the first boxer to win gold medals in three successive Olympics. Just seventeen years old, Australian swimmer Murray Rose won three gold medals.

Several women could easily have been candidates for the hero of the Melbourne Olympics. Hungary's Ágnes Keleti dominated the gymnastics events to win four gold and two silver. Australia's Dawn Fraser was outstanding in the pool with two golds and one silver medal. But in the 1950s, regardless of sporting achievements, women were not in the running to be *the* hero of the Olympics. That would come much later when, in 1976, Romanian gymnast Nadia Comăneci captured the world's attention and hearts with seven perfect tens in Montreal.

In 1956 two candidates for "hero" stood out: long-distance runner Vladimir Kuts from the USSR and American sprinter Bobby Morrow. For Cold War warriors, each epitomized the best their country (and political system) had to offer.

The Soviet Contender

To become an Olympic hero, a candidate needs a good story, and Vladimir Kuts's life certainly exemplified values that Soviet propagandists liked to work with.

Volodya, as Kuts was called by his friends, was born in 1927 in Aleksino, a small village in Ukraine surrounded by collective farms. His parents were of sound proletarian stock. His father worked in a sugar beet factory and his mother in a carpentry workshop.

Biographies describe his happy childhood. In summer he swam in the Boromlya River, picked mushrooms and wild berries in the countryside, and hunted sparrows with his slingshot. On Saturdays he walked for over an hour to the nearby town of Trostianets, where he dashed from one cinema to another to see two or three movies in one day. In winter he would ski with skis he had made himself. As a young boy he was plump and awkward, but spending a lot of his time outdoors, Volodya soon grew into a strong, hardy lad.

Volodya went to the village school where he did not distinguish himself academically, and his playmates nicknamed him "*puchtya.*" This translates to "country yokel," which was unfair: they had mistaken his stubbornness for dimness.

The war changed his rural idyll when German soldiers occupied his village. As soon as the Nazis arrived they requisitioned all the chickens, geese, and ducks. They then took anything else they wanted. Resistance was met with the death penalty.

There is a story told in one biography—possibly apocryphal, perhaps invented by Soviet propagandists, conceivably true—that Volodya and some local lads scrawled "Death to the fascists and traitors of Ukraine!" on a fence post.[3] They were locked up and would have been executed had not some village elders bribed the occupiers with eggs and vodka.

When the village was liberated in March 1943, Volodya packed a loaf of bread and a slab of bacon in a linen bag and headed towards the front, where he worked in a hospital and even saw some fighting. When an officer discovered he was just 16 years old, Volodya was sent home, where he worked for the Pivnenkovskaya Machine and Tractor Station and helped bring in the harvest.

In the winter of 1944 Kuts enlisted in the Red Army, where he became a tank mechanic and then a driver. Later, he joined the Red Banner Baltic Fleet and became a gunner. During a German bombing run, Kuts lost all his identity documents. When he returned home, he saw his framed photo on the wall, surrounded by black crepe. His family had been told he'd died in the raid.

Such tales (whether true or not) are the raw materials that make a Soviet hero.

As many older athletes had perished during the Second World War, sporting clubs were looking for new talent. Kuts had many interests: boxing, running, skiing, football, weightlifting, and swimming. He had tried them all and showed he was a gifted all-around athlete.

Of all these sports, skiing and boxing suited his physique. He was short, just 5 feet 8 inches, and at nineteen, he weighed 188 pounds (85 kg), with muscled legs and a barrel chest. But fate intervened. It was 1949, and Kuts was at the stadium in Tallinn with other sailors from his fleet. They had come to watch the sporting competition to celebrate May Day. When one of the athletes on the Navy team fell ill, Kuts was asked to stand in. It was the 5,000 meters race. Unexpectedly, he stayed with the leaders and, on the last lap, sprinted to the finish line and won. That resolved his question of which sport to pursue. He was to be a long-distance runner.

Over the next few years Kuts lost 28 pounds, achieving a weight more suited to a long-distance runner, and soon he was breaking world records over 5,000- and 10,000-meter distances. In 1956 he was selected to represent the Soviet Union in the Olympic Games.

A few days before his first race, it looked like Kuts might have to pull out. An avid car enthusiast, he had test-driven a Chevrolet and crashed it into an inconveniently placed telephone pole. Kuts knocked his knee—not something an

Olympic runner wants to happen just a few days before their big race. Kuts was later quoted as saying that he was not accustomed to driving on the left side of the road and that he had instinctively turned the steering wheel to the left rather than right when the car lurched forward. If truth be told, even at home, Kuts was a terrible driver with a lead foot, which he applied enthusiastically to both the accelerator and brake.

To dispel the rumor he was seriously injured, that evening he went to the Recreation Hall in the Olympic Village. As he entered he was applauded, and any thoughts that Kuts would not compete were dispelled when he danced the foxtrot with Australian sprinter Shirley Strickland.

Showing no ill effects from the accident, the day after the opening ceremony Kuts limbered up for the 10,000 meters race. The swelling in his knee had gone down, and he was feeling good.

The race was held late in the day, and the weather was fine but cool—ideal racing conditions. The starter's pistol fired, and in bright sunshine, twenty-six athletes, three deep, started on the first of twenty-five circuits of the main stadium's running track.

Kuts, wearing a bright crimson vest, set a punishing tempo at the head of the field. From the start, British runner Gordon Pirie was at his heels, as if the two were joined by an invisible elastic band. Pirie's plan was to stay behind Kuts until the final lap and then outsprint him to the finish.

Kuts, his blond hair flying in the light breeze, could see Pirie's long shadow cast by the late afternoon sun, and he could hear Pirie's loud panting, which had earned him the nickname "Puff Puff" Pirie.

In the fifth lap Kuts accelerated sharply for 150 meters, and at one point was eight meters ahead. While surprised, Pirie stuck to his game plan and sprinted to catch up. "We pounded round, lap after lap," explained Pirie. "Kuts ran terrific lung-searing dashes but slowed up dangerously between, causing me to stumble on occasions."[4] Nevertheless, the invisible elastic band between Kuts and Pirie held.

After 3,000 meters it was becoming apparent the changes of pace were unsettling Pirie by breaking his rhythm, just as Kuts had hoped. While Kuts had trained for sudden changes of pace, Pirie had not, and was caught unprepared. Kuts hoped that this punishing regime would leave Pirie in no condition to run him down in the home straight, assuming Pirie lasted that long.

"Such uneven running is not the way to break records but it certainly breaks hearts," wrote Roger Bannister, who reported the race for *Sports Illustrated*.[5] It was clear Kuts intended not only to test Pirie's stamina but also his mental fortitude.

Reporting the race, Chris Brasher and Herb Elliot wrote that it was a contest between "two courageous men torturing themselves because neither would give up."[6] The race had gone beyond a footrace to something more brutal, more primeval, bordering on lethal. "If Kuts has to kill himself in order to kill off the opposition, he has enough suicidal dedication to run himself to death," wrote Arthur Daley in his account.[7]

At one point, Kuts slowed down so that Pirie could overtake. Pirie refused the first time, but on the second occasion, when Kuts almost came to a stop, Pirie had no choice but to take the lead. "I felt that I must see his face," Kuts explained. "I saw only agony and I knew that the gold medal was in my hand."[8] Having seen what he wanted, Kuts retook the lead and pulled ahead. The invisible band finally snapped. "I was now free, free to choose any tempo, any speed," recalled Kuts after he watched Pirie drop back. "It was damn good to be free!"[9]

As the gaps between Pirie and Kuts widen, Pirie was demoralized. He eventually came in eighth.

Kuts crossed the finishing line, one arm raised in victory, well ahead of the second group of runners. Grinning from ear to ear and waving, Kuts did a victory lap. As he ran around the main stadium, the applause went up a notch when the scoreboard announced that he set a new Olympic record. Moreover, they were amazed that he was still running after such a grueling race. Few doubted that they were watching an athlete with superhuman abilities.

"He murdered me," confessed Pirie immediately after the race. "It wasn't the fact that he beat me—it was the way he did it. It was torture—utter torture."[10]

The next day the headline in Melbourne's morning newspaper, *The Sun*, read, "Everybody loves a sailor."[11] There were also some contrite articles. Writing before the race, *Sports Illustrated*'s Roger Bannister had called Kuts "a ruthless machine." Now he wrote, "Kuts is not a machine. His brain is as finely tuned and his thinking as perfect as his body."[12] The *Daily Mail*'s Peter Wilson took perverse pleasure in the way Kuts had dispatched his opponent. "He runs like a bear squeezing the sweat out of your skin, the marrow out of your bones, the breath out of your lungs, the light out of your eyes, and the hope out of your heart."[13]

Kuts did not want to compete in the 5,000 meters. The days after his 10,000-meter victory his pulse was dangerously high, and there was blood in his urine. Sports minister Nikolai Romanov caught up with Kuts when he heard he wanted to withdraw. "Vladimir, you should run because our country needs you!"[14] As a sweetener, he promised him a general's pension should he win.

Once Kuts decided to compete, he took on the field in the qualifying heat, setting a blistering pace, but Kuts eased up once he had opened a gap. To everyone's surprise, Australian runner Allan Lawrence caught up on the back straight, in sight of the finishing tape. Kuts turned his head sideways towards Lawrence and said something in Russian, which the Australian did not understand. Then Kuts slowed down. Lawrence, wary that this may be a trick, also eased up. Kuts slowed down further, and then the penny dropped for Lawrence. "Kuts wanted me to win the heat in front of the Australian crowd."[15] As Lawrence pulled up next to Kuts, the Soviet runner feigned fatigue in a performance worthy of an Oscar. To the crowd it looked like he was struggling to finish as Lawrence passed him to break the tape. The gesture was not lost on the press. Journalist Gavin Souter saw through the charade, writing in the *Sydney Morning Herald*, "He [Kuts] also delighted Melbourne by letting the Australian Alan Lawrence win a heat in the 5,000 metres."[16] If the Australian public had admired Kuts after his earlier victory, they now looked on him with affection.

Two days later, twelve athletes lined up for the 5,000-meter final. The day was fine and cool, with just a whisper of a breeze.

Soon after the start, Kuts muscled his way to the front so he could dictate the pace. If the British runners expected him to repeat the tactics of "ragged" running he had employed in the 10,000 meters they were in for a surprise. Instead, Kuts decided to maintain a fast pace in the hope of burning off the opposition.

After four laps, only three British runners, Pirie, Derek Ibbotson, and Chris Chataway, could keep up with Kuts. The rest of the field was already 20 meters behind.

In the last five laps Kuts began a series of short punishing sprints and crossed the finishing line 75 meters in front of his closest rival, setting a new Olympic record. Pirie showed great character coming second, with Ibbotson finishing a few meters behind. Chataway finished last.

After the race there was a rumor that the three British runners had conspired to beat Kuts. According to Pirie, Ibbotson saw him before the race and proposed that "we three Englishmen should box Kuts in."[17] In his memoir, Ibbotson denied this account, claiming that they

Vladimir Kuts marking his victory in the 5,000-meter race on November 28, 1956.

"had no intention of helping each other."[18] But he would say that, as ganging up on Kuts would be unsporting.

The American Contender

Kuts was not alone in vying for the distinction of being the hero of the Melbourne Games. He was up against American sprinter Bobby Morrow for that singular honor.

The 100 meters final was held just 24 hours after Kuts's 10,000 meters win, and 21-year-old Morrow was the favorite, having twice equaled the world record in the qualifiers.

A sterling example of American manhood, he stood a little over six feet, had boyish good looks, and a shy grin. He looked like an American out of central casting, with a backstory to match.

Bobby was raised on his family's 600-acre cotton and carrot farm in San Benito, situated on the Texas side of the Rio Grande, where he learned to drive a tractor long before driving a car. Bobby developed his love of running when racing against his cousins in the sprawling fields of the farm. And when his cousins were not around, he would race against black-tailed jackrabbits. His was a carefree childhood of hunting and fishing.

Showing an early talent for sprinting, Morrow could have chosen any college, many of which would have been keen to offer him a generous athletics scholarship. But as a member of the evangelical Churches of Christ, he chose nearby Abilene Christian College, which was associated with his church and reflected his deep religious values.

At college he joined the Frater Sodalis fraternity where the mildest off-color remark attracted a monetary fine. Their idea of blowing off steam was to join arms for a rousing rendition of the club's song, *Drink Milk*. After an evening of Christian fellowship, they would head off to the Dixie Pig café for a generous helping of pecan pie and vanilla ice cream.

It was at Abilene Christian College that his natural abilities as a sprinter were refined, and during the early part of 1956 he equaled the 100 meters world record twice. That year he was not only the fastest man alive but also one of the most graceful. "He could run a 220 [yards] with a root beer float on his head and never spill a drop," observed Coach Oliver Jackson.[19]

Certainly, he had the résumé of an all-American hero. The question was could he win to complete the dream and become an Olympic gold medalist?

As Morrow lined up at the starting line for the 100-meter final, he realized that breaking any records was unlikely as there was a brisk wind blowing in his face and the cinder track was in poor condition, already breaking up after just two days of competition.

Bobby Morrow crossing the finishing line in the 200-meter race on November 27, 1956.

Crouched on his blocks, Morrow never tried to outguess the starter to get the jump on his opponents. It offended his idea of what was fair; it was un–Christian. Nevertheless, he made a good start, but not as fast as Australian Hector Hogan and fellow American Ira Murchison. Hogan led for about three-quarters of the race before being overtaken by Morrow, who took the lead and crossed the finishing tape ahead of the field.

There was no victory lap or Kuts-like theatrics. A humble man, Morrow quietly packed up his starting blocks, put on his tracksuit, and walked off the main arena; he would only return for the medal ceremony. Asked afterward whether he was not disappointed at failing to break the world record, he replied, "Nuts to the time, I just wanted to win."[20]

Three days later the 200-meters final was held. This time Morrow was less confident. During the previous race he had suffered a slight groin pull, and his left thigh was bandaged.

Anxious, he had not slept a wink the night before, and to calm himself down before the race, Morrow, in a cold sweat, lay on an old mattress that had been stored beneath the stands.

Once he was called into the arena he went through his routine, meticulously checking his starting blocks and trying to calm himself down, without much success. He was shaking so badly at the start that he almost fell off his starting blocks. Nevertheless, he started well, and at the 120-meter mark Morrow took the lead. He won in Olympic record time, which was a splendid achievement considering the poor state of the track. Now he had two gold medals to his name, and he still had a chance for one more.

Morrow's final event was the 4 × 100-meters relay. He would run the anchor leg. Having not been beaten in an Olympic sprint relay since 1920, America's record was under threat from a strong Soviet team, which had equaled the time of the Americans in the semi-finals.

The U.S. sprint coach believed his charges were faster than the Soviets. However, he was worried they could lose if they messed up any baton changes. So he took a conservative approach to the baton changes, which chewed up precious split-seconds, in the hope his sprinters could make up the time. The Soviets took the opposite approach. They had practiced their changes, which were slick, and they hoped would give them a sufficient edge to beat the faster Americans.

The race was won in the second leg when American Leamon King opened up the widest margin over the Soviet team—three meters, which was also the winning margin. The Americans set a new world and Olympic record, which would stand for twenty years. For Bobby Morrow, it was his third gold medal.

Judgment

In the head-to-head contest between Kuts and Morrow, both sides of the Cold War predictably crowned their own as the hero of the Olympics.

Sports Illustrated presented Morrow its "Sportsman of the Year" award in 1956 because he was an outstanding athlete with three gold medals in the trophy cabinet. Moreover, he raced with "grace and beauty," as opposed to "machine-like" Kuts.[21]

Equally partisan, Romanov said of Kuts, "He attracted universal admiration achieving outstanding results."[22] He was supported by Petr Sobolev, Soviet Olympic attaché, who declared that the world consensus was that Kuts was "hero of the XVI Olympic Games,"[23] and Russian journalist Alexei Adjoubei wrote, "Vladimir Kuts became a legendary hero of Melbourne."[24]

Putting aside such biased tributes, most pundits came out in favor of Kuts. Australian journalists were fulsome in their praise of the Soviet runner. Gavin Souter wrote that Kuts was undoubtedly "the outstanding athlete of the 1956 Games,"[25] and Peter Banfield declared Kuts "man of the Games."[26] An English newspaper reported that Kuts's two wins had made him a "legend" and described his performances as "almost superhuman."[27] Even Bob Giegengack, assistant coach for the U.S. track and field team, said, "Vladimir Kuts typified the spirit of Melbourne."[28]

There were many reasons why Kuts's reputation soared while Morrow's achievements have largely been forgotten.

Kuts was fortunate to have excelled in long-distance races. The 10,000 meters lasts almost 30 minutes, allowing the sporting public to appreciate the mental and physical strength needed to win. In longer races, tactics are much more critical. As lap follows lap, spectators immerse themselves in the tense drama unfolding before them as athletes engage mind and body to wear down their opponents. Those watching Kuts's races in Melbourne could not help but be astonished by his tactical genius, indomitable spirit, and physical power.

On the other hand, while Morrow was undoubtedly a beautiful athlete to watch (much more so than Kuts), his races were over in seconds and therefore lacked drama. This was also a time in which there was more interest in longer races. This has changed, and today the 100- and 200-meters dashes produce Olympic heroes like Jamaican sprinter Usain Bolt. His races are more suited to the public's short attention span and easily fit in between television commercial breaks.

In addition, Kuts was the showman in the stadium, and he charmed Australians wherever he went. There were his victory laps in which he expressed his gratitude to the spectators. And then he allowed the homeboy Allan Lawrence to win a heat in the 5,000 meters. It is such acts of generosity that make an Olympic hero. While not speaking much English, he was always ready to sign an autograph and was a genial figure around the Olympic Village, smiling and fooling around in front of the media. On the other hand, Morrow was naturally shy and kept to himself.

Five years after the Melbourne Olympics, Kuts's reputation was tarnished by his great rival, Gordon Pirie. In 1961 Pirie wrote an article that appeared in *People* magazine. It accused Kuts of taking Benzedrine, a synthetic amphetamine. As well as exhibiting symptoms consistent with drug use, Pirie also observed that Kuts was "using women's make-up to hide scars on his legs," which led him to believe that "those scars were caused by hypodermic needles."[29]

Australian Alan Lawrence, who ran against Kuts, believes it was a case of sour grapes. "Gordon Pirie's view of the world was simple: No runner in the world was capable of running him into the ground as Kuts did in the 10,000 meters in Melbourne. The fact that Kuts had done exactly that was the only evidence needed to conclude Kuts was obviously drugged."[30]

There is evidence to the contrary from Emil Zátopek, who trained with Kuts during the Games. After a few laps, Zátopek noticed that Kuts's coach gave him a tonic. "Then suddenly phhhhhhew—he was away, speeding up from 66–68s quarters [66–68 second runs over 400 meters] to 60–62s," Zátopek recalled.[31]

Kuts also suffered from other symptoms consistent with amphetamine use. His stomach ulcers became worse, and he required hospitalization. He suffered heart failure and needed sedatives to help him sleep. Also, amphetamines are appetite suppressants. Kuts, who had a naturally stocky frame, constantly had problems keeping his weight down. In early 1955, Kuts weighed 187 pounds (85 kg), and twenty months later he had dropped an astonishing 17 lb. After Kuts stopped competing, his weight ballooned to 265 pounds (120 kg). It is unclear when he stopped using amphetamines, but his sudden weight gains suggest that he did stop.

In the Soviet Union, though, nothing could tarnish Kuts's reputation as the hero of the Melbourne Olympiad. However, Soviet newspapers were instructed not to print recent photos of him. The older and much fatter Kuts was airbrushed out, and if photos of him were needed, it was of the trim Kuts, circa 1956. For the public, Kuts would remain forever a young man, an Olympic hero, with unruly blond hair, crossing the finishing line in Melbourne with one arm upraised in victory.

CHAPTER 13

The Lovers Who
Came in from the Cold

"Too Friendly" Games

A note, signed "Mickey Mouse," was left at the U.S. compound in the Olympic Village. It was addressed to beefy American athlete Harold "Hal" Connolly. He quickly realized the cryptic message was from Olga Fikotová, a vivacious Czechoslovak discus thrower. She did not want anyone to know that they were becoming friendly—very friendly—so she used a codename only Hal would know.

Olga was aware that members of the secret police were keeping a keen eye out for possible defectors, and they would do everything they could to discourage her fraternizing with an American.

When the Czechoslovak team arrived in Melbourne, the head of the delegation warned athletes to

> avoid unnecessary contact with any outsiders who approach you because those are the people who might attempt to harm your performance in the Games or even try to bribe you into defection. You are socialistic men and women, and the imperialistic world judges you without mercy; therefore, be careful about your every step and what you say in public—don't give Western sensationalists anything they could use against us or any other brotherly socialistic nation.[1]

Two weeks earlier, Olga had completed an intense training session and had just returned her discus to the equipment trailer. Brimming with joie de vivre, she bounded down the two wooden steps of the trailer and stumbled into the arms of an athlete who was about to enter. Not much taller than Olga, Hal was massive, weighing 234 pounds (106 kg), all of it hard muscle. He was square-jawed with a mop of unruly black hair, and she noticed a sprinkling of freckles across his nose gave his face a boyish look that she found attractive. Olga quickly apologized in her diffident English, to which he playfully replied, "I quite enjoyed it."[2] He introduced himself, telling her he was a hammer thrower. "I thought all hammer throwers have no hair and have big bellies," she joked.[3] Hal was not in the least offended.

Instead, he was beguiled by this exotic nymph, slim but muscular, with a yellow ribbon in her dark, curly hair, cropped short. And then there was her impish smile that began in her eyes, the color of honey, and spread over her pretty face.

While she would have liked to have kept chatting with this handsome American, Olga cut the conversation short when she noticed her "chaperone," Miroslava Doubravová, was hovering. She was a member of the secret and political police, the Státní bezpečnost, also known as the StB. A small, stout woman with gray eyes and brown hair, Doubravová diligently reported the activities of "Truhla," which was the codename used by the StB for Olga. A bad report from Doubravová could damage Olga's career. So, if she was to meet Hal again, she knew it would need to be away from Doubravová, whose job was to ensure no Czechoslovak athletes were enticed to stay in the West.

On the other hand, Doubravová was aware of statements by communist officials, who had publicly spoken of the Olympic Games as a festival of youth that promoted socialist values like mutual understanding, peace, and friendship between sportspeople. While this was just convenient rhetoric used for propaganda by communist states, Doubravová could not come down hard on Olga, who was, after all, just making friends with a sportsman from another country. Nevertheless, Doubravova knew that she had to discourage Olga's growing friendship without attracting attention. That required subtlety, not a skill StB officers like Doubravová had much practice mastering.

On the following Sunday, Olympic organizers had arranged an afternoon excursion to the Melbourne Zoo. Olga was delighted when Hal hopped onto the bus leaving the Village. She also noticed Doubravova was less than pleased.

At the entrance gate Olga gave Doubravová the slip and caught up with Hal at the goanna enclosure. The lizards slept on warm spots on the concrete floor and paid the athletes no heed.

As they chatted, Olga discovered Hal was a teacher, but he was less committed to this vocation than his sport. Olga told him about her ambition to become an orthopedic surgeon. This surprised Hal as women in the United States seldom aspired to such prestigious professions as medicine. It was the 1950s after all, and American women's main aspirations, according to the prevailing mores, were to find husbands and produce children.

As time was running out before they would have to be back at the bus, Hal asked Olga whether she liked movies, hoping to set up a proper date. Olga had not seen many American films; however, she had seen a Mickey Mouse cartoon, which she quite liked. This greatly amused Hal and provided him with an opening. He suggested that one evening they go to a movie theatre that showed Disney cartoons.

As they approached the bus, Doubravová was glaring out the window. To allay her suspicion Hal and Olga did not sit together during the return trip back to the Village.

Since both athletes were intent on their training, they saw little of one another until the opening ceremony. They decided to stay back at the Village and listen to the ceremony on Hal's transistor radio. With Doubravová at the main stadium, they could now speak freely, and Hal was keen to find out more about this sprite from behind the Iron Curtain.

In September 1948, Olga's family fortunes took a dive when the StB took her father away late one night, without explanation. When summoned by the school principal to explain why her father had been arrested, Olga insisted he was innocent. In "our People's democracy nobody is held anywhere by mistake, Comrade Fikotová,"[4] explained the principal. With tears cascading down her cheeks, Olga ran out of the school, intending never to return. She was just 17 years old, and it looked like her dream of becoming a doctor was at an end. A few days later the principal summoned her back to his office. He had received a petition, signed by her classmates, insisting she be readmitted so she could take her matriculation exams.

While her father languished in prison, the government confiscated the family's Prague apartment, which went to a loyal Communist Party member. Olga and her mother moved to Libiš, a small village 17 miles (28 km) from the Czechoslovak capital, where they lived in a cramped two-room flat. Her father was released in February 1949, but the government had not finished punishing him. He lost his army pension, and to make ends meet both Olga's parents worked in the nearby chemical factory.

To wipe away the disgrace of being the daughter of a "class enemy," Olga took a job in a machine shop, where she labored for more than a year. This gesture, plus the fact she was a gifted athlete, helped her gain admittance to the Univerzita Karlova, so she returned to Prague to study medicine.

When the opening ceremony came to an end, Hal turned off the radio. They then walked through the Village towards the dormitories. Before they went their separate ways, Olga shyly confided, "Hal, I'm afraid! I don't know if I can do it. Everybody else is so very good. I want to win!" Seeing how vulnerable she was, Hal had an urge to kiss her. Instead, he took her hand and gave it a reassuring squeeze. She then asked whether Hal would be at the main stadium to watch her compete. "I can't, Olga," he said. "I'd be too nervous. It's too close to my own competition. But I'll be thinking of you every minute and listening on the radio."[5]

Olympic Contests

East v. East

The next morning an olive-green shuttle bus picked up Olga outside the gates of the Olympic Village. The bus was very quiet as many of the athletes who were due to compete that day were wrapped in their own thoughts. In her rush to catch the bus, Olga had forgotten to put on her competition tracksuit and instead was wearing the old, a rather shabby one she trained in.

The day was quite hot, and as Olga came into the main stadium she noticed the men in the stands already had their jackets off and had improvised, shaping newspapers into makeshift sunhats. Women wore light summer frocks, and children had dabs of white zinc cream on their noses to prevent sunburn. It was the first day of competition, and the excitement in the arena was palpable.

Favorite to win the discus was Nina Ponomareva, who had won the Soviet Union's first gold medal in Helsinki.

It was probably only through the kindness of Nina that Olga was in Melbourne. They had met a year earlier at the Progressive Youth Festival in Warsaw. Olga's performance was woeful. That evening she walked back to the throwing ring and sat down, trying to analyze what she had done wrong. Darkness was falling, and a group of Soviet athletes was walking past. At the time, there was little fraternization between Russian and Czech athletes, and Olga was surprised when one of the Russians peeled off from the group and introduced herself. While the other Soviet women walked off, Nina took pity on Olga when she explained that she had come second last out of twenty-eight competitors. "No wonder. You are so skinny," complained the Russian.[6] Nina suggested they meet the next day when she promised to help Olga.

Back in the dormitory, Olga told her teammates about the meeting. They told her not to trust any Russian. The experience of Czechoslovak athletes was that for sports in which they were world champions, they were expected to share their training secrets with their Soviet comrades, but they were never given any help in return.

The next morning Nina spent two hours with Olga, giving her tips on training, conditioning, and technique. "Ninotchka, I don't know how to thank you. Yesterday I thought I couldn't do anything!" Olga said as they parted. "*Vsevo kharoshevo*, all the best, Olga," Nina replied. "One year is a short time for you, but I believe we will meet in Melbourne."[7]

As Nina had predicted, Olga was in Melbourne, and winning a gold medal would mean having to beat her mentor.

Olga almost did not qualify, as she lost her balance during her spin and her discus fell well short of the qualifying mark. Olga did her best to relax before her second throw, which was good.

Afterward, Olga pulled out from her sports bag Méd'a, her good luck mascot. "We're half done," she told her stuffed bear and tenderly returned him to her bag.[8] The bear was a gift from her father, who had put it in her crib the day she was born, and over the years it had become a constant companion, her confidant, and good luck charm.

By the final round the field had been trimmed to six, who would compete for the medals.

As Olga joined the other competitors, she silently started to recite the Lord's Prayer. After mouthing "Our Father, who art in heaven," she became a little too absorbed in her own situation and looking to the heavens for divine intervention she beseeched the Lord to "give me very fast and perfect footwork and a good release at the end." After a little more thought, she added a postscript, asking the Almighty to provide her discus with a favorable wind.[9] She could but hope her two Soviet opponents were better Marxists than she was and were not on speaking terms with the Good Lord.

To win, Olga had to beat two formidable Soviet competitors, Irina Beglyakova and Nina Ponomaryova. The only American among the finalists was Earlene Brown, but she was well short of the leaders. The fight for gold, therefore, would be an East-East rather than an East-West battle.

Olga's first throw set an Olympic record and put her in the lead.

Hal was listening to the contest on his transistor radio. When Olga took the lead he leaped to his feet shouting, "Go! Go! That's the way!"[10] But as Hal waited for Olga's next throw his radio died. He scoured the Village for new batteries without any luck. He would have to wait for the athletes to return from the main stadium to find out whether Olga had won.

Her final throw was even better, and Olga cried for joy when she realized she had won the gold medal. Irina Beglyakova took silver and Nina Ponomaryova bronze.

The medal ceremony was delayed by an hour because no one could find Nina. When she finally arrived at the victory podium, Nina's eyes were puffy and her nose red. She had been crying, not only for missing out on the glory of a gold medal but because she would miss out on a bonus of 20,000 roubles for coming first. A third place attracted a bonus of just 7,000 roubles, and, having grown up dirt poor, money was important to Nina.

After the medal ceremony, even though she was still upset, Nina turned to the gold medal winner and said, "Bravo, Olga," at which the younger woman enthusiastically embraced her. "Thank you, Ninotchka," she said,[11] knowing she would not have won the gold medal had she not received help from the Russian at a crucial point in her career.

As she left the podium, photographers snapped a grinning Olga as she hugged Méda, certain the little bear had brought her luck.

When Olga returned to the Olympic Village, she walked to the American compound. Finding Hal, she handed him her precious Méda. Hal was touched by the gesture. "I'm not much for good luck charms, but I promise he'll be with me right in the stadium, and I'll take good care of him."[12] After wishing him good luck, she rushed off.

East v. West

The next day, Hal was ready for an epic encounter with Mikhail Krivonosov in what promised to be a classic battle between East and West.

Over the previous two years the two men had exchanged the world record three times. In Melbourne, they were both keen to prove who was the best hammer thrower in the world, and there was no better arena than the Olympic Games to settle the matter.

Olga missed the qualifying rounds as she had to see the team doctor because of an infected heel. With her right foot tightly bandaged, she arrived at the main stadium for the final.

Hal was sitting on the grass, winding tape around his feet so they would fit snugly into his ballet slippers, a gift from his Aunt Mary. She had modified them with thin rubber soles to help him with foot speed during his spin. Olga also saw Krivonosov warming up. He was effortlessly swinging two hammers at once around his head to loosen his shoulders. She could not help but be impressed, but she was confident Hal would beat his formidable opponent.

Conditions were not ideal for hammer throwing; there was a strong gusty wind blowing as the final six competitors lined up. Each finalist was given six throws, the best of which would take out the gold medal.

After winning the discus competition, Olga Fiko-tová holds up Méďa, her good luck bear (PROV VPRS 10742/P0, item A169).

Hal made a bad start, fouling on his first throw. Krivonosov's first throw put him in the lead, while his next two broke the Olympics record. Hal could do no better. Hal could not believe his luck when Krivonosov fouled on his next two throws. Now behind after four throws, as Hal approached the cage his thoughts turned to Olga. "I had to win for us."[13] Everything went well for his fifth throw, and he beat Krivonosov's Olympic record. As Krivonosov approached the concrete circle for his last throw, Hal tried to look away but could not. The Russian's first two spins were fast and precise. As Krivonosov's powerful muscles in his upper body rippled, ready to release the hammer, he faltered on his last spin, and his hammer crashed into the ground. This was just as well as Hal fouled on his final throw.

At the moment of victory, Hal went to his bag and pulled out Olga's bear, Méd'a, and thanked him for bringing him good luck.

As Hal stood at the top of the podium, he scanned the stadium to see if he could see Olga.

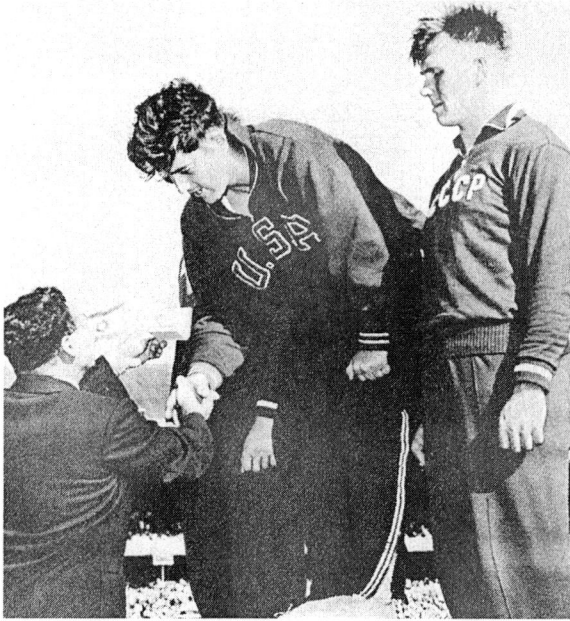

Hal Connolly (left) receiving his gold medal for the hammer throw. Next to him is the Soviet competitor Mikhail Krivonosov (right).

He turned around when he felt a light touch on his hip, which was Krivonosov warning him he needed to face the U.S. flag being raised in honor of his victory.

Afterward, photographers asked Hal to raise his arms as a gesture of victory. He was able to lift only his right arm. "Come on. Raise 'em both," one of the photographers urged.[14] Hal tried, but his left arm rose no higher than his shoulder. He could not fully extend his left arm, which had been damaged when he was born, making his win even more remarkable.

He was a large baby weighing nearly 13 pounds. A difficult delivery dislocated his shoulder and crushed nerves in his cervicobrachial plexus. As a result, he suffered Erbs-Jackson's Paralysis. While surgeons repaired his partially frozen face, his left arm never grew normally and was four inches shorter than his right and much weaker. In and out of hospital during his childhood, Hal developed a fierce desire to succeed. "The thought of being patronized made me sick. I wanted to play by the rules, not rules adapted for me because I was disabled."[15]

Passionate about sport, in college he took up weightlifting, baseball, football, discus, and shot put.

One day Hal's coach asked him whether he would like to earn a few dollars by helping retrieve hammers during a practice session. When Hal started to toss back the hammers beyond where the athletes stood, he realized that here was a sport in which he was a natural. In hammer throwing, the left hand is important in guiding the projectile, which Hal could still do with his damaged arm. He soon became the best hammer thrower at Boston College. As Hal started winning college competitions, he set his sights on the Melbourne Olympics. And now, with a gold medal hanging around his neck, Hal had proven to the world that he was the best in the world.

When Hal got back to the Village, he looked everywhere for Olga. He could not enter the women's dormitories, however, because they were surrounded by a two-meter fence, a measure taken by the Olympic organizers to frustrate the raging libidos of the athletes.

Having had no success in finding her, at midnight he unhappily returned to the U.S. dormitory. That is when he saw an unsigned note that read, "Mickey Mouse is happy." Initially, he was puzzled. And then it struck him. Mickey Mouse was Olga. "What a strange girl," he chuckled. "First she gives me her mascot, now hides behind a cartoon character."[16] Was she playing with him, or was she serious, he wondered. Nevertheless, the note gave love-sick Hal hope, and he hardly slept that night.

Romance Is in the Air

The next day Hal attended an outdoor Mass at Como Park. A devout Catholic, Hal believed that "inside my soul lay the supremely assuring conviction that I had won because of God's will." And so "my participation in the High Mass completed my profound happiness over my Olympic victory."[17]

Later that day Hal finally caught up with Olga, and they went to the movies. Hal remembered he had promised to take her to see a Mickey Mouse cartoon. After they had checked out a few movie theaters, Hal admitted defeat, and they had to settle for a small cinema that was showing some Bugs Bunny shorts. They also saw a newsreel on the Olympic Games. One item showed Hal and Olga receiving their medals. When members of the audience recognized them, they received a round of applause.

In the taxi back to the Village, with his arm around Olga, Hal gently kissed her, and she eagerly returned his kiss. For the first time they realized they shared the same feelings.

They arrived back at the Village a few minutes before 10 p.m. and, worried she would break the curfew set by the ever-watchful Doubravová, Olga dashed for the Czechoslovak dormitory.

Over the next few days they went to parties, the beach, and restaurants, but Olga continued to be wary, keeping out of Doubravová's line of sight. This upset Hal. "Why then are you so afraid to be seen with me?" he asked. "Am I bad or dangerous just because I'm from the United States?" No less frustrated by Cold War games being played by Czechoslovak officials, she explained, "You could be a saint, but if you come from a place on the map that's in the camp of the enemies of socialism, they don't care what kind of a person you are. Hal, I know it's hard for you to understand and I know it's unjust, but please just do this for me."[18]

If Olga had hoped to keep their relationship secret, she failed. As a result, she faced attacks from officials. "You want to run away with that American fascist abroad," said one. "We sent you to the Olympic Games and now you betray us," said another.[19] These barbs hurt because Olga saw herself as a patriotic Czechoslovak. Still, she was not going to cave in and stop seeing Hal. She was too much in love.

Keen to raise some funds, the American Amateur Union hastily organized a meet in Sydney against Commonwealth countries on the Tuesday before the Games ended. Hal realized his time with Olga would be even shorter than he had anticipated. Was this to be just a summer romance, or was there more? They had little time left together to find out.

A few days before Hal left, he and Olga were downtown. As they walked past Foys, a four-story department store in central Melbourne, she stopped to stare at a model kitchen in the display window, with all sorts of wondrous appliances. This was his opportunity. "Olga, when I return home, I'll get a place with a little kitchen just like this one, and then I'll come to Czechoslovakia to ask you if you'll marry me." Stunned by his unexpected proposal, Olga accepted. In the taxi, as they returned to the Village, using her pet name for him, she sighed, "*Halítchku*, I love you."[20]

As the euphoria of their declarations of love wore off, they faced a multitude of sobering questions. Was Olga willing to come to live in the United States? If so, would her government allow her to leave Czechoslovakia? What would happen to her medical studies? How would their families react? And then there was the question of religion: Hal was Catholic, and Olga belonged to the Evangelical Church of the Czech Brethren, a Protestant denomination. But the most immediate problem was how to obtain permission from the Czechoslovak government to marry.

The Horrid Journey Home

Czechoslovak Olympic officials knew that if Olga defected to marry Hal, it would be a propaganda disaster. Newspapers around the world would make much play of the Czechoslovak athlete who fled to the West to be with her American lover. What followed shows just how far communist officials were willing to go to prevent this from happening.

The very first step was to get Olga away from Hal. Unfortunately for the

Czechoslovak officials, they did not know that Hal had already gone to Sydney, because this was where they intended to send Olga to get her out of harm's way.

The day before Hal was to leave, the Czechoslovak Consul-General Dr. Miloslav Jandík and his wife, Ludmilla, arrived in Melbourne and invited Olga to accompany them on their drive back to Sydney so she could see more of Australia. Although the offer meant Olga might see Hal again in Sydney, she declined. Olga preferred to stay in Melbourne for the closing ceremony. As Czechoslovakia's only gold medal winner, she gave herself a good chance of being given the honor of carrying the flag. Soon after, Olga was summoned to a meeting by the head of the Czechoslovakia Olympic Committee, Richard Nejezchleb. He insisted she accepts Jandík's kind offer. Understandably, Olga became suspicious at the lengths that were being taken to get her out of Melbourne. When she refused again, Nejezchleb issued her with a direct order. "Comrade Fikotová, you are going to Sydney. Get out and pack."[21] Given just 30 minutes to get her things together, she was then ushered into the Consul-General's Mercedes for the journey north.

What Olga did not know was that Jandík was an StB officer, using the code name "Kučera." He had been sent to Sydney in June 1954 to run Czechoslovakia's spy network. Following the defection of Vladimir and Evdokia Petrov in April 1954, the Soviet Union's embassy was closed, and so Jandík also ran Soviet agents in Australia.[22] Jandík's sudden appearance in Melbourne and insistence on taking Olga sightseeing was a tactic to keep her under constant surveillance without being too obvious.

They drove via the Princes Highway, which runs along the coast and is more scenic, but would take longer than the direct route to Sydney via the Hume Highway. Evidently, Jandík was in no hurry. Their route took them through sweet-smelling eucalyptus forests and along the spectacular eastern coastline. Despite Olga's initial reluctance, she enjoyed herself. She could not help relishing the irony that rather than taking her away from Hal, Jandík was bringing them together.

On the second day of the trip, with just eight hours to reach Sydney, the Mercedes broke down near Cobargo, a pretty little village near the coast. After Jandík spoke to the local mechanic, he told Olga it would take two days for a spare part to come from Sydney. This meant she would arrive in Sydney after Hal had left for the United States. During the trip, Jandík discovered that Hal was in Sydney and about to leave. So he wanted to delay their arrival.

They stayed at the Cobargo Hotel, a comfortable two-story red brick building on the main street. After the Jandíks had gone to sleep, Olga crept downstairs and asked the proprietor Forbes Bills whether she could make a collect call. When she rang Hal's hotel he wasn't there, but the operator promised to pass on her message. Bills insisted on paying for the phone call, saying, "If you marry your young man, remember who came up with the first wedding gift."[23]

Once the car was ready, Olga asked the mechanic why he had taken two days to repair the car. "If we had known you were in a hurry we could have made the repairs much faster," he said.[24]

Such trips would usually take two to three days. Instead, they arrived in Sydney six days after leaving Melbourne. It was a Saturday, and Olga spent a pleasant afternoon sightseeing with Ludmilla. The following day Jandík roused Olga at 5 a.m. and told her to get ready quickly as she was leaving in ten minutes. A plane was waiting to take her to Melbourne to join the team for the journey home on a French charter airplane.

At Sydney airport Jandík handed Olga over to two men, presumably StB agents, who escorted her onto the plane and stayed with her for the whole journey. Olga became even more anxious when the car that picked them up in Melbourne did not go to the Olympic Village. Instead, it headed toward Appleton Dock, where the Soviet ship the *Gruzia* was moored. When Olga asked what was going on, one of her escorts brusquely answered that she and the rest of the team would be returning by sea. "Yes, Comrade, the terrorists—the boycotters—they damaged the French plane because they wanted the plane to crash with you and everyone, and our Soviet brothers saved us by allowing us to travel back home by their ocean liner."[25] In fact, the plane needed some minor repairs and would only be delayed for a day. The story about sabotage was an excuse, an improbable excuse, to force the athletes on board the *Gruzia*.

Was this an elaborate plot by Jandík to stop Olga from defecting? Certainly. Was she being abducted? Technically, not. But she was undoubtedly coerced into the Sydney trip and continuously kept under the watchful eyes of the Jandíks.

At 10 p.m. the day before Olga arrived back in Melbourne, the rest of the Czechoslovak team had been called together. An official told them to pack quickly because a bus was waiting for them. Like Olga, they were surprised when the buses took them to the harbor rather than the airport.

Was it a mass kidnapping of the Czechoslovak team? Caught by surprise, the athletes did not have a chance to resist being taken on board the *Gruzia*.

Once they were on the ship, Soviet sports minister Nikolai Romanov announced that the Australian government was angry Soviet athletes had beaten those from capitalistic countries, and it had refused to allow anyone ashore before the *Gruzia* sailed. While not under lock and key, everyone on board the ship was effectively imprisoned.

The *Gruzia* did not leave immediately, despite all the passengers—most of the Soviet and Czechoslovak teams, a few Bulgarians and Poles—being on board. They remained in port for the next two days. No reason was given for the delay.

As the ship was about to leave, Czechoslovak officials bustled Olga onto the deck. They ordered her to face the journalists waiting on the wharf and wave a newspaper with the headline "Czechs on red ship. Gold medallist missing. Fikotová to receive Australian asylum." Olga was clearly being used to make a political point to the capitalist press that she was not defecting but willingly returning to Czechoslovakia. The headline was pure speculation, based on the fact that Olga's "disappearance," namely her trip to Sydney, had coincided with Hal's departure from the Village. Even many of the Czechoslovak athletes half believed the story, as they told her later, "We thought you had run off with Connolly to Hawaii."[26]

As the ship left Melbourne, Captain Gogitidze welcomed everyone on board. He cheerfully described the *Gruzia* as "the Ship of Friendship" and told them he was sure they would enjoy the trip home.

It did not take the Czechoslovak athletes long to realize they were not in for a pleasant ocean cruise, and they renamed the ship the *Hrůzia*, which translates to the "horror."

The horror started from day one when Captain Gogitidze allocated cabins on F-deck to the Czechoslovaks. These were emergency berths, not meant to be occupied in normal conditions. Their accommodation was cramped and stuffy. And they were near the ship's engines, which were loud and smelt of diesel. This alone gave the Czechoslovaks good cause to be unhappy. But in the days to come, they would have many more reasons to complain.

Although the *Gruzia* had been in port for over a month, the ship started to run out of essentials after nine days at sea. This provided indirect evidence that the decision to take the Czechoslovak team was made at the last minute and did not allow time for adequate provisions to be taken on board.

First, drinking water was rationed. It was available for just two hours in the morning and two hours in the evening. If anyone wanted to take a shower, they had to use buckets filled with seawater.

The next shortage was announced by the Czechoslovakian shot-putter, Jiří Skobla, who the athletes had elected as the "Admiral" of the *Hrůzia*. "Pirates, we no longer can hush up the fact that *Gruzia* is out of toilet paper. The men's john has been depleted since yesterday, and our women report having shared their final packet today. The time has arrived when collectivization of all notebooks, stationery, and other paper of suitable quality is a must."[27] Before the vote was taken, Olga made a desperate appeal for a dispensation—her love letters from Hal. A few days later, the Czechoslovaks discovered a clean toilet with toilet paper in first class. Soon after, Soviet guards appeared outside that toilet to stop its unauthorized use. Evidently, they had not heard the slogan of "each according to his needs," or else they believed the needs of the Soviet officials were greater than those of the Czechoslovaks. The next day, Czechoslovak athletes turned up at the ship's library to borrow the collected works of Marx, Lenin, and Stalin.

Oddly, they were never seen reading the weighty tomes they had borrowed and never returned them at the end of the journey.

Had they taken the plane, the Czechoslovak athletes would have been home for Christmas. Instead, they were still on the ship, which only added to their misery. Many wept, while others drank. As he became more maudlin, boxer František Majdloch tried to strangle Frantisek Kroutil, a member of the Czechoslovakia Olympic Committee. "It's your fault that we're here on this boat and not home for Christmas."[28] He never competed in another Olympics.

After three weeks at sea, the *Gruzia* reached Vladivostok the day before New Year's Eve. On the dock, a brass band played as thousands of well-wishers welcomed the athletes. They were then taken to the city's central square, where they listened to tedious speeches of welcome. The temperature was -30°C (-22°F), and Olga was dressed for the Australian summer; she was saved by a Russian athlete, who loaned her his jacket. When the speeches ended, Olga bought herself a pair of warm mittens and a brown fur hat.

The athletes then boarded a train on the Trans-Siberian Railway. The journey to Moscow took eight days, but this time the athletes enjoyed much better conditions. The beds on the train were hard but clean, and the food was edible. And the toilets had a plentiful supply of toilet paper.

Unfortunately, Olga caught a terrible cold in Vladivostok and was unable to leave her berth. News of her illness must have got around, and on the first day of the train journey Nina Ponomareva came to see her. Nina brought a small bottle containing a thick green liquor made from bitter herbs, a home remedy she said was a powerful cure. It tasted awful. "You either got instantly well or expired on the spot," explained Olga.[29] Over the next two days Nina nursed Olga and brought her meals. As they spent time together, a genuine friendship developed between the two women. "Olga, this is the first opportunity I've had to tell you how proud I am that you have become such a fine athlete since the time we met in Warsaw," Nina told her former pupil.[30]

When they reached Moscow, most of the Czechoslovaks were allowed to catch a plane home. Several medalists, including Olga, were asked to stay behind for a reception in their honor. The reception was held in the Kremlin's Georgievsky Hall. Children from the Moscow Ballet Academy entertained guests, and then a small orchestra played music by Tchaikovsky and Khachaturian.

The Tsars had once used banquets in this hall to impress supplicants with the richness and power of the Russian Empire. The new masters of the Kremlin used this occasion in much the same way. Certainly, Olga was impressed by the lavishness of the entertainment and awed by the grandeur of Georgievsky Hall.

Late in the evening Premier Nikita Khrushchev swept into the hall, accompanied by a delegation of Chinese political leaders, led by Premier Zhou Enlai. Khrushchev used the welcome home for the victorious Olympians to show his

Chinese visitors the unity that existed within the Soviet sphere. However, it is unclear what Zhou Enlai made of the absence of Hungarian athletes at the banquet.

Invited to address the guests, Olga made a short speech graciously thanking her hosts. The head of the Czechoslovakia Olympic Committee, Richard Nejezchleb, was next. Alluding to the defections of the Hungarian athletes, he boasted there were "no traitors among our athletes, and, as you can see, they are all here in Moscow."[31] Nejezchleb's speech made Olga feel uneasy as this comment could only be directed at her, and it made her wonder what her reception would be like in Prague.

Three Weddings and an Act of Contrition

As Czechoslovakia's only gold medal winner, Olga would normally be fêted on her return and showered with rewards. Instead, she quickly discovered her relationship with Hal had not gone unnoticed, and there were consequences.

At a reception at the Ministry of Interior, Olga met the deputy minister, who handed her a watch (a men's watch, she wryly noted).

> It might, or might not have occurred to you, comrade Fikotová, that deciding on that gift for you was something of a problem. We couldn't quite go all out, because while you gave us a reason to rejoice, at the same time you also so embarrassed us and Czechoslovakia. We may say, comrade Fikotová, that you managed to fulfill the plan of your production on fifty percent. Your involvement with the American fascist was a terrible blunder.[32]

It took all her will not to fling the watch in his face.

On his return home, Hal's reception could not have been more different. He was personally welcomed as a conquering hero by the mayor of Boston. Archbishop Cushing sent him a telegram of congratulations. And his alma mater, Boston College, named an annual four-year scholarship in his honor.

As much as he appreciated these honors, as an amateur, he could not accept monetary rewards, and none were offered. How would he raise money for the airfare to Prague, he wondered.

Hal had promised Olga he would come to Prague to marry her, but he was broke when he arrived in Boston. So he approached the State Department for help. It agreed he would make an excellent goodwill ambassador and bankrolled a tour of Europe—Norway, Finland, Yugoslavia, Iceland, and Ireland—where he would give sports clinics.

At the end of the tour Hal caught a plane to Prague, where Olga met him at the airport. Although they had not seen one another for more than ten weeks, it was clear the chemistry was still there, and Olga told him, "I never was more happy than I am now, and I never want to be separated again."[33]

Together once more, they spent most of their time trying to obtain permission from the Czechoslovak government to marry. When Olga visited the Marriages to Foreigners Department and asked what forms she needed to fill in, the official haughtily replied, "You must be joking, Comrade Fikotová. We're not about to let our Olympic champion run away."[34]

While Olga remained optimistic they would eventually obtain permission, Hal had his doubts. He was keen to put pressure on the government by telling the press about their plight. Olga disagreed with these tactics and persuaded Hal that publicity would make matters worse.

In the weeks that followed, while they worked their way through the red tape, they also enlisted the help of their friend Emil Zátopek, who they hoped might speed up the process. Despite being a triple gold medal winner in Helsinki and a sporting god among Czechoslovaks, his efforts failed. Olga decided to try herself and was able to obtain an audience with President Antonín Zápotocký. After initial hostility, Zápotocký softened as she politely answered his questions and explained there were no political motives to her request. She simply loved Hal and wanted to marry him. "I tell you what, you have my blessing, but all I can do for you is put in a kind word," Zápotocký said.[35]

Zápotocký faced considerable political pressure, which worked in favor of the young lovers. The international media had latched onto the story, which was being presented as thwarted love with the Czechoslovak government in the role of the villain. Playing up to the international media, Secretary of State and Cold War warrior John Foster Dulles remarked, "Well, we believe in romance," when questioned at a press conference.[36] The implication: Marxist Czechoslovakia was against romance. His opportunistic exploitation of the love affair was a clear winner in the psychological war against the communists.

Western reporters also framed the romance in Cold War terms. "It is the Czechs who must stand before the world in the universally despised role of an enemy of young love," thundered the *Toledo Blade*. "How can anyone say that, in this instance, the Communists have made it appear they are for all the good things in life, and we're against them?"[37] On the front page of a Frankfurt evening newspaper, a bright-red headline in the Czech language appealed to the government, "Mr. President Zapotocky, Please Help Olga and Harold to Happiness."[38] This was followed by an emotional article in German, detailing the frustrations Hal and Olga had encountered in their efforts to marry.

Soon after Hal and Olga met with the president, the permit to marry arrived. There were, however, two conditions. The wedding ceremony could go ahead as long as it was conducted quietly, with no fanfare. Second, Olga should leave for the United States immediately after the ceremony on a one-way ticket. Olga had hoped to continue to represent Czechoslovakia in international sporting competitions, but the government had made it quite clear this would not happen.

There was one more obstacle for the lovers to clear. Having navigated the Cold War between East and West, they now faced another cold war, one that had been raging for over four hundred years and was no less vicious. That was the hostility between Catholics and Protestants. This was the next minefield Olga and Hal would have to cross if they were to marry.

A devout Protestant, Olga wanted to be married in the St. Salvator's Evangelical Church of the Czech Brethren, but Hal raised a serious problem. As a Catholic, "I would be excommunicated if I did so, and everyone in Boston would believe I had given up my faith," he explained.[39] But Hal was already asking Olga to give up much to marry him. She would be leaving her family, her friends, her beloved Czechoslovakia, her studies, and she accepted their children would be raised as Catholics. Although it seemed impossible, Hal finally agreed: "Of course we must be married in both churches."[40] However, he was not sure he could convince the Catholic Church to take a compassionate approach to their plan.

First they visited St. Salvator's, where the pastor said he was happy to officiate at their wedding.

Next they visited Father Reinsberg in the rectory at the Church of Our Lady before Týn. While he sympathized with the young couple, he explained he could do little. Hal was bewildered. How could the Catholic Church tell him that if he married the woman he loves in her church, he'd "be committing a mortal sin against God."[41] He appealed to Father Reinsberg to help them find a way around the seemingly intractable problem.

The Vatican soon became involved and Hal and Olga hoped its intervention would overcome the impasse. At their next meeting, Reinsberg had some good news. "Because of the extraordinary circumstances of your marriage, you will be granted a special dispensation and be reaccepted into the church if you comply with two conditions. You are not to participate actively in the Protestant ceremony, and you will have to confess your sorrow for the transgression you have committed."[42] Based on this assurance, Hal and Olga decided to go ahead.

By holding the wedding on a Wednesday, a workday, Olga believed they would not attract attention. She had assured President Zápotocký the wedding would be low-key, just a family affair, and she intended to keep her promise. They were married on March 27, 1957, in three ceremonies.

As the American ambassador's limousine, with Olga inside, approached the Staroměstské náměstí (Old Town Square), it was blocked by a large crowd. There were around 30,000 well-wishers who had taken the day off to witness what promised to be a Hollywood wedding.

Word had got out, and even though it was a weekday, people came for various reasons. One attraction was the presence of Emil Zátopek and Dana Zátopková, both sporting royalty; he one of the world's greatest distance runners, and she a gold medalist in the javelin. They were the best man and woman. Olga herself was an attraction as the only gold medal winner in Melbourne. And then there was Hal; Czechoslovaks were curious to see the American. However, it was more than just idle curiosity. In a tightly controlled communist country like Czechoslovakia, many of those who came were quietly demonstrating their support for a couple who represented détente between East and West. They were also rejecting the steady diet of propaganda that attacked evil American capitalists. This is precisely why the government did not want the ceremony to be publicized, as it would provide a public outlet to the latent opposition to the communist system. The events in Hungary five months earlier undoubtedly made the government nervous. Having 30,000 people in the center of Prague did little to allay its fears.

While there probably was a political undercurrent to the wedding, sight-seers were also in the square to enjoy the spectacle and share in the fairy-tale romance.

Clutching her bouquet of purple baby orchids to her breast, Olga and the rest of the wedding party left the safety of their cars. They then made their way to the town hall, where a civil ceremony would take place. A Pretorian guard of Olga's uncles surrounded her to protect her from the crush of people. As they got closer to the square, one of them shouted, "Away from the bride or you'll strip her to her bloomers!"[43]

Olga was wearing a white, three-quarter-length dress with a tight bodice. On her head she wore a flat, broad-brimmed white Florentine hat but no veil. Hal wore his good navy-blue suit and a tie from Ambassador Johnson's wardrobe.

On the second floor of the town hall, a fine Gothic building with magnificent stained-glass windows dating back to the Renaissance, Hal and Olga were met by the civil celebrant who conducted a civil ceremony with Marxist austerity. After the ceremony Hal turned to Olga, tipped her hat slightly back, and gave her a lingering kiss.

As they emerged from the town hall they were once again greeted by the crowd, who showered them with rice, and well-wishers presented them with the traditional Czech wedding gift of salt and bread.

As it became clear the crowd might stop them from reaching the church, a small contingent of police officers came to their aid. They too were infected by the joy permeating the crowd and were grinning as they cleared a path to Týn church.

As they entered, they saw the place was packed, and the priest officiating was pleading with the congregation to be careful. Some people were standing on the pedestals of statues, and one of the angels had already lost a wing. As the couple made their way to the front of the church, Olga noticed her mother was

Olga Fikotová and Hal Connolly marry in the Church of Our Lady Before Tyn (Prague) on March 27, 1957 (Alamy).

nowhere to be seen. She had been locked outside. Olga rushed up the aisle and told the guard on the door to let her mother in. Bemused, he explained he had already allowed five women into the church who claimed to be her mother. Once Olga found her real mother, the ceremony proceeded.

When the priest intoned "*ego conjungo vos in matrimonium,*" they were married a second time.

With a protective escort of police officers, the wedding party exited the church by a back door to avoid the crowd. A car was waiting for Hal and Olga and took them to their third and last wedding.

During the ceremony Hal heeded Father Reinsberg's advice. He participated minimally in the Protestant service while silently repeating the "Act of Contrition." It was soon over. And once more, Hal said, "Yes, I do," and Olga, "*Ano.*"

Ambassador Johnson's gift to the young couple was to pay for the wedding reception at the embassy. Around 200 wedding guests enjoyed a Boston-style buffet washed down with Californian wine, after which the happy couple ceremoniously cut a three-layered wedding cake. There was also a telegram from Secretary of State John Foster Dulles congratulating the newlyweds.

Undoubtedly, Ambassador Johnson was genuine in helping the young couple. Still, it would stretch credibility if his generosity did not have a political motive. In Prague, American support for Hal and Olga was highly visible. They had use of the embassy's limousine to collect the necessary approvals for the marriage permit. They traveled to the wedding ceremonies in a car with the U.S. flag prominently displayed on its bonnet. The reception at the American Embassy demonstrated once again a very public display of support.

After the wedding, newspapers again picked up the Cold War theme. According to an editorial in the *New York Times*:

> Harold could have married any girl who was willing and able to marry him. Secretary Dulles said so. But Olga couldn't marry Harold unless the Czechoslovak government said she could. The Czechoslovak Government now says yes. We say yes. The hearts of all who have ever known romance say yes.[44]

Life magazine wrote that their marriage represented "the triumph of human rights over ideology, of love over politics."[45] *Paris Match* suggested the Czechoslovaks were "celebrating a day of independence."[46]

Three days after the wedding, Hal received a papal dispensation and was readmitted to the Catholic Church. The following Sunday he attended Mass and received Holy Communion. This was very important to Hal as he explained in a letter to his mother, "I am in the state of grace now and, with God's help, until the day I die."[47]

Even though Hal had made his peace with the Vatican, Catholic Boston was not as forgiving. Soon after his return, Hal was summoned to the Chancery at Boston's Cathedral of the Holy Cross, where he was handed a message from Archbishop Richard Cushing. His note read, "Your marriage in Prague has caused a public scandal in Boston, and until there is a full inquiry, you are to make no public appearances with your wife. In addition, you are not to attend Mass or Holy Communion after 10 a.m."[48] More bad news followed. Boston College canceled the scholarship in Hal's name. And after Hal was seen coming out of Mass, his mother received telephone threats.

The Czechoslovak government never forgave Olga. When she approached the Czechoslovak Olympic Committee and offered to compete for her country at the next Olympics, they rejected her offer. They then spread rumors among her former teammates that she had refused to represent her country.

CHAPTER 14

Sport über Alles?

Shotgun Wedding

Two days after Hal Connolly's victory in the hammer throw, Christa Stubnick lined up in the heats of the women's 100-meter race. She was part of the combined German team and the first athlete from communist East Germany to compete in a Summer Olympic Games.

Few spectators in the main stadium appreciated the historical significance of Stubnick's presence. Instead, they were anticipating their own historical event: Australia's first gold medal on home turf, with Betty Cuthbert and Marlene Mathews the favorites.

Stubnick represented the Australians' greatest threat; two months earlier, she had equaled the Olympic record in Dresden.

Stubnick was a short, slim woman with black hair and a dimpled smile. She wore glasses, even when she raced.

Christa's career as an athlete almost ended before it started. In 1950 she was in Grünau, a forested area on the edge of Berlin, for a cross-country race. She was 17 years old and was accompanied by her father. During a routine pre-race health check, the doctor told Christa she had a heart defect and could not race. Christa was devastated and burst into tears. After she calmed down, she told her father she wanted to catch up with some girlfriends and disappeared into the crowd. The next time he saw his daughter, she was in front of the field of runners. A keen sportsman himself, her father understood Christa's competitive spirit. When she returned, holding the winner's ribbon, he could not bring himself to scold her. Instead, they came to an agreement. She could continue to compete but only in sprints—no more long-distance races.

Possessing raw talent, she lacked technique and had earned the nickname of "penguin" because of her ungainly stride, with her arms flapping at her side. Soon after, she was taken under the wing of Coach Max Schommler, who helped her correct her running style. Before long, she was breaking records.

Watching the race in Melbourne from the VIP box was Avery Brundage.

The IOC president, more than anyone, could take credit for giving Stubnick the opportunity to compete. As East Germany's Olympic committee had not been recognized by the IOC,[1] the only way she could compete was as part of a combined German team, which Brundage championed. This proposal was born out of his belief in *Pax Olimpica* (although he never referred to it by that name), in which sport provided the magic elixir that would bring out humanity's better angels and surmount political squabbles. "Where amateur sport with its high ideals flourishes, there civilization advances," he once declared.[2]

When Brundage first proposed that the two German states cooperate, he faced opposition from both East and West Germany. As implacable enemies in the Cold War, they had conflicting agendas.

West Germany, whose seat of government was in Bonn, believed the German Democratic Republic was a puppet state, which it contemptuously called the "Soviet Occupied Zone." Excluding it from international competition was one way to deny East Germany's existence as a separate country.

The communist regime in East Germany insisted it was a sovereign nation, and therefore had a right to compete in the Olympic Games under its own name—the Democratic Republic of Germany. It should be allowed to march in the opening ceremony behind its flag and have the victories of its athletes marked by the playing of its national anthem. By competing in the Olympics, the East German government could announce, in a very public way, that there were now two Germanys.

For both sides, participation in the Olympics was all about politics and had nothing to do with sport.

The combined team was the result of a shotgun wedding, in which the bride and groom felt they had little choice. For East Germany, it was the only way they could participate in the Olympics. West Germany worried that if it did not agree, the IOC might change its mind and recognize East Germany's Olympic committee. This would clear the way for East Germany to compete as a separate country. While the gun was loaded and cocked, the path towards getting both parties to the altar was fraught.

Negotiations commenced in Hanover on May 17, 1951. On one side of the table sat Karl Ritter von Halt, a tall, heavy-set man with graying hair swept back off a high forehead. A sports administrator and skilled diplomat, he had also been Reichssportführer during the Nazi period (something he hoped would be forgotten).

On the other side of the negotiating table sat 31-year-old Kurt Edel. A former athlete, he was a successful functionary within the communist sporting establishment. This required him to display an unwavering commitment to Marxism-Leninism and loyalty to the Party. Operating in a totalitarian regime, however, had ill-equipped Edel with the skills to negotiate with equals. When frustrated by von Halt's obstructionist tactics, Edel easily lost his temper. This was a bad look in the gentil world of the Olympic movement.

From the start of negotiations it was clear Edel was out of his depth, as the more experienced von Halt ran rings around him. Frustrated, Edel resorted to insults, calling von Halt an "incorrigible old Nazi."[3] Even if true, such crude denunciations did not go down well with executive members of the IOC. At the time, the IOC had more than a passing resemblance to an English gentleman's club where chaps did not call other chaps beastly names. For local consumption, Edel also crudely vilified the IOC. Not one to miss an opportunity, von Halt sent Brundage cuttings from East German newspapers that quoted Edel. These cuttings had the desired effect of upsetting the IOC president. It did not take long for Brundage to conclude Edel was the blame for the failure of negotiations to progress.

This was not totally fair as von Halt was negotiating in bad faith. He was just able to conceal his intentions much better than Edel. While his manner was calm and measured, the positions he took during negotiations were often unreasonable. For example, von Halt wanted East German athletes to compete as part of the West German team and its victories to be celebrated with a rendition of the West German anthem *Deutschlandlied*. Such conditions denied East Germany's existence as an independent state and could not be accepted by Edel. This is precisely what von Halt hoped for. Updating Chancellor Konrad Adenauer, von Halt explained he had conducted negotiations in a way "so that they would be unsuccessful."[4] If he could force Edel to walk away from the negotiating table then von Halt could claim that East Germany was not interested in reaching an agreement. More importantly, East Germany's athletes would not compete in the Olympics, and its government would remain a pariah in the international community.

As the 1952 Helsinki Games approached, under pressure from the IOC, the from the two Germanys and IOC officials arranged to meet in Copenhagen. Again, the West Germans were intent on sabotaging the negotiations. Using diplomatic back channels, the government in Bonn convinced the Danish government to delay granting visas to Edel until the eve of the meeting, so he would miss the meeting. It worked, and IOC members were furious, believing that Edel's late arrival was a deliberate effort to derail negotiations. Taking advantage of the animosity towards Edel, von Halt was able to convince the IOC that East Germany was not interested in being part of a united German team, and in 1952 West Germany competed in its own right.

After these Games discussions resumed, with the objective of sending combined teams to the Cortina d'Ampezzo Winter Games and Melbourne Summer Games in 1956. Bad faith on both sides continued to hamper negotiations. It was only pressure by the IOC that saw them move forward, albeit at a glacial rate.

In May 1954, at the IOC's Athens meeting, East Germany once again tried to have its Olympic committee recognized. Edel was unable to be present to support his country's application because the Greek government would not give him a visa, at the urging of Bonn. The vote was fourteen votes for and thirty-one against.

Brundage was increasingly frustrated by the lack of progress. Seeing Edel as the problem, the IOC president had a quiet word with Konstantin Andrianov, the Soviet member on the IOC, to see whether he would intervene.

Clearly the message got through. At the start of 1955, Edel was replaced by Heinz Schöbel. He was a smooth operator, and his appointment marked the moment when real headway was made, but it was not fast enough for the IOC.

In a successful effort to outflank the IOC, East Germany applied for membership to international sporting federations. By 1955 East Germany had been recognized by nineteen, fourteen of which governed Olympic sports. By refusing to do the same, the IOC was looking foolish.

Responding to this changed landscape, the Olympic Committee Congress, held in Paris in June 1955, voted to provisionally recognize East Germany's Olympic committee. There was a rider: East Germany had to agree to join West Germany in forming a combined team that would compete in the 1956 Olympiads.

This decision sent a signal to von Halt. If he did not reach an accommodation with East Germany on fielding a combined team, the IOC might allow a separate East German team to compete. This maneuver had the desired effect, and afterward both sides showed a greater willingness to compromise.

Sundae in Cortina d'Ampezzo

The West German government had only been willing to allow negotiations to take place, provided the final agreement contained "a minimum of concessions," Minister of State Walter Hallstein told von Halt.[5]

When Hallstein discovered that the agreement did not preclude the playing of East Germany's anthem, should one of its athletes win, he worried that it would confer de facto recognition to East Germany and undermine the Bonn's fiction of referring to it as the Soviet Occupied Zone.

A crisis meeting of West German government ministers was held in Bonn, just twenty days before the Winter Games were to commence. To repair the damage, the Ministry for Foreign Affairs dispatched a special emissary to Italy to convince IOC to expel the East German team participating in Cortina. The mission was entrusted to Fredy Müller, vice-president of the West German Athletics Association.

After arriving in Cortina, Müller cabled his findings to Bonn. His telegram was coded—it was the Cold War after all, and coded messages were de rigueur for the times. It read: "THE SON RECEIVED SUFFICIENT AUTHORISATION FROM THE BOWLING ALLEY TO NEGOTIATE WITH THE LEADER ABOUT THE BEARS CONCERNING THE KANGAROO JUMPING IN THE RAIN. WISHES FROM NUMBER ONE ON THE WINDOW HAVE TO BE ENFORCED. SUNDAE PROBLEM FOR CORTINA NOT REALLY URGENT BECAUSE SINGLE WIN BY ANY BEAR IS NOT EXPECTED." Deciphered, Müller reported that von Halt had been unable to convince the IOC to expel East German athletes. In any case, Müller reported, it was highly unlikely that an East German would win a gold medal, and so its national anthem would not be played.[6]

Müller's prediction was tested on the last day of competition when a field of fifty-one competitors lined up for the ski jump. There were two East Germans: Harry Glass and Werner Lesser. The favorites were the Norwegians and the Finns. But Glass was a chance for a medal, but probably not gold.

It was a fine day, without even a hint of a breeze, and 43,000 spectators sat in the stands at the bottom of the Trampolina. One of them was von Halt, accompanied by Müller. Both were desperately hoping neither of the East German competitors would win.

The competition started late morning, and spectators were well rugged up against the cold; it was -10°C, although they were promised the temperature would rise to a balmy -4°C later that day.

The winner would be decided by the sum of two jumps.

Von Halt had to wait until almost the end to see Harry Glass take his first jump. He kept his body straight, leaning as far forward towards the skis as possible, with arms straight down by his side to reduced aerodynamic resistance. It was a great jump, and he was in the lead. Now von Halt was worried. Very worried.

Glass's next jump was good but not good enough. He was beaten by two Finns: Antti Hyvärinen and Aulis Kallakorpi. Glass came third.

Later that day, Avery Brundage handed the winners their medals. And much to von Halt's relief, it was the Finnish national anthem that was played. Had Glass kept his lead and won gold, East Germany's national anthem *Auferstanden aus Ruinen* (Risen from Ruins) would have been played. At this moment, Glass was just happy to have been placed, and his medal was the first won by an East German at an Olympic Games.

After the near-disaster of Cortina, there was pressure on von Halt to prevent East Germany from displaying its national symbols as part of the combined team in Melbourne.

As the Melbourne Olympics approached, negotiations finally made real progress. Five weeks before the opening ceremony, the two sides finalized protocols under which the combined team would operate.

The issue of which anthem would be played continued to be particularly delicate. East Germany's position was that if one of its athletes won a gold medal, its anthem would be played, and victories by West German athletes would be marked by its anthem. Von Halt was adamant that under no conditions would the East German anthem be played. Finally, both sides agreed Beethoven's melody to Schiller's poem, *Ode an die Freude* (Ode to Joy), would be played, regardless of whether an East or West German won a gold medal.

They also agreed they would march as a single team in the opening ceremony, wearing neutral beige uniforms. And competitors would not be allowed to wear badges displaying their national emblems. Up until 1959 both Germanys had the same flag, so that was not an issue. In Melbourne, the white Olympic rings would be incorporated into the center of the German tricolor.

Selecting athletes for the combined team presented new problems. West Germany was unwilling to allow soldiers attached to NATO, officers in its police force, or public servants, to compete in qualifying events in East Germany, fearing espionage. East Germany pursued the same policy, fearing its athletes would be encouraged to defect to the West. So, neither side could put forward all their best athletes.

Once the composition of the combined team had been decided, East Germany's leader Walter Ulbricht was keen to draw attention to the political significance of his country's participation. At a farewell for his athletes, Ulbricht told them, "A while ago some circles in the capitalist world thought it would be possible to deny the existence of the GDR [German Democratic Republic]." However, East Germany's participation in the Olympics now made it "increasingly difficult for those who wanted to ignore the GDR to do so."[7]

While the East German government saw benefits from the compromise, the government in Bonn was livid. Two days before the start of the Olympics, the West German Cabinet declared that the presence of the East Germans as equal partners in the combined team was an insult to its "national dignity."[8] Some at the meeting even supported ordering West German athletes to return home immediately. Instead, Cabinet decided that "for the moment the Federal government will not decree a non-participation, but under certain circumstances this might have to be taken into consideration."[9] The West Germans may have been angry, but they had little choice but to allow their athletes to compete. Had West Germany boycotted the Games, then East Germany would no longer have been restrained by the arrangements made for the combined team. Its national anthem would have been heard for the first time at an Olympic Games, which, from the West German viewpoint, would have been much worse.

Brundage preferred to ignore such Cold War gameplays, and in Melbourne he welcomed the combined team, citing it as an example of "Olympic power; the answer to a problem that has baffled the Chancelleries of the world."[10] For him it was an example of sport *über alles*—sport over everything.

Combined German team at the opening ceremony in Melbourne on November 22, 1956.

With the politics out of the way it was now up to the German athletes to prove Brundage was right to champion the combined German team. For East Germany, it hoped that Stubnick would win its first medal in a Summer Olympics.

History's Silver Lining

After the heats of the 100 meters, Christa Stubnick was in the final, having equaled the Olympic record in one of the heats.

The day was fine, but the runners would face a stiff headwind, and a record was unlikely. As the competitors entered the stadium, a deafening cheer met the two Australians—Betty Cuthbert and Marlene Mathews. For Stubnick, "it was as if they were the only two runners competing."[11]

All six settled into the blocks and tensed as the starter, Julius "Judy" Patching, commanded, "On your mark!" Then "Set." The knees of all the competitors were now off the ground, ready for take-off. Rather than hearing the starter's pistol next, they were abruptly told, "Stand down." Patching then came over to Stubnick and had words to her. Stubnick, speaking just a few words of English, did not have a clue what he was saying, but she was worried. For a second time the runners lined up, and as the competitors waited for the starter's gun, Patching again told them "Stand down," and then spoke to Stubnick once more. Still no wiser to what she had done wrong, Stubnick was unnerved. "I wondered why he didn't disqualify me," she said. For the third time the competitors lined up. This time the pistol sounded and they were off.[12]

Stubnick's start was poor, and Mathews' was even worse. After 50 meters Cuthbert took the lead. With her mouth agape and her short blonde locks flying, she broke the white tape. The American, Isabelle Daniels, and Stubnick were close on her heels but were surprised when they were joined by Mathews, who had made a remarkable recovery from her poor start.

Spectators went wild when they saw the large stadium scoreboard announce that Cuthbert had won.

Stubnick assumed she had not won a medal when Cuthbert, Mathews, and Daniels were ushered towards the winner's podium.

While unplaced, Stubnick wanted to understand why Patching had spoken to her. She found a German journalist who spoke English, and they approached Patching to ask why he had cautioned her. "Your knees were trembling so much it was putting off the other athletes," he explained.[13]

Having satisfied her curiosity, Stubnick headed for the exit. What she did not know was that a photo had been called for, which took around five minutes to process. As soon as the photo was available, a red-faced official had to tell Daniels, who was waiting by the podium, that she was unplaced, humiliating her. Mathews was told she had come third, not second. Another official chased after the German, yelling, "Frau Stubnick, Frau Stubnick," and then escorted her to the podium where she was awarded the silver medal.

Stubnick would win another silver medal in the 200-meter race, once again beaten by Betty Cuthbert.

In the 4 × 100-meter relay Stubnick found herself once more pitted against Cuthbert. They were both to run the last leg.

The East German team had broken the world record in Leipzig three months earlier, and this was Stubnick's best chance for a gold medal.

But like much else in the combined team, politics intruded. West Germany insisted the team include one of its athletes, Erika Fisch, leaving out East German Gisela Henning, even though she was part of the world-record-breaking team. The reason was that the West Germans did not want East Germany to claim the glory of a gold medal in its own right.

Fisch had no time for these Cold War games. Although the teams of the two German states were accommodated in separate parts of the Olympic Village, she insisted on staying with her relay teammates. This upset von Halt, who insisted Fisch move back with the rest of the West Germans. When she refused, he had some of his athletes physically transfer her gear out of the East German compound.

Unfortunately, Fisch injured herself in the long jump and could not line up for the relay. This forced a last-minute substitute, and West German steeplechaser Maria Sander-Domagalla replaced her.

In the final, the Germans were among the leaders until the second change when the inexperienced Sander-Domagalla badly botched the baton change, and her team came last.

Cuthbert was part of the winning team and collected her third gold medal.

Australians were justly proud of their hometown sprinter. In the wake of Cuthbert's victories, it is worth asking why she was unworthy of being named the hero of the Olympic Games rather than Kuts. After all, she had won three gold medals to his two. Also, she broke the world record in the 200-meter race and was part of the relay team that broke the world record

A survey of the newspaper coverage of Betty Cuthbert after her wins shows why the best she could hope for was to be remembered as the "Golden Girl."[14] At the same time, Kuts was allowed to scale the summit of Olympus as one of its greatest heroes. While profiles of Kuts covered his war experiences and then his struggles against the odds to become a world-class athlete, articles on Cuthbert dwelt on the domestic rather than on her remarkable athletic feats. An article reporting her first gold medal led the story with her fondness for her budgerigars before mentioning her victory.[15] Few people are likely to see a caregiver for seventy budgerigars as a hero. The overseas coverage was no better. In the British *Daily Express* there was a photograph of a grinning Cuthbert with the caption remarking, "more woman, less superwoman."[16]

Striking Gold

A couple of hours after the women's relay, another East German had a chance to mount the winner's podium. He was bantamweight boxer Wolfgang Behrendt, who looked more like a cheeky pageboy than a pug from Berlin's mean streets. He was not, however, the favorite. Most thought the Russian, Boris Stepanov, would win.

After having a bye in the first round, Stepanov came up against Freddie Gilroy, a fighter from Belfast. "He was a hot favorite to lift the gold," said Gilroy, "but I caught him with a sweet left hook in the third round and I knew he was not getting back up."[17]

In this round, local champion Bobbie Bath, a shy country lad from Buninyong, was outpointed by Song Soon-Chun, an aggressive slugger from South Korea.

Song Soon-Chun was born in 1934 during the Japanese occupation of Korea. It was not a good time in Korea: hunger was widespread, and his mother died when he was two years old. In 1952, soon after the Korean War broke out, Song Soon-Chun was on the front line in Paju, just south of the thirty-eighth parallel, and saw fierce fighting as the North Korean troops overran South Korean positions. He escaped uninjured.

After the war he took up boxing, winning many of his fights with a lethal overhand right that often left his opponents on the canvas tallying stars.

After beating Bath, Song Soon-Chun beat Argentina's Carmelo Tomaselli and Chile's Claudio Barrientos to qualify for the final.

The Korean's opponent was Wolfgang Behrendt, who had won his bouts against Danish boxer Henrik Ottesen by a knockout in the second round, and then had points wins against Glasgow's Owen Reilly and Gilroy.

Like Song Soon-Chun, Behrendt had lived in the shadow of war. He was raised in working-class Prenzlauer Berg in the Soviet Occupied Zone of Berlin, and his father was a POW, who was not released until several years after the war ended.

As a kid, Wolfgang loved sport but had to make do with a ball made of rags to play football, with bricks used to mark out the goalposts. And there were a lot of bricks lying around his neighborhood, as much of it had been leveled by Allied bombing. One day a friend brought a pair of boxing gloves to school, and Wolfgang was given a chance to box. However, with just two gloves, he would take one and his opponent the other.

Soon after this, he found a local boxing school set up in the basement of a butcher's shop. It was run by Karl Schwarz, who told Wolfgang he would train him for 25 marks a month. Wolfgang earned some money after school collecting bottles that he sold to Russian soldiers, who took them to an army supply center to be filled with beer. He also found casings from spent grenades and incendiary bombs, which he sold as scrap metal. Unfortunately, he could only earn enough to pay half the monthly fee and asked Herr Schwarz whether he could train at the gym every second day. The trainer agreed. After two weeks Herr Schwarz saw Wolfgang was a natural talent, and he waived the monthly fee.

Behrendt's cherubic looks belied his dangerous left and quicksilver speed.

All the boxing finals were held on December 1, and the competition started at 7:30 p.m. The bantamweight fight was second on the program, and by then the stadium had filled to capacity.

Before coming to Melbourne, Behrendt never believed he was good enough to compete in the Olympics, let alone win a medal. Yet here he was facing Song Soon-Chun in the final.

Behrendt's trainer had warned him that Song Soon-Chun wore down his opponent in the first two rounds before taking him out in the last. The Korean had not lost any of his previous forty-five fights and had won over half of them by knockouts. Behrendt decided to score as many points as possible in the first two rounds but have enough in reserve for the last round to counter the barrage of punches he expected Song Soon-Chun to unleash.

The finals were held in the newly built Western Stadium, with 7,000 fight fans looking forward to a feast of Olympic boxing. As Behrendt and Soon-Chun faced one another, a thickening fug of cigarette smoke rippled under arc lamps, embracing the boxers in an unforgiving glare as the referee issued his pre-fight instructions.

For the first round Behrendt was content to box, scoring heavily with his left to the head and body to accumulate points, while the Korean defended grimly against his faster opponent. In the second round Behrendt landed a couple of hard punches that stunned the Korean. As Behrendt sat in his corner preparing for the last round, his trainer reminded him to expect Song Soon-Chun to come out fast and hard. Behrendt assured him he was still feeling fresh and was confident he could keep his opponent at bay. As the round started Song Soon-Chun unleashed a full-out attack, but Behrendt was fast enough to stay on his feet.

As the judges tallied their scores, many spectators cried out, "Korea! Korea!" The stadium was momentarily silent as the referee just stood there, uncertain who had won. Eventually, he was told who had won and raised Behrendt's arm, declaring him the winner on points, 60–58. Immediately some of the spectators started to boo. But there were also cheers, particularly from German-Australians in the stadium. It was a hard-fought match, and it was difficult not to admire the courage and skill of both fighters.

Behrendt's gold medal was important to the German Democratic Republic. It made the world notice it was now a part of the international community. And as a gold medalist, he was an ideal material for East German propaganda. There was another reason why sporting success mattered. In a country where its Stalinist leaders were unpopular and the economy a basket case, sporting victories provided a bright spot for the communist regime.

To make the athletes from the combined team feel welcome, two days before the closing ceremony, the local German Tivoli Club held a party in inner-suburban Windsor. After some introductory remarks from their host the national anthem was played, and everyone was expected to stand. It was the West German anthem, *Deutschlandlied*. As soon as the East German officials realized what was happening they stormed out. This was provocative and showed that Cold War politics was never far below the surface. The athletes remained, not quite realizing what the fuss was all about.

Later that evening, as Stubnick danced with a German-Australian, her partner tried to persuade her to defect. "Within two years you will have your own house and a car," he promised.[18] She was not interested, nor was any other East German interested in seeking asylum.

On his return home, Behrendt was fêted as a national hero. And East

Germany's leader Walter Ulbricht personally awarded the boxer the *Verdienter Meister des Sport* (Deserving Master of Sport), his country's highest sports award. Stubnick's achievements were also rewarded, and she was promoted within the People's Police.

All the East German Olympic medal winners toured around the country over the next four months, visiting factories and schools, where they described their achievements. And, of course thanked their benefactor. "We are so grateful for the generous support of our State, equaled only by other socialistic countries," Stubnick repeated countless times to crowds who had come to see her as she toured around the country.[19]

Pax Olympia?

Was the formation of the combined German team a victory for Pax Olympia? Certainly Brundage thought so. "I must admit that we were pleased with ourselves with having reunited Germany at least in sport, a thing the politicians have been unable to do," he preened.[20] Afterward, he modestly suggested the IOC be awarded the Nobel Peace Prize for its efforts.

President of East Germany's Olympic committee, Heinz Schöbel, was positive about the experience. "The joint German team at Cortina d'Ampezzo and Melbourne, representing the lofty ideas of friendship and peace in front of the whole world, also manifested the concept of accord between Germans."[21]

But what was it like on the ground? The athletes of the two Germanys stayed in separate dormitories in the Olympic Village and seldom mixed. This was not surprising, as East Germany's security police, the Stasi, kept an eye on its athletes. The feeling of mistrust was also prevalent among the West Germans. "Here, each side is the devil of the other," observed sprinter Inge Fuhrmann.[22]

While the IOC and the international media were happy to hail the combined team as a victory of sport *über alles*, those who had followed the situation closely were not fooled. "It was a nice depiction, yet a mirage," concluded West German sports journalist Guido von Mengden.[23]

Private cables also reveal that serious political games were being played between the two Germanys. West Germany's Australian ambassador Walther Hess, in a telegram to the Department of Foreign Affairs in Bonn, described the Melbourne Games as an occasion in which the "battle for Olympic medals was a political struggle."[24] A second cable from an embassy attaché Baron Götz von Groll lists the final medal counts: West Germany won three gold, six silver, and five bronze to East Germany's one gold, four silver, and one bronze. He concluded that the poor showing on the medal table would "deprive Soviet propaganda of the opportunity to demonstrate through arithmetic dissimulation of medal distribution the superiority of the people's democratic society [German Democratic Republic]."25

Events in Melbourne had wider geopolitical significance.

The Melbourne Games occurred when Bonn was determined to isolate East Germany, raising tensions in the region. In December 1955, the West German government introduced the Hallstein Doctrine in which Bonn threatened to cut diplomatic relations with countries (other than the Soviet Union) that recognized the German Democratic Republic.

Almost as soon as this doctrine was announced, its effect was weakened by the existence of the combined German teams in Cortina and Melbourne. This is why the West German government was so upset when it realized how the Olympics would undermine its efforts to isolate and delegitimize the East German state.

According to historian Andy Streck, considering the weak position East Germany was in, "the choice of sport as a method to force international diplomatic recognition was a stroke of brilliant genius and one for which the West was totally unprepared."26

CHAPTER 15

Blood in the Water

Unprepared

In the run-up to the Olympics, Hungary was the favorite to take gold in water polo. That changed after the revolution, which had interrupted the players' training so that they had become soft and sluggish. More worrying, when they arrived in Melbourne, they were psychologically fragile, and their morale had hit rock bottom.

Realizing that his charges were in no mental state to mount a successful Olympic campaign, Coach Béla Rajki called the players together in the Olympic Village. Addressing them, he delivered perhaps the most important speech of his career. "Whether you stay out here, whether you go home, be sure to take this opportunity to win the Olympic championship." Winning, he argued, was important for those who intended to seek asylum because it would provide them with credentials with which to build a new life, as a coach or even playing for their adopted country. For those returning to an uncertain future in Hungary, the gold medal would protect them from recriminations, particularly for those players who had publicly supported the revolution. At the end of his speech, each player swore a solemn oath, "We will work together, and we will win."[1]

His speech had the desired effect. The team was re-energized, and Rajki ramped up their training. When a pool was not available, they headed to a local Melbourne beach to work on their skills in its chilly waters.

Slowly, the team started to gain match fitness. However, the players knew that they would still struggle when they faced the top teams, particularly the USSR, Italy, and Yugoslavia.

Game On

Fortunately, once the competition got underway, Hungary found itself in Group B, with relatively weak sides. They had comfortable wins against the

United Kingdom and the United States. While they won by wide margins, the Hungarian players were on autopilot and lacked their usual flair and polish.

Hungary could not afford to drop a game as the gold medal was determined by the win-loss ratio over the course of the competition.

In the next round, the Hungarians faced the Italians, who had won bronze in Helsinki. For the first seven minutes the young Italian team kept the Hungarians scoreless. What the Italians lacked in experience they made up for in enthusiasm and vigor.

In Melbourne the Hungarians wore new swimsuits made of Lastex, a body-hugging textile woven from fine threads of chemically modified latex rubber. They hoped this new swimwear would reduce their opponents' ability to pull them off the ball by their swimming trunks, which was easy to do with the old woolen ones. The Italians, however, were up to the challenge, and two Hungarian players needed to have their swimming trunks replaced during the game. Eventually the Italians were outclassed, overrun by more mature bodies, with the Hungarians winning easily.

Germany was their next opponent. While in name they were the United German team, the Hungarians faced a side made up of only West German players, which had beaten an East German side in six elimination matches held in April and May 1956.

Having analyzed the Hungarians' game in preliminary rounds, the Germans played defensively, holding the Hungarians scoreless. But they were unable to score themselves. Lacking the skill and discipline of their opponents, the Germans started to lose concentration, and mistakes were punished by the more polished Hungarian players, who overwhelmed them for a convincing win.

War in the Water

The next game was the semi-final against the USSR. For the Hungarians it was more than just another game of water polo. "We fanatically wanted to win, at all costs," recalled the captain Dezső Gyarmati. "We felt that we were the ones that could get some measure of satisfaction for our country. The odds were even; it was seven people struggling against seven people. Unlike at home, where the Russians were in control, here we could show the superiority of the Hungarian people."[2] A decisive win would be a form of payback. Some felt guilty at having left Budapest during the crisis, and so beating the Soviets would be their way to symbolically defeat the enemy. Losing, of course, would be the final humiliation.

Before the game commenced, Gyarmati gave his players one last piece of advice. "Don't do anything above the waterline that might attract a penalty. But underwater, do as you please."[3] The objective was to make the Soviet players retaliate, hopefully in full view of the referee, and be sent off. With just seven men in a team, the loss of a player could be disastrous.

The game was played in the Glasshouse. The pool had stands on two sides, with the north-west and south-east sides of the stadium made of glass, providing a fine view of trees on one side and the Yarra River on the other. It was a sultry day, and fat gray clouds seemed determined to block out the sun, infusing the pool with a soft, luminous light.

The Glasshouse quickly filled with spectators, with many turned away. Such was the demand that scalpers sold tickets at up to twenty times their face value.

As Gyarmati entered the Glasshouse, he was heartened to see the vast majority of spectators were Hungarian-Australians. Quite a few women wore traditional costumes, hand-embroidered in colorful floral patterns with red lace trim. Their hair was adorned with coronets of small red and white flowers.

As teams lined up on the concourse, Gyarmati glared at his opponents' tracksuits, emblazoned with the initials CCCP (Cyrillic for USSR). These were the very same letters that he had witnessed a little over a month ago, painted on the side of the tanks wreaking havoc in Budapest. Over the loudspeaker the name of each player was announced. As the Hungarians were introduced, spectators rose to their feet and roared their support. The Russians received desultory applause, mainly from officials and Australians scattered around the stands. The air crackled with ill-will when some of the Hungarian players turned their backs on their Soviet opponents.

When Soviet captain, Petr Mshveniyeradze, faced Gyarmati, he was surprised at the intense hostility from the man he thought was a good friend. Whenever he played a Friendly in Budapest, he would always visit Gyarmati at home, who affectionately called him "teddy bear." He would play with Gyarmati's daughter, Andrea, who would giggle as he threw her into the air. But something had changed. What he saw in the Hungarian's deep cobalt blue eyes was a hardness he had never seen before. Mshveniyeradze was further hurt when Gyarmati refused to shake his hand, a usual courtesy between captains before any game started.

The Soviet side was built around Mshveniyeradze, who was born in Tbilisi in Georgia. As a teenager, he played football and took on the high jump. In the summer of 1943, when he was 14 years old, he discovered a nearby pool, where he developed into a world-class breaststroke swimmer. After the war he became interested in water polo and soon found himself in Moscow, playing for Dinamo. An amiable giant of a man with an inoffensive mustache, outside the pool he made friends easily. His fans called him "Tsar Peter" for his command of the pool, where he used his 245 pounds (110 kg) of muscle to barrel through the opposition. He was the team's best striker, able to score with either hand.

In the past, contests between the two were epic as Gyarmati lined up against Mshveniyeradze and always beat him. Both men were 6-feet 1-inch (186 centimeters) tall, but the Georgian was 37 pounds (17 kg) heavier than Gyarmati. However, the Hungarian was teak-hard, fast in the pool, and technically superior to the Soviet captain.

In the more than five years that the two teams had played each other, "we were losing all the time," remarked Mshveniyeradze. "And then we began to slowly, slowly catch up, slowly tightening the noose around their necks."[4] Could this semi-final be the day that the Soviets beat their nemesis?

Mshveniyeradze knew that only a win would do if his team was to have any chance for gold. In an earlier game the Soviets had lost to Yugoslavia 2–3. At the same time, the Hungarians were undefeated, so the Soviet's win-loss ratio was inferior.

With the formalities over, the Soviet players, wearing dark blue caps, and the Hungarians, wearing white, entered the water.

Next to Gyarmati, the most important Hungarian player was Kálmán Markovits. He was the team's tactician as well as being a fine player.

So far, the Hungarians had been lucky, coming up against relatively weak opposition. Realizing that the team would struggle to beat the Soviets, Markovits had come up with a radical new strategy to confound, and hopefully beat the Soviets. It was based on the zone defense that Markovits had seen employed in basketball. Markovits called the new strategy *retesz* (lockdown) and unveiled his plans the night before the semi-final. The Hungarians were a well-drilled and disciplined team, and he was confident his teammates would quickly master his new game plan.

Markovits was lucky to be on the team. His full name was Count Kálmán Markovits de Spizza et Kisterprest, and, as an aristocrat, he automatically became a "class enemy." In communist Hungary there was no need to be guilty of any crime to become a class enemy. People whose parents had been wealthy, capitalists, or, even worse, aristocrats, were automatically guilty by the misfortune of their birth. For Markovits, however, there was a way to redemption, one of the few available in the communist system: excel in sport. Hungarians adored elite water polo players, as did the country's Stalinist leaders, who hoped public support of the country's sporting heroes would translate into support for their regime. And so, Markovits did not suffer unduly.

Markovits was nervous as he entered the pool knowing that the team's success depended on his radical and untried strategy of *retesz*.

Deathly pale, Markovits looked spent before the game had even started. Taking deep breaths to calm himself, Markovits inhaled the pungent smell of chlorine. This was in stark contrast to Császár, the outdoor pool he trained in at home. Like all the pools in Budapest, it was fed by natural springs, each with its own unique sweet taste. All this did was to remind him how far he was from home.

Unlike Markovits, Ervin Zádor could not wait for the game to start. The youngest player on the team, he had already shown prodigious talent and had been spoken about as a future captain. This was no longer possible. In Darwin he told his teammates that he was not going home. In appearance, Zádor showed a remarkable resemblance to a young Marlon Brando—and as he entered the pool, an angry Brando. As Russian was a compulsory subject taken by all Hungarian schoolchildren, Zádor decided to verbally abuse his opponents in their own language "because when you are on edge and you fight you cannot play."[5]

As Swedish referee Sam Zuckerman blew the whistle, a huge roar came from the stands, "*Hajrá Magyarck!*" (Go Hungarians!). Within the first couple of minutes of the game the Soviet players saw that Zuckerman had no intention of giving them a fair go.

Soon after the game started, Gyarmati was within scoring distance. He swung his arm back to shoot, smacking his opponent in the mouth. Accidentally, of course! The referee awarded the penalty to Gyarmati. His shot, however, was deflected by the Soviet goalkeeper. Deciding that the goalkeeper had jumped too early, Zuckerman gave Gyarmati another shot. As the goalkeeper turned to the referee to protest, the Hungarian captain fired the ball into the back of the undefended net. The score stood at 1–0.

Water polo has never been a game for angels. Still, the Soviet players were taken aback by the ferocity of their opponents. According to Soviet center-forward George Lezin, "the Hungarian players decided to not only beat us on the scoreboard but to give us a physical thrashing in the pool."[6] Even after he was hit in the face, Lezin did not retaliate. He felt he had no choice after hearing the voice of Nikolai Romanov, who was on the coaches' bench, crying out, "*Nyet, nyet!*" The minister of sport did not want his players to escalate the game into a bloody war in the pool, which would undoubtedly draw attention to the tense political situation in Hungary. And knowing that the Australian press was hostile to the Soviet invasion, his players would surely be blamed, even if it wasn't their fault.

It was not long before Soviet players were hanging from the side of the pool, gasping for breath after they had been dragged under or briefly incapacitated by low blows.

And Romanov continued to scream "*Nyet, nyet!*" to his battered and bruised players.

Every time the Soviets went forward they found their best scorer, Mshveniyeradze, so closely marked by Gyarmati that it looked like he was sitting on his lap. And whenever the ball came near them, Gyarmati outmaneuvered the much larger man.

In another part of the pool, György "Little George" Kárpáti (the smallest player in the pool) and his opponent were trying to drown one another. Suddenly, turning his back on his opponent, Little George headed toward the Soviet goal face. He had heard Gyarmati yell out *"retesz,"* and he and the rest of the Hungarian team quickly took their places in front of the goal, in accordance with Markovits's plan. At the same time Mshveniyeradze was caged in by Gyarmati and another defender. As the Soviet players swam forward they were faced with a phalanx of defenders. This move was unexpected as water polo had always been played man on man. With the Soviet captain blanketed, the ball was passed to another Soviet attacker. He was too far away to shoot, but he could not move closer as the Hungarian defenders had created an impenetrable wall. The Soviet attacker shook his head; he had never seen anything like this before. Confident that the zone defense would work, Zádor screamed at him, "Go ahead and shoot!" The Soviet player rose out of the water as if to shoot. Then he dropped the ball in front of him, still uncertain whether to shoot or try and penetrate the zone defense. He also expected a Hungarian player to confront him and block his shot. This did not happen. Finally, he decided to have a shot from where he was. He rose out of the water once more, but the ball never made it through the thicket of Hungarian hands. Accurately shooting at this distance with a leather ball that was now water-logged and heavy was almost impossible, as the Soviets soon discovered.

During the next attack, Little George was so confident that his defenders and his goalkeeper would stop the shot that, as the ball left the Soviet player's hand, he had already started to sprint to the other end of the pool. Now in the hands of a Hungarian defender, the ball was thrown the length of the pool where it was gathered by Little George. Now a body length ahead of the nearest Soviet defenders, with an open goal ahead of him, he scored, extending Hungary's lead to 2–0.

Throughout the first half every Hungarian goal was greeted with rapturous cheers. In contrast, every attempt by their opponents to score was greeted with groans and catcalls. The Soviet players were relieved when Zuckerman blew his whistle to mark half-time, giving them time to regroup.

Gathering around their coach—some standing, some sitting on the edge of the pool—the Soviet players looked despondent. Desperately, their coach tried to motivate his players, but he could not answer the question uppermost in their minds: how could they counter the Hungarians' new strategy?

While keeping an eye on Romanov—Mr. Nyet—the players were also aware that a senior KGB man was in the stand. He was Vasili Mitrokhin, wearing a brown overcoat, broad-brimmed hat, and a scowl on his face. He was signaling them to fight back in the second half. For the players, this was welcome news.

At the other end of the pool, the Hungarians were looking self-assured. They were ahead on the scoreboard and confident that their opponents had no answer to their zone defense. And they were winning the fights.

Zuckerman blew the whistle and the second half commenced. The Soviet players quickly showed that they would no longer tolerate being treated like punching bags and started to retaliate. Both sides were also engaging in verbal abuse. "You dirty bastards," yelled Zádor to his opponent. "You come over and bomb our country." In return, the Soviets called their opponents "traitors."[7]

A stray elbow to the face was seen by Zuckerman, and a Soviet player was sent off. This allowed Zádor to score from a penalty. The scoreline was now 3–0, and the game was turning into a rout.

More fights broke out around the pool. In one incident Gyarmati rose out of the water up to his waist and sucker-punched Mshveniyeradze, breaking his nose. As the Soviet captain was washing the blood off his face, Gyarmati hit him in the face again. Wisely, he immediately took off, with Mshveniyeradze in hot pursuit and referee Zuckerman looking the other way. It is not clear what would have happened had Mshveniyeradze caught Gyarmati, who was a fast swimmer. Not by nature a violent man, either in or out of the pool, Mshveniyeradze soon gave up the pursuit. He realized that he risked Zuckerman sending him off, which would do nothing for the team.

This encounter signaled a melee in which players started to wrestle, hit one another, and drag their opponents underwater.

When the game resumed, Gyarmati fired a pass to Antal Bolvári, who had given his opponent Valentin Prokopov the slip and had scored Hungary's fourth goal. The Hungarians were now 4–0 up. With the game was well and truly lost, at least the Soviet players could do is win the fights.

Perhaps smarting from the goal scored against him, Prokopov took out his frustration on Bolvári. After a violent encounter and suspecting he had a burst eardrum, Bolvári swam over to Zádor and asked him to take his man, Prokopov.

To needle Prokopov, Zádor abused him in Russian by saying, *"pyos yop tvoyu mata"* (a dog fucked your mother). This enraged Prokopov, and the two men exchanged blows, oblivious to the ball, which was near the Hungarian goal, 30 meters away.

Facing away from the play, Zádor heard the referee's whistle and assumed that Zuckerman had seen them fighting. At the same time, Prokopov, who could see that Zuckerman was looking the other way, rose out of the water to smack Zádor with a round-arm left. As he turned back, Zádor saw Prokopov's body rising above him. "What in the earth are…. Oh my God," he exclaimed as he was hit.[8] Prokopov's blow struck Zádor just above the right eye. The skin above the eye socket is quite thin, and the cut bled profusely.

The sound of bone on bone was loud, and Zádor's scream of surprise was even louder. This drew the attention of spectators to the incident. For a few seconds they were silent as they took in the scene. Then Hungarian-Australians in the stands started to jeer and abuse Prokopov.

Gyarmati and Markovits immediately swam over to their wounded teammate to inspect the damage. Injuries like this happen all the time, and Gyarmati had seen much worse. Seeing blood seeping between Zádor's fingers, Gyarmati's first impression was that he had been hit by an ax. Here was an opportunity, Gyarmati thought, to use the incident to draw attention to what was happening in Hungary.

When he was hit, Zádor was very close to the stairs that led down to the changing room, where he could receive first aid. Instead, Gyarmati told him to swim to the other end of the pool so that he would color the water with his blood. "And when you get out of the water make sure you turn the bleeding side of your face towards the photographers," Gyarmati told Zádor.[9]

As Zádor pulled himself out of the pool, the spectators went wild when they saw the full extent of his injury. "Kill the damned Russians!" cried one of the Hungarian spectators,[10] and another challenged the Soviets, "Come out and fight!"[11]

Appreciative of Gyarmati's choreography, the clouds parted and let the afternoon sun in through the city side of the pool, bathing the injured water polo player in brilliant light.

Watching this scene was the Soviet player, Boris Markarov. He later recalled, "He just stood posing for photographers, with blood flowing down his face, showing everything."[12]

Rather than risk a

Hungarian water polo player, Evin Zádor, after being struck in the face by his Soviet opponent in the semifinal, held on December 6, 1956 (Alamy).

full-blown riot, Zuckerman declared the Hungarians the winners, 4–0, even though there were still 90 seconds on the clock.

Afterward, Soviet players pulled themselves up onto the apron of the pool, where they were met by angry spectators. Some had jumped over barriers and were shaking their fists, shouting abuse, spitting on them, and hurling missiles, mainly bottles and coins, in their direction. There were no police in the Glasshouse, and so Olympic officials went outside to find some. When the police arrived they did not know who they should be protecting from whom. After a quick conference with Olympic officials, the police shepherded the Soviet players down to the dressing rooms before the Hungarian spectators could tear them apart.

Hissing, booing, hooting, and whistling continued for around ten minutes before order was restored.

While Zádor's cut was being attended to by a first aid attendant—it required thirteen stitches—the atmosphere in the dressing room shared by the teams was tense. Each of the Hungarian players went up to Zádor to commiserate, knowing he would not be playing in the final against Yugoslavia the next day. Zádor was bereft.

One of the Soviet trainers tried to approach Gyarmati to apologize, but he was angrily waved away.

Ray Smee was also in the changing room. The Australian water polo captain was angry at the brawling, which he worried would tarnish the carefully cultivated image of the "friendly Games." He launched a tirade at both sides, whom he blamed equally for the violence. The players were absorbed in their own thoughts and, in any case, none spoke English, and Smee did not speak Hungarian or Russian, so his scolding came to naught.

Once they were dressed the Soviet players skulked out of the Glasshouse and boarded a bus that was waiting outside. The sun was going down as their bus made its way through peak hour traffic, with the players crouching down to avoid further attacks by Hungarian spectators. It was only after the bus reached Hoddle Street, well away from the Glasshouse, that the athletes could take their seats.

As the bus turned into Upper Heidelberg Road, the team manager noticed that they were going past the Orient, a cinema advertising Disney cartoons. Taking pity on the battered and bruised players, he asked them if they were interested. They were much too early for the evening session, which started at 7:40 p.m. Anxious to show the friendly face of Melbourne to visiting athletes (and knowing nothing of what had happened in the pool 30 minutes earlier), the cinema manager put on a special screening.

Walking into the Orient, the Soviet players could not help being impressed with its lush red carpets, molded ceilings, and papier-mâché statues of gaudily painted Indian gods in the alcoves. Cartoons did not need much English, and this break relieved the tension among the team. Coming out of the cinema they were met by ticket-buying picture-goers, bustling ushers in white shirts and bowties, teenagers selling candy and ice creams from trays, and a scrum of newspapermen, who had followed them.

Anticipating hostile media coverage of the water polo semi-final, the Soviet hierarchy was in crisis mode. At 3 a.m. the players were roused from their beds for an urgent meeting with Romanov. They knew they were in trouble for defying Mr. Nyte by retaliating. The fact that Romanov had waited until the middle of the night to call a meeting could mean only one thing—that Romanov had been in touch with the Kremlin for instructions. Over the next half hour Romanov berated the team, "You have damaged Soviet-Hungarian friendship, and it is necessary to show dignity, even in a loss, and not sacrifice your honor by fighting."[13] The KGB man, Mitrokhin, was also present. Contradicting Romanov, Mitrokhin told the players, "You should have hit the Hungarians harder."[14]

On his return to Moscow, Mitrokhin was demoted and put out to pasture in the KGB archives for his failures in Melbourne. He would later defect to the West, taking copies of large parts of the archives with him.

The next morning, a photo of Zádor was splashed over the front pages of Australian newspapers. It had also been reported around the world. Blood coursed down Zádor's face and onto his lean, muscular torso. Although the photo is in black and white, Zádor's blood glistens with indignation against his pale body. The photo brooks no argument. Zádor was no longer an unfortunate athlete injured in the course of a game but a wounded warrior from a wounded country.

Quick thinking by Gyarmati had allowed the Hungarians to ruthlessly exploit this unfortunate incident and write the first draft of history. "Cold War violence erupts at Melbourne Olympics," shrieked the *Sydney Morning Herald*.[15] All the newspapers depicted the Hungarians as blameless, quoting Gyarmati at length. For example, the Hungarian captain told *The Argus* that his players were under strict instructions from the coach not to fight, box or wrestle in the pool. "The Russians started very dirty tactics when we led 4–0," he claimed. "I myself received a terrific kick in the stomach."[16] Then he told *The Argus*, "If anybody is justified in starting a fight it would have been us, after what the Russians have done in our country."[17]

The game has become known as the "Blood in the Water" match, an irony that would not have been lost on Mshveniyeradze, whose blood mingled with Zádor's in the pool that day.

The Final Hurrah

The next afternoon, even though the Soviet players had had a difficult night, they played Germany for the bronze medal, winning 6–4. They then had to wait around for the medal ceremony, which would occur that evening after the final between Yugoslavia and Hungary. So they got to see Hungary play again, this time from the safety of the stands.

One man not in the final was Zádor, who could barely see out of his swollen right eye. Nevertheless, he tried to convince the coach that he could still play. "I was sure we were going to lose the Olympics because I wasn't there," lamented Zádor.[18]

Over the PA system the names of the players were announced. Then Gyarmati shook the hand of the Yugoslavian captain. Both teams were greeted with loud cheers from the spectators, in stark contrast to the previous day.

The Hungarians were not the favorites as they had been beaten by Yugoslavia in five of their previous six encounters since the Helsinki Olympics. This time, however, they were confident that Markovits's zone defense was effective and could win them the game.

The Hungarians were also in luck as the Yugoslavs could not pick their best players for the final, with Cold War politics getting in the way. Prior to the competition their top defender, Ivo Štakula, announced at a team meeting that he intended to seek asylum in Australia, ending his chance of playing. The head of the Yugoslavian delegation and communist hardliner, Miljan Neoričić, was shocked at the support Štakula attracted from his teammates. Ignoring dissenting voices from the team, Neoričić told the defiant Štakula, "If you stay, you will be denounced as a traitor!"[19]

A few minutes after the game commenced Hungary scored the first goal, and soon after another, from a corner.

The Yugoslavian strikers were frustrated as the game went on. Whenever they went forward they faced the Hungarian zone defense. And when they had an opportunity to shoot they were some distance from goal, making Hungary's goalkeeper task much easier.

At the break the score was 2–0, with the Hungarians looking unbeatable.

Early in the second half, one of the Hungarian players was sent off until the next goal. When the Yugoslavs scored he returned, but soon after Gyarmati fouled and was sent off. The Hungarians were again one man down and were vulnerable.

Seething from the sidelines, Gyarmati watched his team desperately hold off the Yugoslavs. The hero of this half was Markovits, who kept possession of the ball, denying the Yugoslavs a chance to score.

With just three minutes to go, Gyarmati noticed that his team members were starting to tire and cramp. This opened up an opportunity, and the Yugoslavs were able to penetrate the Hungarian defense, with their goalkeeper isolated. He panicked and jumped early, while attacker Kačić delayed his shot. The goal face was now undefended. Perhaps a little too anxious and not realizing that he had ample time, Kačić hurried his shot and missed, with the ball flying over the top of the goal. Kačić direct opponent was Little George, who swam up to the devastated Yugoslavian offensive player and said, "*Köszönöm!*" (Thank you for your help!). The game ended a minute later, the Hungarians the winners at 2–1.

As the final whistle sounded, Gyarmati jumped into the pool to embrace his teammates. It was a sweet, sweet victory. As they got out of the water they were mobbed by joyous spectators.

Afterward, the Hungarian players received their medals. They were all wearing dressing gowns over their swimming trunks, except for Zádor, who was in dark pants and a white shirt. By this time tears were coursing down Zádor's face: "I was crying for Hungary because I knew I wouldn't be returning home."[20] Gyarmati also felt the emotion of the moment. "That day, we were a team, and we were happy together," he recalled. "The next day, however, we all became individuals and went on our separate ways. In that moment, you could see a small country's national tragedy reflected and repeated over and over again."[21]

CHAPTER 16

Political Football

The Specter of Tampere

At the Melbourne Olympics, the football competition started two days after the opening ceremony and ended on the day of the closing ceremony. For the Soviet Union, it would be an opportunity to redeem its pride after the humiliating defeat to Hungary in the water polo.

Just a month before the Olympics, though, Soviet sports minister Nikolai Romanov had second thoughts on whether to send his football team to Melbourne.

Football was one sport that was popular around the world (other than in the United States, Ireland, and Australia, where it is called "soccer" so it is not confused with their local codes). Success at the Olympics would be noticed, particularly in developing countries that the Soviet Union was trying to win over.

The Kremlin also needed football to bolster its own legitimacy at home. Having denied religion to the masses, the Kremlin used sport as an alternative opiate. It helped distract the populace from dwelling on the deprivations of daily life, and football was one of the few inexpensive pastimes citizens could enjoy as they waited for the socialist utopia to arrive.

A year before the Melbourne Olympics, Romanov appointed Gavriil Kachalin to manage the campaign. He was a romantic by nature when it came to the beautiful game of football. At the same time, he was ruthless when it came to winning. If he had to leave out a star to execute his game plan, he did so without a moment's hesitation.

Coach Kachalin knew a win in football was particularly important to the Kremlin, and members of the Politburo would be closely following the team's progress in Melbourne. Not surprisingly, he wondered what might happen should they lose, as they had in Tampere four years earlier. "Without Stalin and Beria around, what happened after Helsinki was unlikely, he believed."[1] Like everyone in the football world, he was shocked when Stalin ordered the disbandment of the army team, blaming its players for the loss. While the political atmosphere

had calmed down under the leadership of Nikita Khrushchev, Kachalin was uncertain how the Kremlin might react to another failed campaign.

Rather than bringing together the best players from different teams just before the Games, Kachalin decided to create a permanent national team, which would become "a single organism, with its own history, traditions, and most importantly—its own creative principles strategy."[2]

As a new coach, Kachalin's first task was to recruit talented footballers and mold them into a cohesive national team. The 1950s was a golden age for Soviet football, and Kachalin was fortunate to draft some outstanding players. Spartak proved a fertile recruiting ground for Kachalin, and the fifteen-man national side included ten players from the club. The coach preferred to use players from the same club as they already had a good understanding of one another's playing style.

To prepare his team and bring them together as a single organism, Coach Kachalin embarked on a series of Friendlies in the year running up to the Olympics. He started with games against India. While the competition was not as strong as Kachalin might have found elsewhere, the visit to India served an important political purpose. The Soviet Union was trying to win over postcolonial countries, and India was a prime target. Games were played in Bombay (now Mumbai), New Delhi, and Calcutta (now Kolkata) during February and March 1955, and another in September in Moscow. They generated goodwill that undoubtedly helped pave the way for Khrushchev's visit to India at the end of that year.

Back in Europe for the summer, the Soviet team had mixed success. Losses to Hungary and France caused Romanov to question sending a football team to Melbourne. He could not afford another debacle like the humiliating loss to Yugoslavia in Helsinki.

Looking for reassurance, Romanov called a meeting of all the players and coaches. As they stood in a semicircle around him, he asked each to give him their word the Soviet Union would win in Melbourne. "We gave this oath, and at that time I did not want to think about what would happen if we lost," recalled forward Anatoli Isayev.[3] Coach Kachalin also reassured Romanov his team was good enough to win Olympic gold.

The odds for a Soviet gold medal were improved when strong football countries—Brazil and Uruguay—decided they could not afford to send a team to far-off Australia. Hungary was also absent for the same reason, which must have been a relief to Romanov, as it avoided what could have been a nasty and politically charged game.

By the time the competition commenced, there were only eleven teams that qualified. Many were minnows in the football world. Nevertheless, the Soviet Union would also face three heavyweights—Germany, Bulgaria, and Yugoslavia—that it would have to overcome to be sure of a gold medal.

First Round

In its first game the Soviet Union faced Germany, which had won the World Cup in 1954.

While hyped as the United German team, it had no players from East Germany. Rather than fielding a team of the best players, national teams from East and West Germany played six qualifiers. West Germany won four games, lost one, and drew one, which qualified it to go to Melbourne.

In the run-up to the Olympics, the Soviets invited a West German side to Moscow for an International Friendly, which was played on August 21, 1955. More than just another game of football, it had political undertones.

At a time, the Kremlin was promoting peaceful coexistence with West Germany, and the timing of that game was significant, coming just three weeks before German Chancellor Konrad Adenauer was to visit Moscow, eager to build diplomatic and trade bridges to the USSR. The Kremlin hoped this rapprochement would steer West Germany away from America's sphere of influence.

The Kremlin bent over backward to make the visit a success. As a gesture of goodwill, the Soviet Union had arranged for 1,500 fans to travel from West Germany, and they were accommodated in the best Moscow hotel rooms; some even had adequate supplies of toilet paper and soap.

The game was played in front of 80,000 fans in Dinamo Stadium. German fans arrived at the stadium in buses decked in the flags of the Soviet Union and West Germany. Before the start there were no whistles, just cheers and bouquets of flowers. And during the game Russian spectators called out "Peace, Friendship" in German, to which the visitors called back the same sentiment in Russian, "*druzhba, mir*."[4]

Once the referee blew his whistle it was clear that both sides were desperate to win. The game was of a high standard and played fairly, with the Soviets prevailing, 3–2.

A little over a year later, the two side sides faced off again in Melbourne. The game was played at Olympic Park, a ten-minute walk from the main stadium. The day was warm and sultry, with a disappointing crowd of 12,000 spectators. The "world game" was not popular with Australians, who preferred their own unique football code. So the low turnout was no surprise.

From the start, the German defense was under siege. To counter, the Germans tried to slow the pace to help their defenders. But they were not particularly successful as the Soviets used their speed around the wings to launch attacks. At the end of the first half the Soviets were ahead, 1–0.

After the break, the Germans played more aggressively, and one of the Soviet players was carried off after he took a heavy kick to his shin. Seeing that the Germans were trying to unsettle them, the Soviets tried to avoid physical clashes.

Despite facing a strong wind, the Soviets moved the ball around precisely, like chess grandmasters, and scored a second goal. The Germans replied a minute later. The game ended with the Soviets ahead, 2–1.

While a win was a win, the Soviet players knew they had struggled and would have to improve if they were to beat the competition's other heavyweights.

Quarter-Finals

The game against Germany had been physically taxing. So the Soviet players were looking forward to an easy win against the inexperienced Indonesians.

Their assessments were not unreasonable. A team from the Moscow league, Lokomotiv Moskva, had toured South Asia in November 1955, which included games against Indonesian sides. The visitors won 5–0, 9–0, 4–0, and 3–1. In September 1956, during a tour of Europe, the national Indonesian team had also been convincingly beaten in four International Friendlies against the national teams of Yugoslavia, East Germany, and Czechoslovakia, and against a local side in Yugoslavia, Dinamo Zagreb.

What the Soviets had not taken into account was the tactical genius of Indonesia's coach Toni Pogačnik. He had arrived in Indonesia in 1954 following a personal request from President Sukarno to Yugoslav leader Marshal Tito.

Pogačnik understood that in a physical game his smaller and slightly built players would be brushed aside by the muscular bodies of the Soviets. He therefore concentrated on honing his charges' skills, building their game around speed and accurate passes, giving them a chance of upsetting a physically stronger team.

Unlike the USSR, Indonesia had a bye in the first round when the team from South Vietnam withdrew.

The game was played on Olympic Park, and 3,200 spectators turned up to watch. The day was cool, and the ground was bathed in sunshine.

The Soviet players strutted onto the field, confident of a win. Their complacency vanished when, once the game started, they faced an impenetrable phalanx of defenders.

Coach Pogačnik had watched the match between the USSR and Germany. He noticed the Soviet players were uncomfortable with the Germans' defensive tactics, which stifled their natural propensity to attack. He decided to exploit this weakness by adopting a 1–9–1 structure: the goalkeeper in the penalty area—nine defenders—one player in attack. It was not a formula to win, but against a much better side, particularly one not expecting this tactic, it might just avoid a humiliating loss.

Pogačnik was particularly worried about Soviet striker Eduard Streltsov. His caution was not misplaced. Streltsov was a goal-scoring prodigy who started playing in the Moscow league as a 16 year old. He both frustrated and dazzled fans. He often looked disengaged on the field, showing little interest in the match before suddenly springing to life, rushing forward to kick the match-winning goal. During the game Streltsov was closely guarded, which allow him little room to weave his magic.

The first half was played entirely in the Soviet half of the ground. While there were numerous shots at goal, the Indonesians were able to intercept them, or they were deflected by their goalkeeper.

Football match between Indonesia (dark tops) and the Soviet Union (light tops).

At the end of the first half the score was 0–0. The Soviet players left the field shell-shocked.

In the second half, with six minutes to go, a Soviet shot on goal rebounded, landing at the feet of the solitary Indonesian forward outside the defensive zone. Seeing an opportunity to score, he charged down the field before the Soviet players could organize their defense. Soviet goalkeeper Lev Yashin—called the "black spider" because he seemingly had eight hands that could intercept a ball from any direction—had moved into the center circle to better watch the game and, in an unforgivable lapse, had left his goal undefended. Seeing an Indonesian attacker heading for his goal, Yashin scampered back just in time, deflecting the shot with his fingertips and sending it over the bar.

The game was drawn, even though the Soviets had had twenty-seven corners and sixty-eight shots on goal.

Even during extra time neither side could score.

The Soviet players walked off the field humiliated. Their mood was not improved when they saw Romanov, who had arrived late and was livid when he saw the scoreboard. It was a propaganda disaster, which *Sports Illustrated* took delight in mentioning in its report of the game. "At Melbourne the Soviet soccer team, two or three years ago the world's best, has been held to a tie by the humble Indonesians."[5]

The next day Romanov held a crisis meeting. Before it could start, a KGB agent searched the furniture, walls, and light fittings for listening bugs. "The authorities believed that imperialists were even interested in our conversations on sports," explained midfielder Alexei Paramonov.[6]

The meeting lasted four hours, and each player's performance was picked apart by the coach and officials. They then discussed ways to counter the Indonesians' defensive structure. Coach Kachalin told the players, "We committed an elementary mistake of underestimating our opponent, falling into an old Russian habit of assuming the game would be a walkover."[7] The players did not have to be warned to give their all next time around. The question in the back of the coach's mind was whether his charges had exhausted their physical and emotional reserves in the previous game.

At the end of the meeting, glowering, Romanov reminded his players what was at stake. "You have to understand that by the end of the Olympic Games if we lose at football, even Kuts's achievements will be forgotten."[8]

When the teams ran onto Olympic Park for the rematch, the sky was cloudless, and the temperature was mild. The size of the crowd had doubled as the surprise draw had attracted spectators who were hoping for an upset.

The Indonesians once again set up their defensive wall. But they were not moving particularly well, drained by the previous match. As their tactics depended on leg speed, holes in their defense started to appear.

Switching the ball quickly from one side of the field to the other and now willing to shoot from long range, the USSR was rewarded with three goals in the first half.

In the second half, the Indonesians quixotically decided they would go down fighting. Abandoning their defensive wall, they started to attack, but to no avail, and another Soviet goal resulted in a final score of 4–0.

Although they had lost, the Indonesian players left with their heads held high. They had done much better than anyone expected.

Yugoslavia, Bulgaria, and India also won and progressed to the semi-finals.

Semi-Finals

With the track and field competition completed, the semi-finals were moved from Olympic Park to the main stadium, which could accommodate more spectators.

The first semi-final was played between India and Yugoslavia, starting at noon.

Before the game started the Indians pleaded with the referee to relax the rule on wearing boots, which had been mandated by football's ruling body FIFA in 1948. For Indian goalkeeper Shankar "Babu" Naraya this was not a matter of choice. As children, he explained, we would "play football barefoot as we could not afford boots and did not dare ask our parents to buy us a pair."[9] As a result, Indian players found wearing boots painful, putting them at a disadvantage. A compromise was reached: they would have to wear boots at the start of the game, but they could remove them if necessary. As the game proceeded, one after another of the Indians discarded their boots. By the end, only their goalkeeper was still wearing them.

After a scoreless first half, to everyone's surprise, India took the lead when the ball dribbled past two defenders into the net. This was a brief moment of glory before an avalanche of Yugoslavian goals. Yugoslavia won the game 4–1 and was into the final.

The next day the second semi-final was played between the Soviet Union and Bulgaria. The winner would play Yugoslavia for the gold medal.

While the Soviet team had played three hard matches, Bulgaria had had an easy run. It had a walkover in the first round when Egypt failed to send its team to Melbourne. It then had an effortless victory against Great Britain in the quarter-finals.

The day was warm and balmy, although by the time the game started it was late afternoon and cooling down. As the players ran onto the field for the second semi-final, they were greeted by a respectable crowd of around 21,000.

The Bulgarians attacked from the start with sharp passes, hoping to break the spirit of the Soviets, who were physically and mentally drained from their previous games. The Soviet goalie, Yashin, an odd sight in his distinctive dark-brown cloth cap, was kept busy as the Bulgarians peppered the goal. While they played with skill and passion in a free-flowing game, the Bulgarians failed to score. The Soviets were no more successful, as their star striker Streltsov was closely guarded and had trouble getting into the game.

Late in the first half, defender Nikolai Tishchenko fell awkwardly and writhed on the ground in agony. He could only get up with help from a team-mate, and, worryingly, his right arm was hanging limp. He was quickly taken off the ground. At first, the team doctor would not allow him back onto the field. He had broken his collarbone and was in no fit state to play. "Do what you can, but I have to play," he told the doctor.[10] With no substitutions allowed, the doctor realized that he had no choice but to comply. He injected Tishchenko with Novocain and bandaged his arm to his body so as not to jolt his broken collarbone. After an absence of five minutes, Tishchenko returned to the field.

At the end of an even first half neither side had scored.

Tishchenko received additional treatment at the half-time break. Still, it was clear he would be of little use for the rest of the game, as the doctor warned him not to risk any physical confrontations.

Having little choice, Coach Kachalin rearranged the team, moving Tishchenko to the flank, hoping he would act as a decoy. Tishchenko was a sad sight. When he ran back onto the field, he was using his left hand to hold his damaged right arm in place and stop it from jarring. Not seeing him as a threat, the Bulgarians left him alone.

Even though the Soviets now were down a man, it was the Bulgarians who were on the back foot as the Soviets attacked aggressively. But they could not capitalize on their dominance. The second half ended with a scoreless draw.

After a short break, the referee called the players back onto the ground for 30 minutes of extra time.

The Bulgarians started better, and after six minutes they were up, 1–0.

Looking defeat in the face spurred the Soviet players on. And with just nine minutes to play, the unattended Tishchenko trapped the ball and, with his teeth clenched in pain, speared a precise pass. It arrived at the feet of Streltsov, who who was able to dodge around and scored a goal. The score was level, 1–1.

This goal dispirited the Bulgarians, and their ball movements became ragged, giving heart to their opponents.

Still unmarked, Tishchenko quietly slipped forward from the right flank and passed the ball to Streltsov, who passed it to Boris Tatushin, who scored. Rather than a liability, Tishchenko was turning into an unexpected game-winner, as was the mercurial Streltsov.

With just four more minutes to go, Soviet players successfully defended against the desperate Bulgarians to take the game 2–1.

The injured Tishchenko was clapped off the field by his teammates. But there was no way he could play in the final, which sadly meant he would not receive a medal.

Finals

The two losers of the semi-finals, Bulgaria and India, played off for the bronze medal. The Indians' style of dribble, pass, and constant movement kept the Bulgarians off-balance. But after 37 minutes of play the Bulgarians finally scored. As their experience came to the fore, they scored two more goals to win 3–0.

The next day, the final for the gold medal was played in the main stadium between Yugoslavia and the USSR. The loser would take the silver.

While previous football matches had been poorly attended, there were 86,000 spectators in the stands that afternoon. The numbers would swell to over

100,000 as people arrived for the closing ceremony, which would follow two hours after the end of the match.

As the players lined up in light rain for the start of the game, many of the Soviet players were apprehensive. After four grueling games, did they have enough strength to overcome the formidable Yugoslavian side?

The Yugoslavs started well. Their forwards executed precise passes, and they were clearly on top. There were shots on goals, but they did not get past goalkeeper Yashin, who made save after save. Soviet attacks were less potent, and they never looked like a chance to score.

Fifteen minutes in, tempers became frayed when the referee failed to penalize a Soviet player who brought down his opponent with an illegal tackle.

The first half ended with neither side scoring.

When they returned to the field, the Soviet players' game changed. Rather than depending on static passes and maintaining possession, Soviet forwards were moving quickly, creating confusion among the Yugoslavian defenders. The stalemate was broken when Anatoli Ilyin headed a high ball toward the goal, which was helped into the back of the net by Anatoli Isayev.

Down 1–0, the Yugoslavian players feared the game was slipping away. They attacked desperately and were finally rewarded with a goal. Shaking his head, the referee signaled offside, much to the anguish of the Yugoslavs. The score remained unchanged.

During the closing stages of the game the Yugoslavian players became frustrated, and their tackling became crude. As tempers flared, two Soviet players were hit in off-the-ball incidents. Soon both sides were executing trips and fouls with scientific precision, and the game had turned ugly.

Up to this point, Romanov, sitting on the sidelines, was well satisfied with the way the game was going. The outbreak of violence, however, gave him reason to be worried. Was this driven by frustration at the score, or was it politically motivated, as had occurred in the water polo game two days earlier?

The relationship between the USSR and Yugoslavia had recently soured when Tito had provided sanctuary for the leader of the Hungarian revolutionary government, Imre Nagy, in the Yugoslavian Embassy in Budapest. Khrushchev was furious with Tito.

After the revolution was crushed, Tito negotiated with the new leader of the Kremlin's puppet government in Hungary, Janos Kádár, for Nagy's safe passage to Yugoslavia. But within minutes of leaving the embassy, Nagy was arrested by Soviet military officials and flown to Romania, where he was imprisoned and later executed. Following this incident, relations between Khrushchev and Tito sank to a new low.

While the Yugoslav players may not have known the details, many had formed friendships with the Hungarian athletes and sympathized with their plight.

When the referee blew his whistle, the game ended with a Soviet victory, 1–0. The Soviet players hugged and kissed one another while the Yugoslavian players looked on sullenly.

By the end of the game, the stadium had filled to capacity, and spectators looked forward to the closing ceremony.

CHAPTER 17

The Games End, for Now

The question left hanging at the end of the Melbourne Olympic Games was how they would be remembered. Each Olympics adopts a sobriquet or has one imposed upon it through a judgment of history. For example, there were the Sunshine Games (Stockholm, 1912), the Nazi Games (Berlin, 1936), and the Austerity Games (London, 1948). Would the Melbourne Olympics be remembered as the Friendly Games, as Australians hoped, or the Cold War Games?

This question undoubtedly occupied the minds of the organizers as the date of the closing ceremony approached. Two days earlier there had been the "blood in the water" water polo match, which was fresh in people's minds. And the organizers were aware that other Cold War tensions simmered just behind the façade of amity and international peace they had promoted during the Games. Might these tensions break out into the open during the closing ceremony? What could be done to reduce the threat of unwelcome demonstrations?

An answer to this last question came in an anonymous letter, signed "John Ian," to the chairman of the organizing committee, Wilfrid Kent Hughes. It proposed that the teams not march under their national flags in the closing ceremony. Instead, athletes would mingle so there would be "only one nation. War, politics, and nationality will all be forgotten. What more could anybody want, if the whole world could be made as one nation? Well, you can do it in a small way." Also, rather than marching, athletes should stroll around the main stadium and wave to spectators. The author of the letter would later be revealed to be 17-year-old Melbourne schoolboy, John Wing.[1]

Kent Hughes was taken by the symbolism of the idea. Moreover, it might reduce the possibility of protests. The day before the closing ceremony, chefs de mission embraced Wing's proposal.

On December 8, 102,000 people packed into the main stadium to witness the closing ceremony. Spectators were pleasantly surprised when athletes entered the stadium. With arms linked, beaming and waving, they half-marched, half-walked around the cinder track to thunderous applause. It appealed to the Australian sense of informality and was described in the official report as a "fiesta of friendship."[2]

Of the original 3,314 athletes who participated in the Games, only about 500 were at the closing ceremony. For various reasons, many had returned home early. Although the day was overcast and a misty rain fell, it did not dampen the joie de vivre among athletes as they marched around the stadium. And they felt the unaffected warmth and friendship radiating from spectators in the stadium. There was also a touch of sadness, as they probably would never again see friends they had made in Melbourne.

Despite the changes to the ceremony that de-emphasized national identities, Cold War politics were present, but not obvious. The flagbearer for the United German team was Klaus Richtzenhain, who was from East Germany. West German Karl-Friedrich had carried the flag in the opening ceremony to give the impression that athletes from the two Germanys bridged the chasm created by politicians. This was a carefully created façade, and during the Games athletes did not fraternize. And secret police kept a watch on the East Germans to ensure that they were not tempted by the lure of the decadent West.

Few spectators would have observed that there was no flagbearer for Hungary or team members in the stadium. One part of the team had left that day for Budapest while the rest were hiding, fearing they could be kidnapped by security police. Most of the Soviet team was also onboard the *Gruzia*, as a precaution against defections, with just a few trusted athletes in the stadium.

Spectators enjoying the Olympics in the main stadium.

And following the announcement of boycotts before the Games, athletes from six countries were not represented during the closing ceremony. Seven if you include the People's Republic of China.

Athletes, grinning from ear to ear, circled the infield, past their flagbearers, who were lined up in a row on the inside of the running track. One of them was Vladimir Kuts, wearing a cream jacket that looked two sizes too large and a gray tie. He was the unofficial hero of the Olympics and personified Soviet domination of the XIV Olympiad.

Kuts had won the first gold medal of the Games in the 10,000 meters, and earlier that afternoon the USSR football team had taken out the last, taking the Soviet Union's tally to thirty-seven gold medals.

When the U.S. team arrived home they saw newspaper reports that dwelt on its failure to beat the Soviets. Not only had the Soviet Union had comfortably beaten the United States in the medal count, but also on points, which was a better measure of each country's performance. Points allocated to the first six position-getters, and the USSR came out on top with 722 points to America's 593, which further underlined its dominance.[3]

This victory crowned a decade-long campaign by the USSR to conquer Mount Olympus. On this journey from the start was sports minister Nicholai Romanov, who could now enjoy the panoramic view from the summit.

In Helsinki, Romanov claimed that the USSR would have topped the medal table had it not been for biased judging. Now it was America's turn to make excuses and take on the mantle of sore losers.

Sports Illustrated devoted many column inches to criticizing biased judges from communist countries, accusing them of a "dramatic violation of sportsmanship." Then there were "humorless, dogmatic" Soviet officials, "a bunch of Molotovs," who were accused of "taking every advantage of referees and judges," bullying them to the "point of crassness."[4] According to U.S. high diver Gary Tobian, "This is the worst judging of any meet I've competed in." He went on to accuse a Russian judge of deliberately lowering the scores for American divers.[5] Gymnasts also believed that Soviet and Hungarian judges treated western competitors unfairly.

American journalists also reported specific examples of unsporting behavior. A Soviet footballer was charged with cowardly kicking a Yugoslav footballer while the referee's back was turned. Soviet shooters used illegally modified rifles. And news reports of the "Blood in the Water" incident painted the Soviets as the villains. "They play their sports just as they conduct their lives—with brutality and disregard for fair play," Hungarian water polo player Miklós Martin told *Sports Illustrated.*[6]

Another excuse for Soviet dominance was offered by Allison Danzig of the *New York Times*, who asked how U.S. amateurs had a "hope to compete on anything like even terms with such subsidized athletes?"[7] While Soviet athletes were unarguably supported by the State, U.S. athletes also received support from colleges and the military. The only legitimate complaint was that the USSR system of support was more generous. Other countries, like third-placed Australia, whose athletes were genuine amateurs, had a much more valid reason to rail against both superpowers, which were surreptitiously skirting around the rules.

The next complaint was about the suitability of events included in the Olympic program. *Life* magazine claimed the Soviet Union was only able to win because it had done well in "minor events" like gymnastics, wrestling, and shooting.[8] Others took the same line. "We don't consider ourselves the second sports nation of the world because of what happened here," said Tug Wilson, president of the U.S. Olympic Committee. "We spread-eagled men's track and field, which after all is the core of these games." The USSR won, he explained, because they did better in "fringe sports" such as football, field hockey, gymnastics, and Greco-Roman wrestling.[9] Wilson failed to mention women's sports, undoubtedly because he also considered them to be fringe events. This was another area of weakness for the United States; its women won just four gold medals compared to the seven won by Soviet women.

Soon after the closing ceremony, U.S. Olympic officials called for a change in the way points were allocated, which they labeled as "unjust." In an unashamed move to boost its totals, they wanted more points for sports like relays, decathlon, and basketball. These just happen to be events where the United States did well compared to their Soviet opponents. The objective, according to the *New York Times*, was to "improve the United States chances of regaining supremacy from Russia."[10]

The complaints of biased judges, bad sportsmanship, and inclusion of so-called "fringe events" were used to diminish the significance of the convincing win by the USSR.

Behind these complaints was anxiety by Americans that the Soviet Union would use its victory to promote communism. This was spelled out by Constantine Brown in the *Washington Evening Star*: "The Communists are well aware of the great propaganda value of the Olympics. As such, the Kremlin and all its satellites employ the games as a political weapon, an easy and readymade avenue for penetration of the free world. The athletes are in reality Communist agents."[11]

Perhaps the most vociferous in addressing the Cold War implications of the loss, and incidentally the least gracious, was *Sports Illustrated*. This was not surprising as, editorially, the magazine was strongly anti-communist. In its final report from Melbourne, its anonymous correspondent bitterly remarked that "to the Kremlin brass hats, sport has long been another form of politics, and the Russians have made it clear that their overriding interest in sports is victory— victory calculated to glorify the Soviet system." The report concluded with two impressions of the Melbourne Games: "First, to the Russian athletes it is not nearly so important what the world thinks as what the Russians' masters think. Second, to the Russian masters it is not nearly so vital to persuade the world of victories truly won as to present—to 200 million Russians at home—the shiny gilt trophy of a 'victory.'"[12]

There is no doubt that the Soviet Union used its victories to validate its system with its own populace. For example, on the day of the closing ceremony, *Sovetii Sport* announced that its Olympic triumphs were due to the "constant maternal care" of the Communist Party.[13]

This struggle for medal supremacy was not just between the United States and the USSR, as East and West Germany followed suit. This rivalry only took off in the 1968 Olympics, which was the last hurrah for the combined team. At those Games, East Germany ranked fifth to West Germany's eighth. In the following Olympiads, when East Germany competed in its own right, its government went all out to improve its medal haul. It lavishly funded its Olympic campaigns, built the best facilities, recruited top coaches, rewarded athletes, and supported doctors who kept athletes pumped up with the latest performance-enhancing drugs.[14] It was a case of win at any cost so that communist leaders could use its haul of medals to wage psychological warfare against West Germany. These investments paid off, as East Germany beat West Germany in every Games, other than the 1980 Moscow Olympics, which was boycotted by West Germany, and the 1984 Los Angeles Olympics, which was boycotted by East Germany. The highpoint for East Germany was the 1976 Olympics in Montreal, where it even beat the United States, with only the USSR ahead on the medal table.

While the United States was embarrassed coming second to the USSR in the medal rankings, there was a bright spot for American Cold War warriors. Soon after the Melbourne Olympics ended, *Sports Illustrated* planned to parade East European athletes, who had defected during the Games, around major U.S. cities. Called the Freedom Tour, it would be an opportunity to highlight communist oppression in Eastern Europe, particularly Hungary.

CHAPTER 18

The Freedom Tour

The Adventure Begins

The offer to join the Freedom Tour was too good to refuse for water polo player György "Little George" Kárpáti. Unlike others, who were committed to defecting, Little George saw it as a bit of fun. "We could first look around the US to see if we liked it or not. If we wanted to stay then jobs or scholarships would be found. However, there was no talk of money, other than three dollars a day per diem and full board."[1] He only agreed because of the amnesty issued by the new government in Budapest, which allowed athletes to stay away from Hungary until March 31, 1957, without risking punishment. I "just wanted to look around the famous USA but never thought of staying there," he admitted.[2] Little George was told the Freedom Tour involved exhibitions and competitions against American athletes and would run for the first six weeks of 1957. This would allow him to return home before the amnesty expired.

Others, however, were committed to staying in the United States. One of them was Ervin Zádor, the cut above his eye now almost healed. In Australia he had been offered a coaching position and a house. Nevertheless, he decided he would have a better life in the United States. "This is where I would like to live, and this is where I would like to die," he said when he arrived on American soil.[3] Water polo teammate Miklós Martin was not interested in pursuing his sporting career. He had explored setting up a ski school in the Australian Alps but had decided he would look around America first to see whether it offered better opportunities. Martin had the advantage of speaking English, and once he had made his decision to defect, he anglicized his name to Nick Martin. Fencer Jenő Hámori had graduated in industrial chemistry from the University of Budapest, and he hoped to pursue a career in research in the United States.

László Nádori would not decide until he knew that his wife and two children in Budapest were safe. Others shared his reticence.

Called the Hungarian National Olympic Team, although it included four Romanians, the athletes' introduction to America could not have been warmer.

Their first stop was Hawaii. As they left the plane, each athlete was garlanded with floral leis and given a traditional Hawaiian kiss, rubbing noses with their hosts. They then watched hula girls gyrate in ways Hungarian girls would never think of doing. They also had their first taste of American cuisine: hamburgers with onions.

They then headed for San Francisco. Water polo player László Jeney was keen to be the first to see the American mainland. So he convinced the pilot, who happened to be Hungarian, to allow him into the cockpit. Arriving on the morning of Christmas Eve, Jeney observed, "the city emerged out of the mist—the Golden Gate Bridge, the blue of the bay, snow-white skyscrapers, sailing boats like small white feathers."[4]

At San Francisco's International Airport they were met by Governor Goodwin J. Knight, who awkwardly greeted each of them with the words "*Isten Hozott Magyarok*" (Welcome, Hungarian), including the four Romanian water polo players. Next, a military band played the Hungarian national anthem. The Hungarians wore their Olympics uniforms and carried small cabin bags, which contained all their worldly possessions.

After the formal welcome, the athletes were then mobbed by a crowd of 150 Hungarian-Americans who were at the airport to meet them. Journalists and photographers were also there to capture the moment. The atmosphere was festive, and the athletes were happy to have finally arrived on American soil.

It was a joyful arrival for other reasons. Fencer Béla Rerrich received news that his wife and two children, Maria, aged four, and Dorathea, aged two, had escaped to Sweden, where he had intended to go before being persuaded to join the Freedom Tour. *Sports Illustrated* was keen for him to stay with the tour and offered to fly his family to meet him in the United States. Rerrich was important because he was one of the few Hungarians who could speak English.

Sixteen-year-old Zsuzsa Ördögh was met at the airport by teenage American swimmer Nancy Ramey and her family. The two girls had become friends in Melbourne. Before she left Budapest, her father told Zsuzsa, "If you can, do not come back."[5] In Melbourne, Nancy had phoned her parents and asked them whether they would look after Zsuzsa if she came to the United States as she was too young to join the tour. Now in the company of her new family, Zsuzsa (rechristened Susie) caught another plane to Seattle, where she would become part of the Ramey family.

The American newspapers lapped up these human interest stories, often reminding their readers that the Hungarian athletes had "elected not to return home to Communist domination."[6]

The team was taken to the Mark Hopkins Hotel in white Cadillacs. The *Sports Illustrated* organizers were aware not all the athletes were committed to remaining in the United States and were keen to create a good first impression.

As the athletes entered the hotel foyer, they were impressed by the giant Christmas tree decorated with green, red, and blue fairy lights. Over a speaker, Bing Crosby crooned "White Christmas." Outside the hotel groups of people sang carols.

They had rooms on the twenty-fifth floor, and Little George marveled at the "skyscrapers, and beyond the main part of the city, bungalows spread like building blocks arranged by children. How clean and fresh it was. The air was so clean." He concluded, "Everything seemed so much bigger than Budapest."[7]

At midnight the next day they boarded a United Airlines plane, arriving at Idlewild Airport in New York on December 26.

It was the occasion of more reunions. Zádor embraced his brother Zoltán, who had escaped Hungary and arrived in the United States two weeks earlier. Through a torrent of tears, Lidia Domôlky hugged her elder brother György. He had swum the Einserkanal River and dodged landmines to reach Austria, and then come to the United States. "It was like a dream," she gushed.[8] A junior fencer, György would join his sister on the Freedom Tour.

Speeding towards Manhattan, the Hungarians were amazed by the number of billboards along the side of the road. This was quite unlike anything they had at home and provided them with their first encounter with American advertising. Soon they were chanting brand names—Goodyear tires, Wrigley chewing gum, Coca-Cola—convincing them of the seductive power of capitalist psychology.

By mid-morning they arrived at the New York Athletic Club, a twenty-four-story building on the south side of Central Park. This would be their home for the next week. This respite gave them a chance to adjust to their new surroundings and enjoy themselves.

After dropping off their bags, they were on the streets exploring the city. They sampled hot dogs and took an elevator up the Empire State Building. They wandered into Woolworths, where they were struck by the range of consumer goods for sale, all at prices that could be afforded by working-class Americans. Nothing like it existed in Budapest. Then, to see how the other side lived, they walked down Fifth Avenue, populated by major banks. "The movement of money is so quiet," marveled Little George.[9]

By late afternoon they'd had enough, overwhelmed by the wild energy and frantic rhythm of the city, disorientated by its noise, and struggling to digest the flood of new experiences. Back at the Athletic Club the water polo players discovered a 25-meter swimming pool on the third floor. The water may not have had the sweet taste of pools in Budapest, but it nevertheless provided a quiet refuge from the alien world in which they found themselves. Once in the water, they did not speak but just tossed a yellow leather ball around.

In the evening they went for another walk, enjoying the bright lights of Broadway. In 43rd Street, they dropped into the Paramount Theatre for a double feature. Zádor sat next to Nick Martin, and in return for feeding him chocolates, Martin explained the plot to him.

After the movies they went to the Basin Street Café, where they were entertained by Louis Armstrong. The night ended at an underground gambling den on Coney Island, where they tried to supplement their meager per diem allowances.

On December 30 the Hungarians water polo team made their first public appearance in the United States on the *Ed Sullivan Show*. After the photo of a bloodied Zádor had been splashed over the American newspapers, there was considerable interest in seeing the water polo players perform. And for *Sports Illustrated,* an appearance of the Hungarian water polo players on the *Ed Sullivan Show,* with its 60 million viewers, would help kick-start the tour.

Before the show, the players sat down with Ed Sullivan, who explained how the network would shoot the match. They would have a five-minute rehearsal followed by the game, which would be given just two minutes of airtime. "I want to show my viewers the whole beauty of water polo," the great showman explained. Through an interpreter Little George replied: "It is not possible to show anything in two minutes." Sullivan replied, "Too bad." After giving this matter more consideration, he said, "All right, let's make it three minutes, but it better be good."[10]

The pool was surrounded by scaffolding, on which cameras were mounted. There were also two underwater cameras.

The game was against a U.S. side. It quickly became apparent the Americans were determined to beat their well-regarded opponents. Needless to say, the Hungarians had their pride and were determined not to lose. In one attack, Little George made a break for the goals. When he was confronted by a defender, he neatly flipped the ball over the American's head and quickly swam around him to resume his attack. The defender turned around and grabbed Little George by his swimming trunks, and with a grin on his face, said, "Sorry, *Ed Sullivan Show*." Little George responded with a swift kick to free himself while yelling back to his opponent, "Sorry, *Ed Sullivan Show.*"

After the game Ed Sullivan interviewed Béla Rerrich, whose English was fluent, about the situation in Hungary. He then urged his viewers to donate to the Hungarian relief effort. On his next show Elvis Presley dedicated his final song, "Peace in the Valley," written by Hungarian composer Béke a Völgyben, to the people of Hungary.

The water polo players spent New Year's Eve with a local Hungarian family, Magdi and Jancsi Simon, and their two children Maud and Johnny. They all sang folk songs from home, and Little George was up and down, replenishing bottles of Tokaji on the table. Another reminder of home was the meal of traditional Hungarian dishes, such as *töltött káposzta*: cabbage rolls stuffed with minced pork and rice, smothered in sour cream. At midnight the athletes shook hands with Johnny and kissed Maud. This reminded Little George how much he missed his little sister, making him more homesick than ever. He was not sure whether he could stick it out to the end of the tour.

The next day, a dozen or so of the Hungarian athletes spent the evening with CD Jackson at his luxury apartment at Central Park West. Interpreting for the athletes, Béla Rerrich told CD the athletes could barely survive on the miserly $3 per diem *Sports Illustrated* was giving them. They had come to America with nothing and had few resources to fall back on, and certainly not enough to buy clothing and other necessities. As amateurs, the American Amateur Union would not allow them to take additional fees for taking part in the Freedom Tour. CD asked his guests whether they played cards. Of course they did. CD suggested they would play poker for money, and by the end of the evening he told them he expected to lose $1,000. And he did. This money was later distributed to the rest of the team.

They were also helped by Jack Kelly, Jr., a rower and two-time Olympian. He took them to John Wanamaker's department store, a dazzling twelve-story emporium of marble and polished granite, which stocked some of the best merchandise America had to offer. In the foyer they were met by its chief executive Richard C. Bond. "The eyes of the free world are upon you," said Bond. "We are proud to have you come to live among us."[11] Each of the athletes was then given a large suitcase, and Bond told them they could fill it with anything they liked, except jewelry.

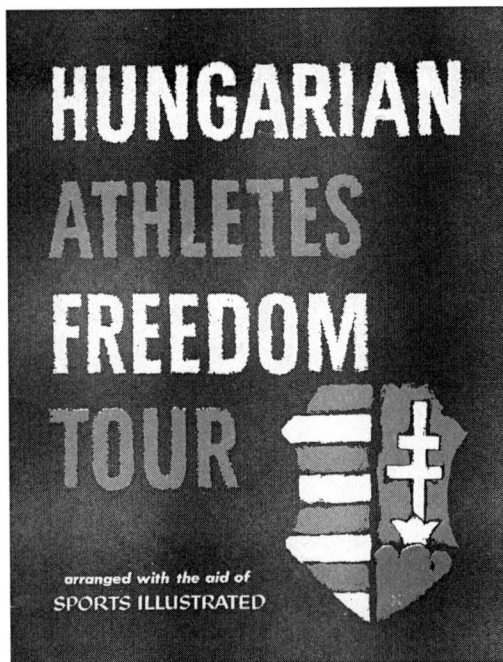

The program for the Freedom Tour of the United States, held during January and February 1957.

On the Road

The Freedom Tour formally commenced on January 2, 1957, and the athletes were divided into three groups. The fencers and gymnasts were in one group. The swimmers, divers, and water polo players had a different schedule. And runner László Tábori and his coach Mihály Iglói joined the U.S. indoor track circuit.

The fencers and gymnasts started in Philadelphia, where their shows sold out. The pro-

Fencing demonstration in Norwalk, Connecticut, between Daniel Magay (right) and American fencer Robert Blum (left), staged during the Freedom Tour (Doug Nichols, Andy Shaw/Museum of American Fencing).

gram started with flag exercises by the three female gymnasts, followed by exercises on the parallel bars by the men. Then fencing coach, György Jekelfalussy-Piller, and gold medalist Dániel Magay provided an exhibition of the finer points of saber technique. Finally, there were matches between local fencers and the Hungarians. No female opponent could be found for Lidia Domölky, so she fought several American men and won "much to their horror," she gleefully recalled.[12]

Unfamiliar with the sport, American audiences saw fencing as a blur of movement, and they were unable to appreciate the subtleties and skill of the sport. Unlike Europe, fencing had a tiny following in the United States, which meant that after the tour, there would be limited opportunities for Hungarians to sustain themselves as fencers or coaches.

As the tour progressed, the fencers added some vaudeville to their shows to keep their audiences entertained. They came up with a simple scenario, which was inspired by swashbuckling films coming out of Hollywood. It would start with a domestic scene with a husband, played by Jenő Hámori, and his wife, played by Margit Korondi, sitting quietly on a couch. The husband then gets up and leaves. A few minutes later, her lover, Dániel Magay, arrives, and they engaged in some staged ardor worthy of a cheesy melodrama. The lovers are interrupted by the return of the husband. His entrance is exciting: with a saber in his mouth, he swings in on a rope tied to the basketball ring. A fight ensues. More fencers appear and join in the sword fight for no apparent reason other than to add to the spectacle. The husband takes on these other swordsmen, whom he dispatches one by one, leaving only the lover. The two men then fight, and the husband disarms his rival. But before he can administer the coup de grâce, Magay pulls out a gun and shoots the husband. The lover leaps up and hugs and kisses the wife (now a widow). End of story, and Errol Flynn wept.

The water polo players started their tour in Miami, where they put on three shows at Hotel Fontainebleau, overlooking Miami Beach.

Before the first game they had to cadge some timber to construct goals. Given the players weren't skilled carpenters, the goals looked terrible. But they had to do. Tickets sold for $35, which surprised the athletes. The organizers explained that wealthy spectators would not come if they charged $5. How odd the rich in American were, thought the Hungarians.

By evening, the terraces around the pool were full, with 3,000 spectators. All the athletes could see were red glowing points of cigarettes, hovering like fireflies, and the glint of jewelry and gold cufflinks.

The show started with some diving, and then Ervin Zádor did a lap of the 50-meter pool, swimming underwater on a single breath.

At the interval, five young girls carrying baskets wandered up and down the stands collecting money. In ten minutes they had amassed over $15,000 (equivalent to $146,000 in 2021) for the Red Cross, which would help resettle Hungarian refugees.

Next came a water polo demonstration. The players passed the ball from one end of the pool to the other without it landing in the water, which took strength and skill that the American spectators did not fully appreciate.

After these exercises, the players divided into two teams to play a match. Because this was an exhibition match there was none of the wrestling and man-to-man contact that was a regular part of water polo. The audience watched politely until Little George forgot himself and, out of habit, cuffed Zádor. This was more like it. Spectators started clapping, shouting, stamping their feet, and the more refined just jangled their jewelry in appreciation.

At the interval, Jim Belse from *Sports Illustrated* suggested that they spice up the game to keep spectators entertained. At first, they were offended. Didn't the audience did not appreciate the skills on display? Little George turned to one of the other players and sarcastically suggested: "Perhaps I should rip your arm off and throw it into the audience." Belse, quite earnestly, responded, "That's a bit too strong, but something like that would be good."[13]

After the game, the water polo players sat down and devised a hybrid game they believed would be enjoyed by their American audiences. It was part water polo, part wrestling, and part soccer, with players even able to pass the ball to players who had jumped out of the pool. In a normal game, goals can only be scored by hand. In their invented game, goals could only be scored by kicking or heading the ball into the net from the apron of the pool. "After ten minutes of artistry," Little George wryly remarked, "we gave them ten minutes of circus."[14]

In Hungary, water polo is a serious sport, and spectators are critical connoisseurs of tactics and technique. And as Olympians, they were treated as celebrities and fêted wherever they went. Not so in America, where the game was not popular. For those Hungarians who had hoped to resume their sporting careers in the United States this did not bode well. Their only other option was to become swimming coaches.

The third part of the Freedom Tour involved the runner László Tábori and his coach Mihály Iglói. They attended indoor track meets in New York, Boston, Philadelphia, Washington, Chicago, and Milwaukee.

By the time the Hungarians had finished the tour, they had seen more of the United States than most Americans ever had. They traveled 4,000 miles, visited fifty-nine different cities and towns, and staged ninety-five performances.

Decision Time

The water polo team arrived in Washington, D.C., at the end of January. Desperately homesick, Jeney and Little George decided to go home. So they called the Hungarian consul to see how they could take advantage of the amnesty.

A few hours later they met consular officials in the foyer of the Willard Hotel. As soon as they shook hands, two men in dark suits arrived and explained they were from the FBI. The consul immediately excused himself and, as he left, he told the athletes, "this is their home, do whatever they demand."[15]

What is remarkable is that the FBI was on the spot. Was there an informer among his teammates? Were their phones bugged? Were they followed?

One of the tour organizers, George Telegdy, was certain that FBI agents were "engaged in supervising the affairs of the Olympic athletes" to prevent the communist regime from "luring" the athletes home.[16] The interception of Little George and Jeney was evidently part of this FBI operation.

They were taken to another room in the hotel, where the agents tried to question them. However, they did not speak Hungarian, and the athletes' knowledge of English was rudimentary. The FBI men quickly found out that detaining Little George and Jeney did not come cheap, as they took full advantage of room service, showing a healthy appetite for champagne and caviar.

At 2 a.m., Little George knocked on Nick Martin's door and asked him to act as interpreter.

"You are our guests. Why do you want to go home?" asked one of the FBI men. Jeney told him he wanted to go home to see his son. Little George wanted to keep playing international water polo, and there were limited opportunities in the United States. He also wanted to be reunited with his fiancée, the actress Éva Gerber. And he missed his grandma. "But it's so bad in Hungary and so good here," one of the FBI agents countered.[17] Unconvinced, Little George and Jeney were adamant they wanted to return home. Both were desperately homesick and wanted to train at the swimming pool on Margit Island, cruise around the night-spots in Old Buda, and watch a football match at the Honvéd ground.

Unable to convince them to stay, the FBI agents bundled the athletes into a car that took them to the airport. They were put on a flight to Vienna, where they would have to make their way back to Hungary. They were not even allowed to say goodbye to their teammates. Instead, they were deported.

The U.S. government feared communist propaganda would claim that having seen America, Little George and Jeney had not liked it and returned home. Instead, the U.S. government could declare they had been expelled from the country.

They arrived in Vienna without papers, and immigration officers took them into custody. When they showed the Austrian officials their Olympic gold medals, frowns turned into smiles. They were then taken to the Hungarian embassy, where they obtained travel documents. Soon they were in a car provided by the ambassador, heading home to Budapest.

In Budapest they were summoned to a meeting with Gyula Hegyi, who scolded them for participating in the Freedom Tour. It was the mildest of rebukes.

While defection of the Hungarians was a win for America—these athletes had chosen freedom over tyranny—re-defections were a win for the Soviet Union. It allowed the Kremlin to argue that having seen what the capitalist West had to offer, the athletes preferred to live under communism.

For this reason, after the Freedom Tour, *Sports Illustrated* and the Hungarian National Sports Federation worked hard to help athletes find jobs or secure university scholarships, with considerable success.

Even with attractive inducements to stay, at the end of the tour several athletes returned home. They preferred the privileges and celebrity that came with being an elite athlete to the relative obscurity they would encounter in the United States. They included swimmer László Magyar and fencers József Sákovics and his wife, Lidia. Others returned for family reasons or because they were homesick. Zoltán Török, the rowing coach, learned his mother was seriously ill and so flew home. László Nádori, a sports administrator, received letters from his family pleading with him to return home.

The question is, why did *Sports Illustrated* organize the Freedom Tour? The exercise did not come cheap, with the tour costing $35,000 (equivalent to

$340,000 in 2021). *Sports Illustrated* argued it was a commercial decision to promote the magazine. Others involved viewed the tour as a political exercise. Andre Laguerre, *Sports Illustrated*'s chief correspondent at the Olympics, explained. "The defection was a major blow to Soviet standing in the world in general and in Eastern Europe in particular."[18] Richard Neale, an assistant publisher for the magazine, stressed: "the importance of this tour, both for keeping the story of Hungary's fight for freedom alive in America, and for its impact behind the Iron Curtain."[19] And photographer Richard Pollard, who traveled with the fencers, wrote, "The propaganda value for the US, particularly in the vast field of international sports, seems obvious to us." By giving Hungarian athletes first-class treatment during the tour, Pollard explained that "when they travel and are interviewed, they can say with assurance that the life in America is what they had been led to believe it would be."[20] This was not, however, a private frolic by *Sports Illustrated* but, according to Neale, had the "active support of the State Department and CIA."[21] For American Cold War warriors, it was just another battle in its psychological war with communism.

The athletes understood they were fodder for the American propaganda machine, and they accepted this. Water polo player Nick Martin remarked that he expected the "Western World would derive some political propaganda value from such a tour."[22] Gymnast Attila Takâcs sourly remarked that *Sports Illustrated* used the defectors to provide "a source of very cheap propaganda, which the Americans exploited at every opportunity."[23] Nevertheless, they were willing to cooperate as the price of helping them settle in the United States.

If judged by the publicity the Freedom Tour generated, it was an outstanding success. There were over 800 mentions of the tour in the media. Movie and television newsreels across the United States showed clips of the athletes. Radio, television, and newspapers were filled with stories about the Hungarian athletes. For example, in one interview, Béla Rerrich said, "It was a great and fateful decision we made to leave our beloved countries to seek asylum in the United States. Your country had always been a symbol of liberty and freedom. We will never forget your help in our greatest hour of need."[24] This was typical, with articles dwelling on the theme that the Hungarians chose freedom by fleeing communism. They were living proof that Hungarians wished to be rid of their Russian oppressors.

Sports Illustrated carried numerous stories, and the organizers of the tour published a special edition booklet that commemorated the Freedom Tour, taking considerable liberties, in the interests of enhancing its value as propaganda, with the stories of the athletes.

> Most of these athletes were actively engaged in the bloody Hungarian revolution against the Communists. They dropped their machine guns and their stretchers to go to the Olympic Games only when it looked as though Hungary had won her

independence from Russia. They were outside the country when Russia reappeared with armies and tanks and, temporarily at least, put down the revolt. Some could not go back because their participation in the uprising was known to the Russians; others simply did not want to go back to living under the domination of the Communists. They all sought a new free life in America.[25]

In another article, which appeared in *Sports Illustrated,* the Hungarian athletes were described as "a living demonstration of the obstinate, furious idea of Free Hungary."[26]

Chapter Notes

Preface

1. An important element of psychological warfare is propaganda, although Americans were coy about using this word, and maintained that their information campaigns were based on the "truth," which, in practice, was their version of the truth consistent with the political aims of the campaign. While not as crude as the propaganda used by the USSR and other communist countries, U.S. psychological warfare was predicated on the same principles and techniques, which is the psychological manipulation of enemies, friends and prospective friends. Depending on the context, it is also known as psychological operations and political warfare. For more, see Phillip M. Taylor "Through a Glass Darkly? The Psychological Climate and Psychological Warfare of the Cold War," in Gary D. Rawnsley, ed., *Cold-War Propaganda in the 1950s* (London: Palgrave Macmillan, 1999).

2. Toby Miller, Geoffrey Lawrence, Jim McKay, and David Rowe, *Globalization and Sport: Playing the World* (London: Sage, 2001), back-cover blurb.

3. Harry Blutstein, *Cold War Games* (Victoria: Echo Books, 2017).

4. Harry Blutstein, *Games of Discontent* (Montreal: McGill-Queen's University Press, 2021).

5. Harry Blutstein, *The Ascent of Globalisation* (Manchester: Manchester University Press, 2015).

Chapter 1

1. George Orwell, "You and the Atomic Bomb," *Tribune*, October 19, 1945. Italics in the original.

2. Neil Allen, "Little Stoker Zatopek Talks

of the Fire in His Heart," *Times of London*, March 14, 1967, 8.

3. "Pourquoi la Roumanie ne participe pas aux Jeux Olympiques," *Journal de Geneve*, August 6, 1948, 6.

4. Andraž Rožman, "Zaradi atletike skoraj izključen iz šole," *Dnevnik*, July 28, 2012. Available at https://www.dnevnik.si/1042544021, accessed November 30, 2020.

5. Ekrem Dupanović, "Neke stvari se dogode samo jednom u životu," *Mediacentar Sarajevo*, February 7, 2014. Available at https://www.media.ba/bs/magazin-novinarstvo/-neke-stvari-se-dogode-samo-jednom-u-zivotu, accessed November 30, 2020.

6. *Przegląd Sportowy*, July 31, 1948, cited by Adam Fryc and Mirosław Ponczek in "An Event of 'Two Heroes': Poland and the 1948 London Olympic Games," *International Journal of the History of Sport* 27, no. 6 (2010): 1065–1079.

7. Dmitry Okunev, "Сталин в спорте: стрелял и разгонял," *Gazeta.ru*, December 19, 2017. Available at https://www.gazeta.ru/sport/2017/12/19/a_11500940.shtml, accessed February 12, 2021.

8. CF. *Kultura i zhizn*, November 1, 1949, cited by Jim Rioden in "More Serious than Life and Death: Russian and Soviet Football," in *The Organisation and Governance of Top Football Across Europe: An Institutional Perspective*, eds. Hallgeir Gammelsæter and Benoît Senaux (New York: Taylor & Francis, 2011), 224–237.

9. Maya Peshkova, "Победа. Одна на всех. К столетию Героя Советского Союза генерал-полковника Глеба Бакланова," *Echo of Moscow*, July 18, 2010. Available at https://echo.msk.ru/programs/time/696164-echo/, accessed December 6, 2020.

10. Allison Danzig, "King George Opens Olympics for 6000 from 59 Nations," *New York Times*, July 30, 1948, 1.

11. Mark Dyreson, "To Dip or Not to Dip': The American Flag at the Olympic Games since 1936," *International Journal of the History of Sport* 25, no. 2 (2008): 163–184.

12. Red Smith, *Out of the Red* (New York: Knopf, 1950), 259.

13. Roger Bannister, *The Four Minute Mile* (New York: Dodd, Mead, 1956), 79.

14. Undated report by Gleb Vladimirovich Baklanov to Deputy Head Department of Propaganda and Agitation of the Central Committee of the CPSU (Boris Nikolayevich Ponomarev) cited in the "Secret Archive of Axel Vartanyan," *Sports-Express*, September 3, 2002. Available at https://www.sport-express.ru/newspaper/2002-09-02/9_1/, accessed December 6, 2020.

15. Václav Dostál, *Provazniková a Šotola o Sokolu* (Prague, 2016). Available at http://vaclavdostal.8u.cz/provaznikova.pdf, accessed December 2, 2020.

16. "XI. všesokolský slet," *Připraven k práci a obraně vlasti! Padesát let českého sportu v totalitní společnosti* (Prague: ÚSTR, Prague City Hall, Czech Olympic Committee, National Museum, 2014), 19. Available at https://www.olympic.cz/upload/files/Sport-totalita-katalog.3RED.pdf, accessed November 29, 2020.

17. Milan Krejčiřík, "Nedáme si diktovat, koho máme milovat! Ať žije prezident Beneš!," undated. Available at http://milan.i-line.cz/gymnazium100let/slet1948.html, accessed December 8, 2020.

18. This account of the slet is based on Petr Roubal's *Spartakiads: The Politics of Physical Culture in Communist Czechoslovakia* (Prague: Karolinum Press, 2019), trans. Dan Morgan, 110–120, and Milan Krejčiřík's article "Nedáme si diktovat, koho máme milovat! Ať žije prezident Beneš!" The rhymes and wit of the chants are lost in the English translation.

19. Pavel Kovář, "Den, kdy zemřela Eliška Misáková. Jediná sportovkyně, která získala olympijské zlato až po své smrti," *Reflex*, August 14, 2018. sportovkyne Available at https://www.reflex.cz/clanek/historie/89193/den-kdy-zemrela-eliska-misakova-jedina--ktera-zi skala-olympijske-zlato-az-po-sve-smrti.html, accessed December 10, 2020.

20. "Zlatí čeští medailisté: prvenství gymnastek a smutek ze smrti Elišky," *Česká televize*, August 18, 2016. Available at https://sport.ceskatelevize.cz/clanek/olympijske-hry/rio-2016/-zlati-cesti-medailiste-prvenstvi-gymnastek-a-

smutek-ze-smrti-elisky/5bdb3ec60d663b6fe 89c7061, accessed December 10, 2020.

21. "Czech Olympic Leader to Go to U.S.," *The Guardian*, August 19, 1948, 6.

22. Editorial, "The Taste of Freedom," *Palladium-Item* (Richmond, Indiana), August 17, 1948, 6.

23. Editorial, "The Iron Curtain Cracks," *Arizona Republic* (Phoenix), August 19, 1948, 6.

24. Robert C. Ruark, Jr., "Another Jolt," *Lansing State Journal* (Michigan), August 18, 1948, 8.

25. Gayle Talbot, "Gripping Ceremony Ends Olympics After Mexico Takes Final Medal," *Albuquerque Journal* (New Mexico), August 15, 1948, 7.

26. Barbara J. Keys, *Globalizing Sport: National Rivalry and International Community in the 1930s* (Cambridge: Harvard University Press, 2006), 178 and note 93 on 253.

27. Stanislav Tokarev, "Портреты на фоне времени," *Ogonyok*, June 10–17, 1989, 30–31. The quote from Alexander Pushkin is taken from his poem "The Miserly Knight."

Chapter 2

1. James Riordan, "The Rise and Fall of Soviet Olympic Champions," *Olympika: The International Journal of Olympic Studies* 2 (1993): 25–44.

2. David Lloyd Hoffmann, *Bodies of Knowledge: Physical Culture and the New Soviet Person* (Washington, D.C.: National Council for Eurasian and East European Research, 2000), 14.

3. This is sometimes spelt "Dynamo" in English.

4. James Nickels, "Dinamo Moscow's 1945 Goodwill Tour of Britain," *Russian Football News*, May 18, 2017. Available at https://russianfootballnews.com/dinamo-moscows-1945-goodwill-tour-of-britain/, accessed February 14, 2021.

5. Frank Keating, "Pale Dynamos Who Shone a Brilliant Light in Postwar Britain," *The Guardian*, November 6, 2000, 6.

6. Tom Jenkins and Jonny Weeks, "Chelsea's Stamford Bridge—Then and Now," *The Guardian*, December 18, 2014. Available at https://www.theguardian.com/football/ng-interactive/2014/dec/18/chelseas-stamford-bridge-then-and-now, accessed February 21, 2021.

7. Brian Glanville, *Soccer Nemesis* (London: Secker & Warburg, 1955).

8. *Ibid.*

9. Victor Peppard and James Riordan, *Playing Politics: Soviet Sport Diplomacy to 1992* (Greenwich: JAI Press, 1993), 57.

10. *Ibid.*

11. Matty Brown, "Boris Arkadyev—The Soviet Genius Behind Total Football and Tiki-Taka," *Russian Football News*, August 6, 2013. Available at http://russianfootballnews.com/-boris-arkadyev-the-soviet-genius-behind-total-football-and-tiki-taka/, accessed July 31, 2015.

12. David Caute, *The Dancer Defects: The Struggle for Cultural Supremacy During the Cold War* (Oxford: Oxford University Press, 2003), 22.

13. Ronnie Kowalski and Dilwyn Porter, "Cold War Football: British-European Encounters in the 1940s and 1950s," *East Plays West: Sport and the Cold War*, eds. Stephen Wagg and David L. Andrews (London: Routledge, 2007), 69.

14. Robert Edelman, *Spartak Moscow: A History of the People's Team in the Workers' State* (Ithaca: Cornell University Press, 2009), 132.

15. Nikolaï Starostin, *Футбол сквозь годы* (Moscow: Sovetskaya Rossiya, 1989), 107–108.

16. Simon Sebag Montefiore, *Stalin: The Court of the Red Tsar* (London: Phoenix, 2004), 185.

17. Starostin, *Футбол сквозь годы*, 113.

18. Nikolai Romanov, *Трудные дороги к Олимпу* (Moscow: Fizkultura i sport. 1987), 57.

19. *Ibid.*, 64.

20. Valery Burt, "Фальстарт Почему советские спортсмены не приехали на зимнюю Олимпиаду 1952 года," *Svobodnaya Pressa*, February 7, 2014. Available at http://svpressa.ru/sport/article/81879/, accessed December 9, 2020.

21. Nikolai Romanov, *Восхождение на Олимп* (Moscow: Sovetskiy Sport, 1993), 40.

22. *Ibid.*

23. Yuri Lukashin, *Хоккей на белых олимпиадах* (Moscow: Sport and Physical Education, 1959), chapter 3.

24. Peppard and Riordan, *Playing Politics,* 67.

25. Riordan, "The Rise and Fall of Soviet Olympic Champions."

26. J. Sigfrid Edström to Otto Mayer, April 24, 1951, Recognition Requests of the NOC of the USSR: Correspondence and Recognition, 1935–51, Box 238, International Olympic Committee Archives, Lausanne, Switzerland.

27. Jenifer Parks, *The Olympic Games, the Soviet Sports Bureaucracy, and the Cold War: Red Sport, Red Tape* (Lanham: Lexington, 2017), 17.

28. *Ibid.*, 20.

CHAPTER 3

1. Red Smith, "The Spirit of the Olympics Could Be Crushed by Small Incident," *Milwaukee Journal*, July 19, 1952, 8.

2. Arthur Daley, "Every Little Bit Helps," *New York Times*, June 10, 1952, 32.

3. Shirley Povich, "This Morning," *Washington Post*, January 8, 1952, 12.

4. Antoni Ekart, *Vanished Without a Trace* (London: Max Parrish, 1954), 207.

5. Carl Posey, *The Olympic Century, XV Olympiad: Helsinki 1952, Cortina D'Ampezzo 1956*, Vol. 13 (Warwick: Warwick Press, 2015).

6. "Muddies Accorded Real Taste of Red Propaganda," *The Times-News*, July 25, 1952, 8.

7. CIA, "Current Intelligence Digest," August 25, 1952, CIA-RDP79T01146A001 200120001–6.

8. "Soviet Hospitality Goes Unreturned," *New York Times*, July 28, 1952, 20.

9. L. Wayne Hicks, "1952 Olympics Telethon," *tvparty.com*. Available at http://www.tvparty.com/50tel.html, accessed 19 June 2016.

10. Michael Prozumenschikov, Deputy Director of the Russian State Archive of Contemporary History, interviewed by Leonid Velikhov for broadcasts, *Games Freedom Sensitive Olympic*. Available at http://www.svoboda.org/content/transcript/25214061.html, accessed February 5, 2016.

11. Radio Free Europe, "Soviet and Satellite Screening Athletes Who Will Go to Helsinki Olympic Games," March 17, 1952, Item No. 3631/52.

12. Robert Pruter, untitled book review of *Olympic Glory Denied, and a Final Opportunity for Glory Restored* by Frank Zarnowski, *Journal of Sport History* 5, no. 1 (1998): 201–203.

13. Toby C. Rider, "Political Warfare in Helsinki: American Covert Strategy and the Union of Free Eastern European Sportsmen," *The International Journal of the History of Sport* 30, no. 13 (2013): 1493–1507.

14. Oleg Matveev, "Тайное Противостояние в Хельсинки," *Trud*, September 6, 2000. Available at http://www.trud.ru/article/06-09-2000/11562_tajnoe_protivostojanie_v_xelsinki.html, accessed October 11, 2016.

15. Mark Whitaker, "Olympics Investigation: How the Russians Tried to Turn Our Star British Sprinter into a Spy," *The Telegraph*, August 4, 2016. Available at https://www.telegraph.co.uk/men/thinking-man/-olympics-investigation-how-the-russians-tried-to-turn-our-star-b/, accessed February 22, 2021.

16. Paul Abarenov, "Наша первая Олимпийская чемпионка Нина Ромашкова-Пономарева," *SovSport.ru*, July 8, 2008. Available at http://www.sovsport.ru/gazeta/article-item/297367, accessed February 18, 2016.

17. "U.S. Breaks 7th Olympic Record," *Daily Times*, July 25, 1952, 10.

18. "Olympics and Politics," *Washington Post*, July 25, 1952, 10.

19. Pat Robinson, "'The Sports Grill,'" *Atlanta Daily World*, May 1, 1952, 7.

20. Harry Schwartz, "Stalin Trains His Olympic Teams," *New York Times*, April 20, 1952, 19, 58–60.

21. Victor Vasiliev, "Железная леди," *Samozashchita bez oruzhiya*, 33, no. 4 (2008).

22. "Пономарева (Ромашкова) Нина Аполлоновна," Modern Sports Museum. Available at http://www.smsport.ru/expo/katalog/legatlet/otkalenko/, accessed December 9, 2016.

23. Ben Phlegar, "Red Amazon Discus Champ," *The Barre Daily Times*, July 21, 1952, 2.

24. Kathryn Jay, *More Than Just a Game: Sports in American Life since 1945* (New York: Columbia University Press, 2004), 55.

25. Vladimir Shteinbatch, *Soviet Sport: The Success Story* (Moscow: Raduga, 1967), 72.

26. Susan Cahn, "'Cinderellas' of Sport: Black Women in Track and Field," in *Sport and the Color Line: Black Athletes and Race Relations in Twentieth-Century America*, eds. Patrick B. Miller and David K. Wiggins (New York: Routledge, 2004), 224.

27. "Olympics and Politics," *Washington Post*, July 29, 1952, 10.

28. Jeronim Perović, "The Tito-Stalin Split: A Reassessment in Light of New Evidence," *Journal of Cold War Studies* 9, no. 2 (2007): 32–63.

29. Aksel Vartanyan, "Три смерти за один матч," *Sports-Express*, November 13, 2009. Available at https://www.sport-express.ru/football/reviews/784816/, accessed February 14, 2021.

30. Vlado Vurušić, "Kako je Tito Pobijedio Staljina," *Jutarnji list*, July 22, 2015. Available at https://www.jutarnji.hr/life/kako-je-tito-pobijedio-staljina-u-oci-utakmice-u-svlacionicu-je-stigao-telegram-od-tita-osobno.-igracima-su-se-noge-odsjekle-283342, accessed February 14, 2021.

31. Vartanyan, "Три смерти за один матч."

32. Vurušić, "Kako je Tito Pobijedio Staljina."

33. Yuri Tepper interviewed by Alexei Kuznetsov, "Воспоминания о Хельсинской Олимпиаде 1952 года," *Radio Liberty*, August 4, 2002. Available at http://www.svoboda.org/content/transcript/24203363.html, accessed March 11, 2017.

34. Richard Mills, "Cold War Football: Soviet Defence and Yugoslav Attack Following the Tito-Stalin Split of 1948," *Europe-Asia Studies* 68, no. 10 (2016): 1–23.

35. Jonathan Wilson, *Behind the Curtain: Football in Eastern Europe* (London: Hachette UK, 2012), 267.

36. "Gold Gives Birth to the Magical Magyars," *FIFA.com*, August 2, 2012. Available at http://www.fifa.com/tournaments/archive/mensolympic/london2012/news/newsid=1673992/index.html, accessed February 23, 2016.

37. Alexander Titeev, "'покрыли своё знамя позором' Чёрная страница в истории ЦСКА—клуб закрыли на два года Подробнее на «Чемпионате," championat.com, May 7, 2020. https://www.championat.com/football/article-4032963-istorija-rospuska-cdsa-v-avguste-1952-goda.html, accessed February 12, 2021.

38. Harrison E. Salisbury, "Russians Recount, Then Recant; Concede Tie to U.S. in Olympics," *New York Times*, August 7, 1952, 16.

39. Boris Burkov, "На XV Олимпийских Играх: крупный успех," *Ogoniok* 33 (August 1952), 9–11.

40. It is unclear how Romanov calculated this total. An audit conducted in 2002 by sports historian Aksel Vartanyan has the U.S. beating the USSR 495 to 487. See Aksel Vartanyan, "Нас Обманывали 50 Лет: Олимпиаду-52 Все-Таки Выиграли Американцы," *Sports-Express*, October 21, 2002. Available at http://www.sport-express.ru/olympic14/newspaper/58024/, accessed February 19, 2016. Whatever the real score was, the USSR would claim a draw in the years to come.

41. "Soviet Control of Sports Activities

and Sports Propaganda," Document Number (FOIA) /ESDN (CREST): CIA-RDP80–008 10A005900310006–0, dated January 1, 1955.

42. *Ibid.*

43. Leonid Mlechin, *Александр Николаевич Шелепин* (Moscow: Molodaya Gvardiya, 2009).

44. Jenifer Parks, "Verbal Gymnastics," *East Plays West: Sport and the Cold War*, eds. Stephen Wagg and David L. Andrews (London: Routledge, 2007), 39–40.

45. Alexander Arkadievich Gorbunov, *Борис Аркадьев* (Moscow: Sport and Physical Education, 1990), 127.

46. Boris Valiev, "CCCP—США: спортивные войны XX века," *Soviet Sport* 56 (March 27, 2004). Available at http://m. sovsport.ru/gazeta/article-item/148562 *Soviet Sport*, accessed December 10, 2016.

Chapter 4

1. "U.S. Shocks Canada, 4–1, in Olympic Hockey," *The Gazette* (Montreal), February 1, 1956, 1.

2. Václav Poživil, "Hokejová Propaganda v Komunistickém Československu v Kontextu Bipolárně Rozděleného Světa" (Master diss., Univerzita Palackého v Olomouc, 2017), 70.

3. Alena Gilbert, "Hokejista Oldřich Zábrodský o životě v emigraci," *Krajane. net*, June 3, 2008. Available at http://archiv. krajane.net//articleDetail.view?id=1329, accessed December 15, 2020.

4. "Tomáš Bouška interviews Augustin Bubník," trans. Olivia Webb, *politicalprisoners. eu*, October 15, 2012. Available at http://www. politicalprisoners.eu/gustav-bubnik-life-story. html, accessed February 8, 2016.

5. "Interview with Mr. Augustin Bubník." Interviewer Tomáš Bouška, trans. Olivia Webb, *politicalprisoner.eu*, October 15, 2012. Available at http://www.politicalprisoners.eu/gustav-bubnik-life-story.html, accessed February 22, 2021.

6. Mikhail Prozumenschikov, "Soviet-Czechoslovak Ice Hockey Politics," trans. Alex Fisher, in *The (Inter-Communist) Cold War on Ice: Soviet-Czechoslovak Ice Hockey Politics, 1967–1969*, Cold War International History Project, Working Paper #69, ed. James G. Hershberg (Washington, D.C.: Woodrow Wilson International Center for Scholars, 2014), 94.

7. Andre Laguerre, "Russia Takes Over," *Sports Illustrated*, February 6, 1956, 17–23.

8. Jeffery Weinstein, "Ikola Remembers Teammate Matchefts, 1956 Winter Olympics,"

mgoblue.com, February 21, 2014. Available at https://mgoblue.com/news/2014/2/21/Ikola_ Remembers_Teammate_Matchefts_1956_ Winter_Olympics, accessed December 12, 2020.

9. Len Taylor, "Only 9 Shots on Goal Bring Russia Victory, Bad Luck Helps Beat Dutchmen," *Kitchener-Waterloo Record* (Ontario), February 6, 1956, 1–2.

10. Jess Myers, "Memories of a Silver Feat Still Shine," *USA Hockey Magazine*, February 2012. Available at https://www.usahockey magazine.com/article/2012–02/memories-silver-feat-still-shine, accessed December 12, 2020.

11. Maxim Makarychev, "Всеволод Бобров. Непревзойденный гений," *RG.ru*, December 28, 2013, Available at http://www. rg.ru/2013/12/28/bobrov-site.html, accessed February 13, 2016.

12. Jack Stepler, "'Gashouse Gang' Wrecked Soviet's Hockey Supremacy," *Ottawa Citizen*, March 7, 1955.

13. "They Are Bad Losers," *Southeast Missourian*, March 19, 1955, 4.

14. "The Year the Russians Took the Gold Away," *MacLean's*, February 14, 1994, 49.

15. Frank R. Corkin Jr., "Propaganda and the Olympics," *The Journal* (Connecticut), January 30, 1956, 4.

16. Austin Conover, "No National Winners," *Los Angeles Evening Citizen News*, February 6, 1956, 16.

17. Editorial, "Are Americans Getting Soft?," *Altoona Tribune* (Pennsylvania), February 7, 1956, 4.

18. Editorial, "Olympic Doldrums," *San Francisco Examiner*, February 8, 1956, section II, 2.

19. Henry McLemore, "Olympic Games Match between U.S. and Reds," *The Daily News* (Pennsylvania), February 7, 1956, 4.

20. "Americans Point to Summer Test," *The Gazette and Daily* (York, Pennsylvania), February 9, 1956, 27.

21. "Russian Say They'll Sweep Summer Olympics, Too," *The Boston Globe*, February 7, 1956, 8.

Chapter 5

1. John Terence McGovern, "We'll Lose the Next Olympics," *This Week* magazine, May 16, 1954, 7–8.

2. Don Canham, "Russian Will Win the 1956 Olympics," *Sports Illustrated*, October 25, 1954, 10–12, 60–65.

3. Arthur Daley, "Will Soviet Union Sweep

the Olympics?," *American Legion Magazine*, June 1955, 16–17, 51–53.

4. Yuri Rastvorov, "Red Amateurs Are Pros," *Life* magazine, June 6, 1955, 93–4, 97–8, 102, 105–6.

5. *Ibid.*

6. *Ibid.*

7. As the director of the Deutsche Bank, it was politically astute for von Halt to join the party, without necessarily embracing its ideology. According to Harold James, "Halt successfully tamed part of the national Socialist threat inside the bank." See Harold James, *The Nazi Dictatorship and the Deutsche Bank* (Cambridge: Cambridge University Press, 2004), 58.

8. Allen Guttmann, *The Games Must Go On: Avery Brundage and the Olympic Movement* (New York: Columbia University Press, 1984), 70.

9. "President Avery Brundage visits the USSR," *Bulletin du Comité International Olympique*, no. 48 (October-November 1954), 13–15.

10. Avery Brundage, "I Must Admit—Russian Athletes Are Great!," *Saturday Evening Post*, April 30, 1955, 109–112, 114.

11. "President Avery Brundage Visits the USSR."

12. *Ibid.*

13. *Ibid.*

14. Joseph A. Marchiony, "The Rise of Soviet Athletics," *Comparative Education Review* 7, no. 1 (1963): 17–27.

15. "Guest at Soviet 'Athlete Day,'" *Intelligencer Journal* (Pennsylvania), July 19, 1954, 10.

16. Avery Brundage, "I Must Admit—Russian Athletes Are Great!"

17. *Ibid.*

18. *Ibid.*

19. Robert Edelman, *Serious Fun: A History of Spectator Sport in the USSR* (Oxford: Oxford University Press, 1993), 137.

20. "Brundage Amazed at Rapid Growth of Russian Sports," *Chicago Sunday Tribune*, August 1, 1954, part 2, 4.

21. Whitney Shoemaker, "Olympics Ban on Russia Demanded," *San Francisco Examiner*, April 4, 1956, 32.

22. Thomas M. Domer, *Sport in Cold War America, 1953–1963: The Diplomatic and Political Use of Sport in the Eisenhower and Kennedy Administrations* (Ph.D. diss., Marquette University, 1976), 162.

23. Congressman Frank Thompson, Jr.,

"Footnotes on the 1956 Olympic Games," *Congressional Record*, April 19, 1955, 101, part 4: 4758.

24. Congressman Michael A. Feighan, "Importance of Sports and Recreation in the Health and Well-Being of Our Nation, Extension of Remarks," *Congressional Record*, March 1, 1956, 102, part 3: 3788–3789.

25. Arthur Daley, "Will Soviet Union Sweep the Olympics?" *American Legion Magazine*, June 1955, 16–17, 51–53.

26. Senator John Marshall Butler, "Participation in the 1956 Olympics," *Congressional Record*, May 17, 1956, part 6: 8334–5.

27. *Sports Illustrated*, December 20, 1954, 71.

28. "International Athletics—Cold War Battleground," September 28, 1954, Jackson Papers, Box 62, "International Sports," Dwight D. Eisenhower Library.

29. *Ibid.*

30. "The Communist Sports Offensive," undated, Jackson Papers, Box 62, "International Sports," Dwight D. Eisenhower Library.

31. Letter from Abbott Washburn to C.D. Jackson, January 11, 1955, Jackson Papers, Box 62, "International Sports," Dwight D. Eisenhower Library.

32. *Ibid.*

33. Toby C. Rider, *The Olympic Games and the Secret Cold War: The U.S. Government and the Propaganda Campaign Against Communist Sport, 1950–1960* (Ph.D. diss., University of Western Ontario), 246. Ralph R. Busick memo of October 20, 1955, to Brigadier General Dale O. Smith.

34. "Brundage Blasts U.S. Hysteria," *Chicago Daily Tribune*, April 8, 1956.

35. Robert Creamer, "Of Greeks—and Russians," *Sports Illustrated*, February 6, 1956, 30–2, 56.

36. *Ibid.*

CHAPTER 6

1. Roland Vegso, *The Naked Communist: Cold War Modernism and the Politics of Popular Culture* (New York: Fordham University Press, 2012), 93.

2. George A. Dondero, "Communist Conspiracy in Art Threatens American Museums," *Congressional Record*, March 17, 1952, 98, part 2: 2423.

3. "Ike Likes the Arts—So U.S. May Export Culture," *U.S. News & World Report*, January 28, 1955, 68, 70.

4. *Ibid.*

5. Joel Sleed, "Dallas Has Come A Long Way," *Sarasota Herald-Tribune* (Florida), February 24, 1980, 9G.

6. Jerry Bywaters, *Seventy-Five Years of Art in Dallas: The History of the Dallas Art Association and the Dallas Museum of Fine Arts* (Dallas: Dallas Museum of Fine Arts, 1978), 55.

7. Francine Carraro, *Jerry Bywaters: A Life in Art* (Austin: University of Texas Press, 2010), 187.

8. "'Red Art' Onslaught Hot," *Texas Observer*, February 15, 1956, 6.

9. Francine Carraro, "Seeing Red: The Dallas Museum in the McCarthy Era," in Elizabeth C. Childs, *Suspended License: Censorship and the Visual Arts* (Seattle: University of Washington Press, 1999), 247.

10. Warren Leslie, *Dallas, Public and Private: Aspects of an American City* (New York: Grossman, 1964), 170–1.

11. Carraro, *Jerry Bywaters*, 189.

12. *Ibid.*, 194.

13. John Rosenfield, "Art's Stillness and Republicans," *Dallas Morning News*, February 9, 1956, Part 2, 8.

14. Helen Bollock, "Banker Opposes 'Patriotic' Fear," *Dallas Morning News*, March 1, 1956.

15. Aline B. Saarinen, "Art Storm Breaks on Dallas," *New York Times*, February 15, 1956, 15.

16. "Dallas Art Dispute Goes On," *New York Times*, March 4, 1956, 14.

17. Charlotte Devree, "The U.S. Government Vetoes Living Art," *ARTNews* (September 1956), 34–35, 54–56.

18. Carraro, "Seeing Red," 243.

19. Carraro, *Jerry Bywaters*, 174.

20. Rual Askew, "Art and Artists: Points of View Clearly Drawn," *Dallas Morning News*, March 25, 1956, 6.

21. Devree, "The U.S. Government Vetoes Living Art."

22. Askew, "Art and Artists."

23. Anthony Lewis, "U.S. Cancels Tour by Arts; Irked Texan," *Des Moines Register* (Iowa), May 26, 1956, 16.

24. "Art in the Heart of Texas," *New York Times*, May 27, 1956, section 4, 10.

25. Jonathan Marshall, "Dondero, Dallas and Defeatism," *Arts* 30, no. 10 (July 1956): 9, 31.

26. Walter Lippmann, "A Political Standard for Art?," *Des Moines Register* (Iowa), June 23, 1956, 4.

27. George A. Dondero, "Communism Under the Guise of Cultural Freedom—Strangling American Art," *Congressional Record*, June 14, 1956, 102, part 8: 10419, 10421.

28. Thomas B. Hess, "Banning Modern Art," *New York Times*, September 11, 1956, 34.

29. Called Ching-hsi in Chinese, which means the "Capital opera," the company was also referred to as the "Peking Opera," "Chinese Opera Company," "Classical Theatre of China," and "Chinese Classical Opera Company" while it toured Australia.

30. "Art and Entertainment: Latest 'Cold War' Weapon for U.S.," *U.S. News & World Report*, July 1, 1955, 57–59.

31. Quoted by Victoria Phillips Geduld in "Dancing Diplomacy: Martha Graham and the Strange Commodity of Cold-War Cultural Exchange in Asia, 1955 and 1974," *Dance Chronicle* 33, no. 1 (2010): 44–81.

32. "A City Of Plays: The Drama of Many Countries," *Times of London*, June 9, 1955, 12.

33. "We'll See Red Opera—AFTER the Games," *The Argus*, October 22, 1956, 3.

34. Robert Menzies, "Chinese Classical Theatre Company," House of Representatives Hansard No. 42, October 18, 1956, 1601.

35. "Storm in a Chinese Teacup," *The Age*, October 19, 1956, 2.

36. George Kerr, "Diplomats Are Posing as Opera 'Stars,'" *The Argus*, October 20, 1956, 3.

37. "Keep Away from Games," *The Argus*, October 18, 1956.

38. "Australian Hits at Mr. Attlee," *The Guardian*, February 14, 1955, 7.

39. "Phantom of the Opera," *The Argus*, October 19, 1956, 1.

40. "Red Faces and Red Opera," *Sydney Morning Herald*, October 19, 1956, 2.

41. Peter Russo, "Through an (Opera) Glass ... Darkly," *The Argus*, October 19, 1956, 2.

42. Judy Joy Davies, "Oh! The Shame," *The Argus*, October 19, 1956, 3.

43. Clive O. Jackson, "Ban Is Provocative," *The Argus*, October 20, 1956, 4.

44. Peter F. Weiner, "Who Whispered in Mr. Menzies Ear?," *The Argus*, October 19, 1956, 4.

45. "What Will Happen if Red Craze Wins?" *The Argus*, October 20, 1956, 3.

46. "Classical Theatre of China," *Australian Women's Weekly*, November 21, 1956, 20–21.

47. "Chinese Players Enthral Large Audience," *Canberra Times*, December 8, 1956, 2.

48. Alistair Shaw, "Telling the Truth about People's China" (Ph.D. diss., Victoria University of Wellington, 2010), 95–96.

49. *Ibid.*

CHAPTER 7

1. Balázs Gabay, "A melbourne-i vérfürdő nem volt reváns ötvenhatért," *MNO*, October 23, 2012. Available at http://mno.hu/belfold/-a-melbourne-i-verfurdo-nem-volt-revans-otvenhatert-1112457, accessed November 20, 2016.

2. György Szepesi, *Búcsú a mikrofontól* (Budapest: Paginarum, 1998), 341.

3. Charles Gati, *Failed Illusions: Moscow, Washington, Budapest, and the 1956 Hungarian Revolt* (Washington, D.C.: Woodrow Wilson Center Press, 2006), 194.

4. Victor Sebestyen, *Twelve Days: The Story of the 1956 Hungarian Revolution* (London: Phoenix, 2006), 127.

5. Attila Arday, István L. Pap, and Gábor Thury, *Vér és aranyak* (Budapest: Ringier Kiadó KFT, 2006), 165.

6. András Kő, *Melbourne 1956* (Budapest: Nemzet Kiadó, 2006), 101.

7. Sándor Kopácsi, *In the Name of the Working Class* (New York: Grove Press, 1986), Kindle edition, chapter 13.

8. Pál Peterdi, *Gyarmati sors, avagy egy bal kéz története* (Budapest: Históriás Könyvkiadó és Értékesítő Betéti Társaság, 2005), 118.

9. András Kő and László Tábori, *A Biography: The Legendary Story of the Great Hungarian Runner* (Sarasota: Design, 2015), chapter 9.

10. Attila Ághassi, "Egy elmaradt kézfogás törte ketté az életét," *Index*, August 19, 2006. Available at http://index.hu/sport/2006/08/19/060816bg/, accessed June 10, 2016.

11. Kő, *Melbourne 1956*, 107.

12. Arday, Pap, and Thury, *Vér és aranyak*, 75.

13. "Sárkány István naplója," *origo.hu*, November 2, 2006. Available at http://www.origo.hu/melbourne1956/re/naplo/20061102sarkany.html, accessed June 11, 2016.

14. Pál Peterdi, *Gyarmati sors*, 122.

15. *Ibid.*

16. Dezső Dobor, *Olimpiának indult* (Budapest: Aréna 2000, 2006), 80.

17. Kő, *Melbourne 1956*, 122.

18. *The Revolt in Hungary: A Documentary Chronology of Events*, October 23, 1956–November 4, 1956 (New York: Free Europe Committee, 1957), 84. Available at https://www.cia.gov/library/readingroom/docs/-CIA-RDP80B01676R001000010035–4.pdf, accessed December 14, 2020.

19. Kő, *Melbourne 1956*, 110.

20. Dobor, *Olimpiának indult*, 84–5.

21. *Ibid.*, 88.

22. András Kő, *Melbourne 1956*, 172.

23. *Ibid.*, 183.

24. Éva Székely, *Sírni csak a győztesnek szabad* (Budapest: Új Mandátum Könyvkiadó, 1992), 75.

25. "Seven Out Now—Norway Will Stay," *The Argus*, November 12, 1956, 17.

CHAPTER 8

1. Geert Mak, "Russische inval in Hongarije; November 4, 1956 door NCRV-radio verslaggever Alfred van Sprang," NOB sound archive, *nrc.nl*, November 2, 1991. Available at http://www.nrc.nl/handelsblad/1991/11/02/russische-inval-in-hongarije-4-november-1956-door-6985824, accessed April 19, 2016.

2. "Primeur van een politieke boycott," *de Volkskrant*, February 17, 2011. Available at http://www.volkskrant.nl/archief/primeur-van-een-politieke-boycott~a1835620/, accessed April 22, 2016.

3. Aad Haverkamp, *De politieke Spelen? De dynamiek van de maatschappelijke discussies over het boycotten van de Olympische Spelen in 1936, 1956 en 1980* (Master's thesis, Rijksuniversiteit Groningen, 2012), 60.

4. *Ibid.*, 62.

5. Rob Bruins Slot and Ad van Liempt, "Terwijl Boedapest brandt dansen de communisten," *De Nederlandse Publieke Omroep*, April 3, 2015. Available at http://www.npogeschiedenis.nl/andere-tijden/afleveringen/2001–2002/Terwijl-Boedapest-brandt-dansen-de-communisten.html, accessed April 19, 2016.

6. "Nederland zal niet aan de Olympische Spele deelnemen," *Leidse Courant*, November 7, 1956, 7.

7. Marjolein te Winkel, *De Verloren Spelen. Nederlandse boycot Olympische Spelen 1956* (Eindhoven: Deboekenmakers, 2008), 74.

8. Marjolein te Winkel, *Holland ist nicht dabei!* (Master's thesis, Universiteit Utrecht, 2007), 50.

9. Cockie Gastelaars, telephone interview with author, May 10, 2016.

10. Te Winkel, *De Verloren Spelen*, 77.

11. Ad van Liempt, "Bij de dood van Puck. Atlete Puck Brouwer werd slachtoffer van Olympische boycot 1956," *NPO*, October 9, 2006. Available at http://www.npogeschiedenis.nl/nieuws/2006/oktober/Bij-de-dood-van-Puck.html, accessed May 3, 2016.

12. Te Winkel, *De Verloren Spelen*, 61.

13. Wichard Woyke, "Olympische Spiele und Fussballweltmeisterschaften—Mega-Events und ihre Bedeutung für die Politik," in *Sport und Politik. Eine Einführung*, ed. Uwe Anderson (Schwalbach: Wochenschau Verl, 2006), 11–34.

14. *Der Bund* (Bern), November 9, 1956, 7.

15. André Rodari, "Oui, Non Oui. Est-ce une farce?," *Journal de Geneve*, November 12, 1956, 7.

16. Colette Muret, "Démission l'espirit olympique," *Gazette de Lausanne*, November 9, 1956, 7.

17. Armand Péclet, "La Suisse n'Ira pas a Melbourne," *Tribune de Lausanne*, November 9, 1956, 11.

18. Josef Renggli, "Das Bauernopfer von Melbourne 1956," *Neuen Zürcher Zeitung*, November 22, 2006, Available at http://www.nzz.ch/articleEN00L-1.77495, accessed May 19, 2016.

19. Colette Muret, "Quoique absente, la Suisse sera presente a Melbourne: la montagne accouche ... d'un escrimeur," *Gazette de Lausanne*, November 16, 1956, 7.

20. "Acuerdos de la Delegación Nacional de Educación Física y Deportes y de sus organismos integrantes. España no concurre a la XVI Olimpiada," *Boletín Oficial de la Delegación Nacional de Educación Física y Deportes*, November 1956, 2.

21. "Brundage Still Can't Understand Why Some Don't Feel Like Holding Play," *Lewiston Evening Journal* (Maine), November 10, 1956, 7.

22. "España participará en los Juegos Olímpicos de 1956," *ABC* (Seville), October 12, 1955, 31.

23. Ian Jobling, "Melbourne 1956," *The Encyclopaedia of the Modern Olympic Movement*, eds. John E. Findling and Kimberley D. Pelle (Westport: Greenwood Press, 2004), 147–8.

24. Will Grimsley "Withdrawals Stun Olympic Magnates," *The Ottawa Citizen*, 9 November 1956, 13.

25. "Egypt Out," *The Strait Times*, August 13, 1956.

26. "Les Raisons du forfait de L'Égypte aux Jeux Olympiques," *Le Monde*, August 17, 1956.

27. D. Richard Thorpe, "What We Failed to Learn from Suez," *The Telegraph*, November 1, 1956.

28. "Iraq Withdraws," *Milwaukee Journal*, November 3, 1956, 12.

29. "Lebanon Withdraws from Olympics," *Tampa Sunday Tribune* (Florida), November 11, 1956, B-2.

30. Vasili Sarychev, "МИГ и Судьба," *pressball.by*, August 7, 2005. Available at http://www.pressball.by/articles/author/sarychev/91039, accessed May 16, 2016.

31. Allen Guttmann, *The Games Must Go On*, 145.

32. "Games Invitation—'Red' China Protests," *The Argus*, February 21, 1955, 3.

33. Liang Lijuan, *He Zhenjiang and China's Olympic Dream* (Beijing: Foreign Languages Press, 2007), 47.

34. Geoffrey Ballard, *Nation with Nation* (Richmond: Spectrum, 1997), 59.

35. Fan Hong and Lu Zhouxiang, *The Politicisation of Sport in Modern China* (London: Routledge, 2015), 15.

36. Ted Bolwell, "Flag Mix-Up as Olympic Village Opens," *The Herald*, October 19, 1956, 1.

37. "National Flag Breaking Ceremony, 29th October, 1956—Breaking of Incorrect Chinese Flag," Memorandum from Geoffrey Ballard to Peter Miskin, dated October 29, 1956. Papers of Sir Wilfrid Kent Hughes (1895–1970), series 19, MS 4856, National Library of Australia.

38. Letter from Jung Kao-t'ang to Wilfrid Kent Hughes, dated November 6, 1956. Papers of Sir Wilfrid Kent Hughes (1895–1970), series 19, MS 4856, National Library of Australia.

39. Letter from Wilfrid Kent Hughes to Huang Chung, dated November 13, 1956. Papers of Sir Wilfrid Kent Hughes (1895–1970), series 19, MS 4856, National Library of Australia.

40. Sarychev, "МИГ и Судьба."

41. Alexei Adjoubei, *Те Десять Лет* (Moscow: Sovetskaya Rossiya, 1989), 154.

Chapter 9

1. "Documentary Chronology," Telegram from Andre Laguerre to Sid James, DC, November 23, 1956, Jackson Papers, Box 104, *Sports Illustrated—Hungarian Olympic Team Defectors*, DDEL.

2. Blanche Wiesen Cook, *The Declassified Eisenhower* (Harmondsworth: Penguin Books, 1984), 203.

3. "Documentary Chronology," Telegram from Andre Laguerre to Sid James, DC, November 23, 1956.

4. *Ibid.*, 179.
5. *Ibid.*, 180.
6. *Ibid.*, 32.
7. Dezső Dobor, *Olimpiának indult*, 146.
8. Kő, *Melbourne 1956*, 112.
9. *Ibid.*, 103.
10. Commonwealth Department of Immigration, Gyorgy Szepesi, Application for Political Asylum in Australia, undated.
11. Csaba Ilkei, *Besúgók, árulók, kalandorok* (Budapest: Szerzői Kiadás, 2013), 13.
12. Miklós Martin, telephone interview with author, December 22, 2016.
13. Dobor, *Olimpiának indult*, 203.
14. "40 Hungarians Will Leave the Team," *The Argus*, December 6, 1956, 1.
15. "Documentary Chronology," Telegram from Andre Laguerre to Sid James, December 6, 1956.
16. Martin, telephone interview.
17. "Documentary Chronology," Telegram from Roy Terrell to Sid James, DC, December 9, 1956.
18. Eric Thomas Chester, *Covert Network: Progressives, the International Rescue Committee, and the CIA* (Armonk: M.E. Sharpe, 1995), 1.
19. Martin, phone interview.
20. "Hungarian Athletes Cutting Ties," *New York Times*, December 6, 1956, 5.
21. The Kossuth emblem was the coat of arms used by Lajos Kossuth when he led the fight for independence against the Hapsburg Empire in 1848. This victory was short-lived and a year later Austria, with the help of its ally Russia, crushed the revolution. The flag was adopted by the freedom fighters as they attacked the Red Army three weeks earlier on the streets of Budapest.
22. Peterdi, *Gyarmati sors*, 130.
23. *Ibid.*, 135.
24. "Gyarmati's Story," *Sports Illustrated*, April 8, 1957, 32.
25. Peterdi, *Gyarmati sors*, 137.
26. "Documentary Chronology," Telegram from Andre Laguerre to Sid James, December 15, 1956.
27. "Documentary Chronology."
28. "Pan Am Can't Give Free Rides to Refugee Olympic Athletes," *Honolulu Recorder*, December 27, 1956, 1.

CHAPTER 10

1. The KGB was likely to have called on the support GRU (Glavnoye razvedyvatel'noye upravleniye), the Soviet Union's foreign military intelligence agency, for its operations in Melbourne.
2. Letter from C.C.F. Spry to R.G. Menzies, dated October 10, 1956, in *XVI Olympiad Melbourne 1956: Grant to Political Asylum to Team Members and Visitors*, National Archives of Australia: A6122, 2782, December 1956.
3. Vladimir Petrov and Evdokia Petrov, *Empire of Fear* (London: Andre Deutsch, 1956).
4. Michael Bialoguski, *The Petrov Story* (Melbourne: William Heinemann, 1955), 65.
5. Peter Wilson, "British Agents Saw Wife as the Quality Catch," *Weekend Australian*, April 4, 2011.
6. "Intelligence Aspects of 1956 Olympic Games in Melbourne," in *Selected Appendices of Unpublished History of ASIO [Security Intelligence]*, National Archives of Australia A6122, 1414.
7. "Olympic Games Soviet State Security Colonel to Hungarian State Security Officer(s) Report," December 8, 1956, in *XVI Olympiad Melbourne 1956 Counter Espionage Targets (TS)*, National Archives of Australia A6122, 2776.
8. *Ibid.*
9. *Soviet Use of Assassination and Kidnapping*, CIA Historical Review Program, September 22, 1993. Available at https://www.cia.gov/library/center-for-the-study-of-intelligence/-kent-csi/vol19no3/html/v19i3a01p_0001.htm, accessed December 8, 2016.
10. Vladimir and Evdokia Petrov, *Empire of Fear*, 222–223.
11. "Intelligence Aspects of the Visit of Soviet and Satellite Teams, Including the Possibility of Defection," in *XVI Olympiad Melbourne 1956 Espionage Use by RIS*, National Archives of Australia: A6122, 2777.
12. Letter from C.C.F. Spry to Prime Minister Menzies, November 29, 1956, in *PETROV, Vladimir 1956 Personal Conduct Incident in Queensland*, National Archives of Australia, A6122: 2757.
13. Letter from C.C.F. Spry to Mr. Petrov, November 29, 1956, in *PETROV, Vladimir 1956 Personal Conduct Incident in Queensland*, National Archives of Australia, A6122: 2757.
14. "Friendship First at Games, Russians assure U.S. Officials," *Sydney Morning Herald*, November 17, 1956.
15. "Intelligence Aspects of 1956 Olympic Games in Melbourne."
16. Arkady Nikitovich Vorobiev, На трёх Олимпиадах (Sverdlovsk: Sverdlovsk Book,

1963). Available at http://olympic-weight lifting.ru/unedited_texts/vorob6.htm, February 12, 2021.

17. "Intelligence Aspects of the Visit of Soviet and Satellite Teams, Including the Possibility of Defections."

18. N. Savin, "Неудачи Аллена Даллеса," *Literaturnaya Gazeta*, April 2, 1957.

19. *Ibid.*

20. *Ibid.*

21. Tibor Takács, Zsolt Krahulcsán, and Müller Rolf, *Állambiztonság és olimpia 1956–1988* (Budapest: L'Harmattan, 2008), 38.

22. Memo, dated December 3 1956, in *XVI Olympiad Melbourne 1956 Counter Espionage Targets (TS)*, National Archives of Australia A6122, 2776.

23. "Suspected Intelligence Workers," in *XVI Olympiad Melbourne 1956 Espionage Intelligence Aspects Volume 1*, National Archives of Australia, A6122, 2791.

24. Joanna Ostrowska and Marcin Zaremba, "Kobieca gehenna," *Polityka* 10 (November 2009): 64–66.

Chapter 11

1. Handwritten note by Arthur Tange, dated November 18, 1956, in *Political Asylum—Nina Paranyuk*, National Archives of Australia A1838, 1606/3.

2. File note by J.C C. Kevin after speaking to Francis Stuart on November 19, 1956, in *Political Asylum—Nina Paranyuk*, National Archives of Australia A1838, 1606/3.

3. David Horner, *The Spy Catchers: The Official History of ASIO, 1949–1963* (Sydney: Allen & Unwin, 2014), 456.

4. "Intelligence Aspects of 1956 Olympic Games in Melbourne," in *Selected Appendices of Unpublished History of ASIO [Security Intelligence]*, National Archives of Australia A6122, 1414.

5. "Woman Vanishes from Russian Games Liner," *The Argus*, November 19, 1956, 1.

6. Lionel Hogg, "Nina Tells: Why I Fled," *Herald Weekend Magazine*, February 9, 1957, 17–18.

7. *Ibid.*

8. *Ibid.*

9. *Ibid.*

10. *Ibid.*

11. Lionel Hogg, "Fear Gripped Me ... but I Found Friends to Hide Me," *The Herald*, February 11, 1957, 5.

12. *Ibid.*

13. *Ibid.*

14. It was probably through the network of members of the Union of Ukrainians, set up in 1953, that Nina found people in this close-knit community to hide her.

15. Lionel Hogg, "Nina Tells: How She Went into Hiding," *The Herald*, November 12, 1957.

16. "The Police Are Not Hiding Nina," *The Argus*, November 20, 1956, 1, 5.

17. "It's an Offence to Hide Nina," *The Argus*, November 24, 1956, 9.

18. "Soviet Defector Tells of Years of Fear," *Canberra Times*, May 29, 1968, 3.

19. "The Riddle of Nina," *The Argus*, December 3, 1956, 6.

20. Lionel Hogg, "Nina Tells: How She Went into Hiding," *The Herald*, February 12, 1957, 5.

21. "Captain to Nina: 'All Is Forgiven,'" *The Argus*, December 11, 1956, 1.

22. "Not a Clue to Nina," *The Argus*, December 13, 1956, 7.

23. Lionel Hogg, "I'll Take a job, a New Name," *The Herald*, February 13, 1957, 5.

24. Eric Nave, unpublished autobiography.

Chapter 12

1. Ron Clarke and Norman Harris, *The Lonely Breed* (London: Pelham, 1967), 65.

2. Christopher McDougall, *Born to Run* (New York: Alfred A. Knopf, 2009), 95–96.

3. V. P. Tennov, *Моряк с Балтики* (Moscow: Physical Culture and Sport, 1987), chapter 2.

4. Gordon Pirie, *Running Wild* (London: Sportsman's Book Club, 1962), 156.

5. Roger Bannister, "Kuts the Cat, Pirie the Mouse," *Sports Illustrated*, December 3, 1956, 16–18.

6. Christopher Brasher and Herb Elliot, "He Who Dares," *The Age*, 23 September 1964, 13, 15.

7. John Kieran, Arthur Daley, and Pat Jordan, *The Story of the Olympic Games* (Philadelphia: J.B. Lippincott, 1977), 303.

8. Brasher and Elliot, "He Who Dares."

9. Tennov, *Моряк с Балтики*, chapter 15.

10. Harry Gordon, "Everybody Loves a Sailor!," *The Sun*, November 24, 1956, 3.

11. *Ibid.*

12. Bannister, "Kuts the Cat, Pirie the Mouse."

13. Peter Wilson, "Pirie's Failure," *The Argus*,

December 1, 1956, 11. This article was syndicated from the *Daily Mail*.

14. V.A. Vlasenko, V.V. Kolotovkin, M.A. Rakitin, and E.V. Yakushina, Они прославили Россию Герои Олимпийских игр (Moscow: Ministry of Education and Science, 2009), 82.

15. Allan Lawrence, *Olympus and Beyond* (Pittsburgh: Dorrance, 2014), 146.

16. Gavin Souter, "Vladimir and his Friends," *Sydney Morning Herald*, November 29, 1956, 2.

17. Pirie, *Running Wild*, 158.

18. Derek Ibbotson and Terry O'Connor, *Four-Minute Smiler* (London: Stanley Paul, 1960), 84.

19. Mike Shropshire, "Blue, Blue Days Bobby Morrow, Who Sprinted to Three Gold Medals at the 1956 Summer Olympics, Is a bitter and All-but-Forgotten Man," *Sports Illustrated*, June 5, 2000, 59–63.

20. Kieran, Daley and Jordan, *The Story of the Olympic Games*, 294.

21. "Golden Melbourne," *Sports Illustrated*, December 10, 1956, 19–29, 35, 37–38, 43–46.

22. Interview with Nikolai Romanov in *Sovetskii Sport* film magazine, no. 15, December 1956. Available at https://www.youtube.com/watch?v=cKnbNUh8s2M, accessed August 19, 2016.

23. Nikolai Lyubomirov and Petr Sobolev, *A Story of Soviet Sport* (Moscow: Progress, 1967), 68.

24. Adjoubei, Те Десять Лет, 154.

25. Gavin Souter, "Vladimir and His Friends," *Sydney Morning Herald*, November 29, 1956, 2.

26. Peter Banfield, "How Kuts the Killer Broke Them—One by One," *The Argus*, November 29, 1956, 20.

27. Lyubomirov and Sobolev, *A Story of Soviet Sport*, 95.

28. Bruce Howard, *15 Days in '56: The First Australian Olympics* (Sydney: Angus & Robertson, 1995), 78.

29. Gordon Pirie, "Pirie Accuses," *The People* magazine, October 15, 1961, 6–7.

30. Alan Lawrence, *Olympus and Beyond* (Pittsburgh: Dorrance, 2014), 201.

31. John Cobley, "Profile: Vladimir Kuts, 1927–1975," *Racing Past*. Available at http://www.racingpast.ca/john_contents.php?id=121, accessed September 25, 2016. The author has spoken to the source of this quote, and while he wishes to remain anonymous, his account is credible.

CHAPTER 13

1. Olga Connolly, *The Rings of Destiny* (New York: David McKay, 1968), 30.

2. *Ibid.*, 5.

3. Harold Connolly, *Olympic Echoes*, unpublished memoir, 2008, 15.

4. *Ibid.*, 69.

5. Connolly, *Olympic Echoes*, 52.

6. Randy Harvey, "A New Love Story: Olga Connolly, Once the World's Darling, Is Giving Something Back," *Los Angeles Times*, January 31, 1989, 157.

7. Connolly, *The Rings of Destiny*, 99.

8. *Ibid.*, 124.

9. *Ibid.*, 127.

10. Connolly, *Olympic Echoes*, 53.

11. Connolly, *The Rings of Destiny*, 134.

12. *Ibid.*, 137.

13. Connolly, *Olympic Echoes*, 270.

14. *Ibid.*, 274.

15. Robert Lipsyte, "At Last, Harold Connolly Raises Both Arms," *New York Times*, December 13, 1991, B21.

16. Connolly, *Olympic Echoes*, 279.

17. *Ibid.*, 279.

18. *Ibid.*, 274.

19. Ian Willoughby, "Olga Fikotová-Connolly: 1956 Olympic Champion Dubbed 'Traitor' in Communist Czechoslovakia Over Romance with U.S. Sthlete," *Radio Prada*, January 5, 2008.

20. Connolly, *Olympic Echoes*, 311.

21. Jeremy Rosenberg, "Olga Connolly: An Amazing Olympic—and American—Love Story," *KCET*, August 23, 2012. Available at https://www.kcet.org/departures-columns/-olga-connolly-an-amazing-olympic-and-american-love-story, accessed March 27, 2016.

22. Peter Hruby, *Dangerous Dreamers: The Australian Anti-Democratic Left and Czechoslovak Agents* (New York: iUniverse, 2010), chapter 8.

23. Connolly, *The Rings of Destiny*, 178.

24. Rosenberg, "Olga Connolly."

25. *Ibid.*

26. Tomáš Macek, "Z her se vraceli měsíc. Lodí "Hruzia" a přes Sibiř," *iDNES.cz/OH*, November 29, 2006. Available at http://oh.idnes.cz/z-her-se-vraceli-mesic-lodi-hruzia-a-pres-sibir-f40-/sport_oh.aspx?c=A06 1129_000649_sport_oh_mah, accessed March 29, 2016.

27. Connolly, *The Rings of Destiny*, 191.

28. Karel Hynie and Pavel Tausig, *Cestovní*

zpráva z lodi Gruzia aneb Není důležité zvítězit, ale vrátit se, Czech Television, 2005.

29. Lewis H. Carlson and John J. Fogarty, *Tales of Gold. An Oral History of the Summer Olympic Games Told by America's Gold Medal Winners* (Chicago: Contemporary Books, 1987), 279.

30. Connolly, *The Rings of Destiny*, 196.

31. "Moszkvában fogadták a Szovjetunió és Csehszlovákia oiimpiai versenyzőit," *Új Szó*, January 10, 1957, 6.

32. Connolly, *The Rings of Destiny*, 205.

33. *Ibid.*, 219.

34. *Ibid.*, 224.

35. Willoughby, "Olga Fikotová-Connolly."

36. "Who's for Romance," *Toledo Blade*, March 18, 1957, 16.

37. *Ibid.*

38. Connolly, *Olympic Echoes*, 406.

39. *Ibid.*, 382.

40. *Ibid.*, 383.

41. *Ibid.*, 412.

42. *Ibid.*, 421.

43. Connolly, *The Rings of Destiny*, 293.

44. "'Tis Love,' 'Tis Love, Etc.," *New York Times*, March 22, 1957, 22.

45. "Love Triumphs Over Ideology," *Life* magazine, April 8, 1957, 50–52.

46. Vick Vance, Charles Courriere and Franz Goess, "Prague dans la rue pour les mariés Olympiques," *Paris Match*, April 6, 1957, 72–79.

47. Connolly, *Olympic Echoes*, 441.

48. *Ibid.*, 447.

Chapter 14

1. In 1951 West Germany's National Olympics Committee (NOC) was first off the mark to obtain recognition from the IOC. IOC then argued that there could only be one committee per country, and it therefore refused to recognize East Germany's NOC. Consistency was not a strong point for the IOC, which went on to recognize the NOCs of the two Chinas.

2. "Remarks of Welcome by Avery Brundage in Behalf of AAU to British Empire Track Team on Arrival in Chicago 1930," quoted by Carolyn Marvin in "Avery Brundage and American Participation in the 1936 Olympic Games," *Journal of American Studies* 16, no. 1 (1982): 81–105.

3. Bernd Walter Raeke, *German-German Relations in the Fields of Sport, with Particular Reference to the Olympic Games 1952–1972* (Ph.D. diss., Plymouth University, 2014), 74.

4. Uta Andrea Balbier, "A Game, a Competition, an Instrument?: High Performance, Cultural Diplomacy and German Sport from 1950 to 1972," *The International Journal of the History of Sport* 26, no. 4 (2009): 539–555.

5. Martin H. Geyer, "Der Kampf um nationale Repräsentation. Deutsch-deutsche Sportbeziehungen und die 'Hallstein-Doktrin,'" *Vierteljahrshefte für Zeitgeschichte* (1996): 55–86.

6. Klaus Ullrich-Huhn, *Der Enflose Politfeldzug Gegen Den DDR-Sport* (Berlin: Verein Fur Sport und Gesellschaft e.V. undated), 33–34.

7. Ivana Veselková, *Společný tým NDR a SRN na olympijských hrách v Melbourne v roce 1956* (Diploma diss., Univerzita Karlova, 2012), 44.

8. Geyer, "Der Kampf um nationale Repräsentation," 71.

9. Raeke, *German-German Relations in the Fields of Sport*, 44, quoting a statement by the speaker of the West German Cabinet in a press conference at Bonn on November 16, 1956.

10. Speech of Avery Brundage at the opening ceremony of the IOC Session in Melbourne on November 19, 1956.

11. Christa Stubnick, "Zwei Silbermedalaillen für Deutschland," *Fünf bunte Ringe—Dynamosportler erzählen* (Berlin: Verlag des Ministeriums für Nationale Verteidigung, 1957), 49.

12. Christa Stubnick, "Christa Stubnick erzählt," *Fünf Bunte Ringe* (Berlin: Verlag des Ministeriums für Nationale Verteidigung, 1957), 49–50.

13. *Ibid.*, 50.

14. Richard Goldstein, "Betty Cuthbert, 79, Sprinter with 3 Golds At '56 Olympics, Dies," *New York Times*, August 8, 2017, B14.

15. "Pets Are Champion's Hobby," *The Age*, October 15, 1956, 6.

16. *Daily Express*, December 4, 1956, 5.

17. Bernard O'Neill, "Irish Boxing at the Olympics," *IABA News*, July 13, 2016. Available at https://iaba.ie/irish-boxing-olympics-4/, accessed October 11, 2016.

18. "Die erste 'Sommer'-Medaille über Christa Stubnick," *Beiträge zur Sportgeschichte*, issue 33 (Spring 2012): 13–20.

19. Stubnick, "Christa Stubnick erzählt," 31.

20. Raeke, *German-German Relations in the Fields of Sport*, 72. Avery Brundage made this statement at the 51st meeting of the IOC at its Paris meeting held between June 13 and 18, 1955.

21. Heinz Schöbel, "Vorwort," *Die XVI Olympischen Spiele in Melbourne 1956* (Berlin: Sportverlag, 1957), 9.

22. "Muskelkater nach Melbourne," *Der Spiegel*, December 19, 1956, 44.

23. Norbert Lehmann, *Internationale Sportbeziehungen und Sportpolitik der DDR* Teil I (Münster: Lit Verlag, 1986), 309.

24. Gerhard Oehmigen, "Die Olympische Spiele in Melbourne und die Deutschen," *Beiträge zur Sportgeschichte—Deutsche Sportgeschichte DDR*, issue 7. See cable from Walther Hess to the Foreign Office, Bonn, December 12, 1956.

25. *Ibid*. See cable from Götz to the Foreign Office, Bonn, December 12, 1956.

26. Andrew Strenk, "Diplomats in Track Suits: The Role of Sports in the Foreign Policy of the German Democratic Republic," *Journal of Sport & Social Issues* 4, no. 1 (1980): 34–45.

Chapter 15

1. Gabay, "A melbourne-i vérfürdő nem volt reváns ötvenhatért."

2. Péter Hardi, "Akik revánsot vettek," *Vasárnapi hírek*, October 22, 2011. Available at http://www.vasarnapihirek.hu/nyomtatas? cikk=/sport/gyarmati_szabad_fold_ vizilabda_forradalom_tortenelem_olimpia_ film, accessed November 20, 2016.

3. Péter Ágh, "Civil életem legszebb eseménye volt, hogy megvertük a szovjeteket, s megnyertük az olimpiát," *Fidelitas*, February 20, 2008. Available at http://www.fidelitas. hu/cikk/civil_eletem_legszebb_esemenye_ volt_hogy_megvertuk_a_szovjeteket_s_ megnyertuk_az_olimpiat, accessed November 21, 2016.

4. Colin K. Gray and Megan Raney, *Freedom's Fury* (Los Angeles: WOLO Entertainment, 2006), DVD.

5. Gabriella Hideg, "Sport és politika az 1956-os melbourne-i Olimpia tükrében," *Sporttudományi Sziporkák*, ed. G. Róbert (Pécs: University of Pécs, 2014), 56–62. Available at http://www.ttk.pte.hu/files/tdk/Sport tudomanyi_Sziporkak_Dijazott_OTDK_ Dolgozatok_2011–2013.pdf, accessed March 13, 2017.

6. Anastasia Kuzmina, 'Призер Олимпийских игр Георгий Лезин: 'Венгры хотели нас убить!,'" *Sport*, June 22, 2012. Available at http://www.sportsdaily.ru/ articles/prizer-olimpiyskih-igr-georgiy-lezin-

vengryi-hoteli-nas-ubit-50940, accessed December 30, 2016.

7. Miles Corwin, "Blood in the Water at the 1956 Olympics," *Smithsonian.com*, July 31, 2008. Available at http://www.smithsonian mag.com/history/blood-in-the-water-at-the-1956-olympics-1616787/, accessed November 21, 2016.

8. Gray and Raney, *Freedom's Fury*.

9. Tamás Sárközy, "A világklasszis döntetlenje a történelemmel," *NOL*, October 2, 2009. Available at http://nol.hu/sport/-20130921-a_vilagklasszis_dontetlenje_a_ tortenelemmel-1414363, accessed March 10, 2017.

10. Hideg, "Sport és politika az 1956-os melbourne-i Olimpia tükrében."

11. Howard, *15 Days in '56*, 180.

12. Maxim Kiselyov, "'Кровавому полуфиналу'—полвека," *ВЕСТИ.RU*, December 6, 2006. Available at http://www.vesti. ru/doc.html?id=114658&cid=7, accessed November 21, 2016.

13. Boris Valiev, "Гойхман: Воспоминания о неразвитом социализме," reprinted in *WaterPolonline.ru* from *Sovetskiy Sport*, no. 53 (April 7, 1994). Available at http://www. waterpolonline.ru/opinions/?id=1173, accessed November 1, 2016.

14. Kuzmina, 'Призер Олимпийских игр Георгий Лезин.

15. "Cold War Violence Erupts at Melbourne Olympics," *Sydney Morning Herald*, December 7, 1956, 1.

16. *Ibid*.

17. "Fists Fly in Pool Fracas," *The Argus*, December 7, 1956, 1, 3.

18. Mike Rowbottom, "Ervin Zádor: Blood on the Water," *The Independent* (UK), December 2, 2006.

19. Jurica Gizdic, *Hrvatska I olimpijska Odlicja* (Zagreb: Grafika Markulin 2003), 153.

20. Oskar Wiktorsson, "Vattenpolomatchen som blev storpolitik," *Fria Tidningen*, February 5, 2013. Available at http://www. fria.nu/artikel/96276, accessed November 21, 2016.

21. Gray and Raney, *Freedom's Fury*.

Chapter 16

1. Yuri Juris, "Тренер Номер Один," *Sport-Express*, no. 7, May 1995.

2. Ivan Grinko, "Гавриил Качалин: первый успех," *NTV-PLUS West*. Available at http://sport.ntvplus.ru/article/15/

gavriil-kachalin-pervyj-uspeh.xl, accessed October 7, 2016.

3. Alexey Patrikeev, "Борис Разинский," *Yezhenedel'nik (Futbol)*, no. 59 (August 1997). Available at http://www.rusteam.permian.ru/players/razinsky.html, accessed December 26, 2020.

4. Manfred Zeller, "'The Second Stalingrad': Soccer Fandom, Popular Memory and the Legacy of the Stalinist Past," *Euphoria and Exhaustion: Modern Sport in Soviet Culture and Society*, eds. Nikolaus Katzer, Sandra Budy, Alexandra Köhring, and Manfred Zeller (Frankfurt: Campus Verlag, 2010), 208.

5. "Golden Melbourne."

6. Alexei Paramonov, "Олимпийская Сборная СССР—1956," *Yezhenedel'nik (Futbol)*, no. 49 (1996). Available at http://www.rusteam.permian.ru/olimp_team/history/1956_00.html, accessed December 26, 2020.

7. Juris, "Тренер Номер Один."

8. Leonid Velikhov, "Непризнанный герой Мельбурна. Анатолий Исаев," *Radio Liberty*, May 31, 2014. Available at http://www.svoboda.org/a/25404364.html, accessed October 5, 2016.

9. Mario Rodrigues, "My Fundays," *The Telegraph* (Calcutta), April 27, 2011. Available at http://www.telegraphindia.com/1110427/jsp/telekids/story_13904927.jsp, accessed October 18, 2016.

10. Anrdei Ivanov, "Просто спартанец. История одного героя," *Chempionat*, June 9, 2015. Available at https://www.championat.com/football/article-3261903-nikolaj-tishhenko-sbornaja-sssr-futbol-olimpiada-1956.html, accessed December 28, 2020.

CHAPTER 17

1. Howard, *15 Days in '56*, 193.

2. *The Official Report of the Organizing Committee for the Games of the XVI Olympiad Melbourne 1956* (Melbourne: The Organizing Committee of the XVI Olympiad, 1958), 26.

3. There were two systems of scoring. The points quoted are on the American system 10–5–4–3–2–1 for the first six places, while the European system in based on 7–5–4–3–2–1. The points quoted use the American method of calculating points. If the European system is used (the one preferred by the Soviet Union) the USSR still beat the U.S., 622 to 497.

4. "In Full View of the World," *Sports Illustrated*, December 17, 1956, 22.

5. "Repeat the Rhubarb in the Games!" *Detroit Free Press*, December 7, 1956, 41.

6. "The Battle of Melbourne," *Sports Illustrated*, December 17, 1956, 23.

7. Allison Danzig, "Russia Far Ahead of 68 Other Nations as Olympic Games End in Melbourne," *New York Times*, December 9, 1956, 23.

8. "How the Russians Won All those Points," *Life* magazine, December 17, 1956, 95–98.

9. "Olympic Flame Dies," *The Victoria Advocate*, December 9, 1956, 10A.

10. "Scoring Change Discussed," *New York Times*, December 9, 1956, 23.

11. Constantine Brown, "New Olympic Victory for Reds," *Washington Evening Star*, June 15, 1959.

12. "In Full View of the World."

13. *Sovetii Sport*, December 8, 1956, 1.

14. To be fair, West Germans were also using performance enhancing drugs. The difference was hey were not administered by the State, but by coaches. See Simon Krivec, *Die Anwendung von anabolen-androgenen Steroiden im Leistungssport der Bundesrepublik Deutschland in den Jahren 1960 bis 1988 unter besonderer Berücksichtigung der Leichtathletik* (Berlin: Logos Verlag Berlin GmbH, 2017).

CHAPTER 18

1. Dobor, *Olimpiának indult*, 250.

2. Gergely Csurka, "A Life of Goals, Gold—and Fun," *FINA* magazine, 102–105.

3. Dobor, *Olimpiának indult*, 254.

4. László Jeney and György Kárpáti, *Melbourne—Miami—Margitsziget* (Budapest: Sport, 1957), 31.

5. "Zsuzsa Ordogh, 'Si tu peux, ne reviens pas!,'" *L'Équipe*, August 8, 2016.

6. "Iron Curtain Olympians Arrive," *The Tennessean*, December 25, 1956, 4.

7. Jeney and Kárpáti, *Melbourne—Miami—Margitsziget*, 32–33.

8. "Athletes to Stay. Big New York Welcome," *Kingston Daily Freeman* (New York), December 26, 1956, 5.

9. Jeney and Kárpáti, *Melbourne—Miami—Margitsziget*, 58.

10. *Ibid.*, 51.

11. Mayer Brandschain, "Hungarian Olympians Feted, Receive Presents," *Philadelphia Inquirer*, January 3, 1957, 19.

12. *Ibid.*, 51.

13. Jeney and Kárpáti, *Melbourne—Miami—Margitsziget*, 74.

14. *Ibid.*

15. Csurka, "A Life of Goals, Gold—and Fun."

16. Rider, *Cold War Games: Propaganda, the Olympics, and U.S. Foreign Policy* (Urbana: University of Illinois Press, 2016), 311.

17. János Sebők, "Elvis Presley énekelt nekünk," *Cultura* magazine, August 7, 2012. Available at http://cultura.hu/szub-kultura/-elvis-presley-enekelt-nekunk/, accessed November 11, 2016.

18. Andree Laguerre, "Down a Road Called Liberty," *Sports Illustrated*, December 17, 1956, 14–18.

19. Rider, *Cold War Games*, 127.

20. Rider, *The Olympic Games and the Secret Cold War*, 315.

21. *Ibid.*, 303.

22. "Note to File" of an interview with Z. Victor Partenyi on November 30, 1956, in *Martin, Miklos*, National Archives of Australia: A6126, 1388.

23. Dobor, *Olimpiának indult*, 262.

24. "Iron Curtain Olympians head for U.S. Homes," *Deseret News*, December 24, 1956.

25. Richard L. Neale, "A Word of Explanation," *Hungarian Athletes Freedom Tour* booklet. Undated.

26. Richard L. Neale, "Across a Free Land," *Sports Illustrated*, April 8, 1957, 37.

Bibliography

Primary Sources

Books and Manuscripts

Adjoubei, Alexei. *Те Десять Лет* (Moscow: Sovetskaya Rossiya, 1989).

British Olympic Association, and Cecil Bear, ed. *Official Report of the XVth Olympic Games: Helsinki, July 19-August 3, 1952* (London: World Sports, 1953).

Bywaters, Jerry. *Seventy-Five Years of Art in Dallas: The History of the Dallas Art Association and the Dallas Museum of Fine Arts* (Dallas: Dallas Museum of Fine Arts, 1978).

Comitato Olimpico Nazionale Italiano. *Official Report of the 1956 Olympic Winter Games* (Rome: Società Grafica Romana, 1956).

Connolly, Harold. *Olympic Echoes.* Unpublished memoir, 2008.

Connolly, Olga. *The Rings of Destiny* (New York: David McKay Company, 1968).

Gray, Colin K., and Megan Raney. *Freedom's Fury* (Los Angeles: WOLO Entertainment, 2006). DVD.

Jackson Papers, Box 104, Sports Illustrated— Hungarian Olympic Team Defectors, DDEL.

Jeney, László, and György Kárpáti, *Melbourne— Miami—Margitsziget* (Budapest: Sport, 1957).

Lechenperg, Harald. *Olympische Spiele 1956: Cortina, Stockholm, Melbourne* (Munich: IM Bertelsmann Lesering, 1957).

Nave, Eric. Unpublished autobiography.

Novotný, Jan, and Oldřich Žurman. *Dopisy z Melbourne* (Prague: Sportovní a turistické nakladatelství, 1957).

Organizing Committee for the XIV Olympiad. *The Official Report of the Organising Committee for the XIV Olympiad London 1948* (London: Organising Committee for the XIV Olympiad, 1951).

Organizing Committee of the XVI Olympiad. *The Official Report of the Organizing Committee for the Games of the XVI Olympiad Melbourne 1956* (Melbourne: The Organizing Committee of the XVI Olympiad, 1958).

Petrov, Vladimir, and Evdokia Petrov. *Empire of Fear* (London: Andre Deutsch, 1956).

Pirie, Gordon. *Running Wild* (London: Sportsmans Book Club, 1962), 156.

Romanov, Nikolai. *Восхождение на Олимп* (Moscow: Sovetskiy Sport, 1993).

Romanov, Nikolai. *Трудные дороги к Олимпу* (Moscow: Fizkultura i sport. 1987).

Sportclub Dinamo Berlin. *Fünf bunte Ringe— Dynamosportler erzählen* (Berlin: Verlag des Ministeriums für Nationale Verteidigung, 1957).

Starostin, Nikolaï. *Футбол сквозь годы* (Moscow: Sovetskaya Rossiya, 1989).

Székely, Éva. *Sírni csak a győztesnek szabad* (Budapest: Új Mandátum Könyvkiadó, 1992).

Takács, Tibor, Zsolt Krahulcsán, and Müller Rolf. *Állambiztonság és olimpia 1956–1988* (Budapest: L'Harmattan, 2008).

Magazines

Brundage, Avery. "I Must Admit—Russian Athletes Are Great!" *Saturday Evening Post*, April 30, 1955, 109–112, 114.

Congressional Record.

Herald Weekend Magazine

Savin, N. "Неудачи Аллена Даллеса," *Literaturnaya Gazeta*, April 2, 1957.

Sports Illustrated

National Archives of Australia

Chinese Opera Company—visit to Australia, NAA: A10302, 1956/1597.

FIKOTOVA, Olga, NAA: A6126, 1389.

GYARMATI Dezso born 23 October 1927; Eva born 3 April 1927; Andrea born 15 May 1954—Hungarian, NAA: A12513.

HEGYI, Gyula, NAA: A6126, 1379.

Hungary—Political refugees, NAA: A1838, 33/2/6 PART 1.

Martin, Miklos, NAA: A 6126, 1388.

Nationales Olympisches Komitee der Deutschen Demokratischen Republik. *Die XVI Olympischen Spiele in Melbourne 1956: offizielles Standardwerk des Nationalen Olympischen Komitees der Deutschen Demokratischen Republik* (Berlin: Sportverlag, 1957).

Operation Robin Red Breast (TS), NAA: A6122, 2881.

Operation Wren, NAA: A6122, 2883.

Papers of Sir Wilfrid Kent Hughes (1895–1970), series 19, MS 4856.

Political Asylum—Nina Paranyuk, NAA: A1838, 1606/3.

XVI Olympiad Melbourne 1956—Communist Front Organisations—Interest in Olympic Games, NAA: A6122, 2775.

XVI Olympiad Melbourne 1956 Counter Espionage Targets (TS), NAA: A6122, 2776

XVI Olympiad Melbourne 1956 CPA interest in Olympic Games, NAA: A6122, 2783

XVI Olympiad Melbourne 1956 Espionage Intelligence Aspects Volume 1, NAA: A6122, 2791.

XVI Olympiad Melbourne 1956 Espionage Use by RIS, NAA: A6122, 2777.

XVI Olympiad Melbourne 1956 Grant of Political Asylum to Team Members and Visitor, NAA: A6122, 2782.

XVI Olympiad Melbourne 1956: Grant to Political Asylum to Team Members and Visitors, NAA: A6122, 2782.

XVI Olympiad Melbourne 1956 Officials Teams intending to proceed to USA, NAA: A6122, 2784.

XVI Olympiad Melbourne 1956 Sovbloc Countries sport and Athletics in USSR and Satellite countries, NAA: A6122, 2788.

XVI Olympiad Melbourne 1956 Transport Russian Ship GRUZIJA aka GRUZIA aka GRUZIYA Volume 1, NAA: A6122, 2764.

XVI Olympiad Melbourne 1956 Transport Russian Ship GRUZIJA aka GRUZIA aka GRUZIYA Volume 2, NAA: A6122, 2765.

XVI Olympiad Melbourne 1956—Volume 2—Officials—Teams from Russia, NAA: A6122, 1257.

XVI Olympiad Melbourne 1956—Volume 3—Officials—Teams from Russia, NAA: A6122, 1258.

Selected appendices of 'Unpublished history of ASIO' [Security Intelligence], NAA: A6122, 1414.

Newspapers

The Age
The Argus
Canberra Times
Dallas Morning News
Gazette de Lausanne
The Guardian
The Herald
Journal de Geneve
Leidse Courant
Los Angeles Times
Le Monde
New York Times
The Ottawa Citizen
Sydney Morning Herald
Times of London
Tribune de Lausanne
Washington Post

Secondary Sources

Allison, Lincoln, ed. *The Politics of Sport* (Manchester: Manchester University Press, 1986).

Anderson, Sheldon. *The Politics and Culture of Modern Sports* (Lanham: Lexington, 2015).

Arnaud, Pierre, and James Riordan, eds. *Sport and International Politics* (London, Routledge, 1999).

Balbier, Uta Andrea. "A Game, a Competition, an Instrument?: High Performance, Cultural Diplomacy and German Sport from 1950 to 1972." *The International Journal of the History of Sport* 26, no. 4 (2009): 539–555.

Ballard, Geoffrey. *Nation with Nation* (Richmond: Spectrum Publications, 1997).

Barrett, Edward W. *Truth Is Our Weapon* (New York: Funk and Wagnalls, 1953).

Belmonte, Laura A. *Selling the American Way: US Propaganda and the Cold War* (Philadelphia: University of Pennsylvania Press, 2013).

Bialoguski, Michael. *The Petrov Story* (Melbourne: William Heinemann, 1955).

Brokhin, Yuri. *The Big Red Machine: The Rise and Fall of Soviet Olympic Champions*. Trans. Glenn Garelik and Yuri Brokhin (New York: Random House, 1977).

Cahn, Susan. "'Cinderellas' of Sport: Black Women in Track and Field." *Sport and the*

Color Line: Black Athletes and Race Relations in Twentieth-Century America, eds. Patrick B. Miller and David K. Wiggins (New York: Routledge, 2004).

Carraro, Francine. *Jerry Bywaters: A Life in Art* (Austin: University of Texas Press, 2010).

Carraro, Francine. "Seeing Red: The Dallas Museum in the McCarthy Era.'" *Suspended License: Censorship and the Visual Arts I,* ed. Elizabeth C. Childs (Seattle: University of Washington Press, 1999).

Caute, David. *The Dancer Defects: The Struggle for Cultural Supremacy During the Cold War* (Oxford: Oxford University Press, 2003).

Chester, Eric Thomas. *Covert Network: Progressives, the International Rescue Committee, and the CIA* (Armonk: M.E. Sharpe, 1995).

Dent, Bob. *Budapest 1956* (Budapest: Európa Könyvkiadó, 2006).

Dobor, Dezső. *Olimpiának indult* (Budapest: Aréna 2000, 2006).

Domer, Thomas M. *Sport in Cold War America, 1953–1963: The Diplomatic and Political Use of Sport in the Eisenhower and Kennedy Administrations* (Ph.D. diss., Marquette University, 1976).

Edelman, Robert. *Serious Fun* (New York: Oxford University Press, 1993).

Edelman, Robert. *Spartak Moscow: A History of the People's Team in the Workers' State* (Ithaca: Cornell University Press, 2009).

Espy, Richard. *The Politics of the Olympic Games* (Berkeley: University of California Press, 1979).

Findling, John E., and Kimberly D. Pelle, eds. *Encyclopedia of the Modern Olympic Movement* (Westport, CT: Greenwood Publishing Group, 2004).

Fursenko, Aleksandr, and Timothy Naftali. *Khrushchev's Cold War: The Inside Story of an American Adversary* (New York: W.W. Norton, 2010).

Gati, Charles. *Failed Illusions* (Washington, D.C.: Woodrow Wilson Center Press, 2006).

Glanville, Brian. *Soccer nemesis* (London: Secker & Warburg, 1955).

Gordon, Harry. *Australia and the Olympic Games* (St. Lucia: University of Queensland Press, 1994).

Guoqi, Xu. *Olympic Dreams: China and Sports 1895–2008* (President and Fellows of Harvard College, 2008).

Guttmann, Allen. *The Games Must Go On: Avery Brundage and the Olympic Movement* (New York: Columbia University Press, 1984).

Guttmann, Allen. *The Olympics: A History of Modern Games* (Urbana: University of Illinois Press, 2002).

Hampton, Janie. *The Austerity Olympics: When the Games Came to London in 1948* (London: Aurum Press Limited, 2012).

Hargreaves, Jenny, ed. *Sport, Culture and Ideology* (London: Routledge, 1982).

Haverkamp, Aad. *De politieke Spelen? De dynamiek van de maatschappelijke discussies over het boycotten van de Olympische Spelen in 1936, 1956 en 1980* (Masters diss., Rijksuniversiteit Groningen, 2012).

Hill, Christopher. *Olympic Politics: Athens to Atlanta 1896–1996* (Manchester: Manchester University Press, 1996).

Hong, Fan, and Lu Zhouxiang. *The Politicisation of Sport in Modern China* (London: Routledge, 2015).

Horner, David. *The Spy Catchers: The Official History of ASIO, 1949–1963* (Sydney: Allen & Unwin, 2014).

Howard, Bruce. *15 Days in '56: The First Australian Olympics* (Sydney: Angus & Robertson, 1995).

Jay, Kathryn. *More Than Just a Game: Sports in American Life Since 1945* (New York: Columbia University Press, 2004).

Kanin, David B. *A Political History of the Olympic Games* (Boulder: Westview Press, 1981).

Kaplan, Karel. *The Short March: The Communist takeover in Czechoslovakia, 1945–1948* (London: C. Hurst, 1987).

Katzer, Nikolaus, Sandra Budy, Alexandra Köhring, and Manfred Zeller, eds. *Euphoria and Exhaustion: Modern Sport in Soviet Culture and Society* (Frankfurt: Campus Verlag, 2010).

Keys, Barbara. "The Early Cold War Olympics, 1952–1960: Political, Economic and Human Rights Dimensions." *The Palgrave Handbook of Olympic Studies* (London: Palgrave Macmillan, 2012), 72–87.

Kieran, John, Arthur Daley, and Pat Jordan. *The Story of the Olympic Games* (Philadelphia: J.B. Lippincott, 1977).

Kő, András. *Melbourne 1956* (Budapest: Nemzet Kiadó, 2006).

Kopácsi, Sandor. *In the Name of the Working Class.* Trans. Daniel and Judy Stoffman (London: Fontana, 1989).

Lendvai, Paul. *One Day That Shook the Communist World* (Princeton: Princeton University Press, 2008).

Leslie, Warren. *Dallas, Public and Private: As-*

pects of an American City (New York: Grossman, 1964).

Lijuan, Liang. He Zhenjiang and China's Olympic Dream (Beijing: Foreign Languages Press, 2007).

Lucas, Scott. "Beyond Freedom, Beyond Control, Beyond the Cold War: Approaches to American Culture and the State-Private Network." Intelligence and National Security 18, no. 2 (2003): 53–72.

Lynn, Katalin Kádár, ed. The Inauguration of Organized Political Warfare: Cold War Organizations Sponsored by the National Committee for a Free Europe/Free Europe Committee (Budapest: Central European University Press, 2013).

Lyubomirov, Nikolai, and Petr Sobolev. A Story of Soviet Sport (Moscow: Progress, 1967).

Mason, John. The Cold War: 1945–1991 (London: Routledge, 2002).

Miller, David, ed. The Official History of the Olympic Games and the IOC: Athens to London, 1894–2012 (Edinburgh: Mainstream, 2012).

Mills, Richard. The Politics of Football in Yugoslavia: Sport, Nationalism and the State (London: I.B. Tauris, 2018).

Montefiore, Simon Sebag. Stalin: The Court of the Red Tsar (London: Phoenix, 2004).

The Olympic Games, Melbourne, 1956 (Melbourne: Colorgravure Publication, 1956).

Parks, Jenifer. The Olympic Games, the Soviet Sports Bureaucracy, and the Cold War: Red Sport, Red Tape (Lanham: Lexington, 2017).

Peppard, Victor, and James Riordan. Playing Politics: Soviet Sport Diplomacy to 1992 (Greenwich: JAI Press, 1993).

Perović, Jeronim. "The Tito-Stalin Split: A Reassessment in Light of New Evidence." Journal of Cold War Studies 9, no. 2 (2007): 32–63.

Peterdi, Pál. Gyarmati sors, avagy egy bal kéz története (Budapest: Histórias Könyvkiadó és Értékesítő Betéti Társaság, 2005).

Posey, Carl. The XV Olympiad: Helsinki 1952, Cortina D'Ampezzo 1956 (Toronto: Warwick Press, 2015).

Posey, Carl. The XVI Olympiad: Melbourne 1956, Squaw Valley 1960 (Los Angeles: World Sport Research & Publications, 1998).

Raeke, Bernd Walter. German-German Relations in the Fields of Sport, with Particular Reference to the Olympic Games 1952–1972 (Ph.D. diss., Plymouth University, 2014).

Redihan, Erin Elizabeth. The Olympics and the Cold War, 1948–1968: Sport as Battleground in the U.S.–Soviet Rivalry (Jefferson: McFarland, 2017).

Rider, Toby C. Cold War Games: Propaganda, the Olympics, and U.S. Foreign Policy (Urbana: University of Illinois Press, 2016).

Rider, Toby C. The Olympic Games and the Secret Cold War: The US Government and the Propaganda Campaign against Communist Sport, 1950–1960 (Ph.D. diss., University of Western Ontario, 2011).

Rider, Toby C. "Political Warfare in Helsinki: American Covert Strategy and the Union of Free Eastern European Sportsmen," The International Journal of the History of Sport 30, no. 13 (2013): 1493–1507.

Rinehart, Robert E. "Fists Flew and Blood Flowed." Symbolic Resistance and International Response in Hungarian Water Polo at Melbourne Olympics 23, no. 2 (Summer 1996): 120–139.

Roubal, Petr. Spartakiads: The Politics of Physical Culture i Communist Czechoslovakia. Trans. Dan Morgan (Prague: Karolinum Press, 2019).

Sebestyen, Victor. Twelve Days: The Storey of the 1956 Hungarians Revolution (New York: Vintage Books, 2010).

Senn, Alfred Erich. Power, Politics and the Olympic Games (Champaign: Human Kinetics, 1999).

Shneidman, N. Norman, The Soviet Road to Olympus: Theory and Practice of Soviet Physical Culture and Sport, Occasional Papers No. 19 (Toronto: Ontario Institute for Studies in Education, 1979).

Shteinbatch, Vladimir. Soviet Sport: The Success Story (Moscow: Raduga, 1967).

Stern, John Allen. C.D. Jackson: Cold War Propagandist for Democracy and Globalism (Lanham: University Press of America, 2012).

Strenk, Andrew. "Diplomats in Track Suits: The Role of Sports in the Foreign Policy of the German Democratic Republic." Journal of Sport & Social Issues 4, no. 1 (1980): 34–45.

Szepesi, György. Búcsú a mikrofontól (Budapest: Paginarum, 1998).

Taborsky, Edward. Communism in Czechoslovakia, 1948–1960 (Princeton: Princeton University Press, 1961).

Taylor, Phillip M. "Through a Glass Darkly? The Psychological Climate and Psychological Warfare of the Cold War." Cold-War Propaganda in the 1950s, ed. Gary D. Rawnsley (London: Palgrave Macmillan, 1999).

Tipping, Edward William. The Tipping Olym-

pics: Melbourne 1956—Rome 1960 (Melbourne: Peter Isaacson, 1972).

Vegso, Roland. *The Naked Communist: Cold War Modernism and the Politics of Popular Culture* (New York: Fordham University Press, 2012).

Wagg, Stephen, and David L. Andrews. *East Plays West: Sport and the Cold War* (London: Routledge, 2007).

Wallechinsky, David. *The complete book of the Olympics* (London: Aurum Press, 1996).

Wiesen Cook, Blanche. "First Comes the Lie: C.D. Jackson and Political Warfare." *Radical History Review* 31 (1984): 42–70.

Wilford, Hugh. *The Mighty Wurlitzer: How the CIA Played America* (Cambridge: Harvard University Press, 2009).

Wilson, Jonathan. *Behind the Curtain: Football in Eastern Europe* (London: Hachette UK, 2012).

Winkel, Marjolein te. De verloren spelen: *Nederlandse boycot Olympische Spelen 1956* (Eindhoven: deboekenmakers, 2008).

Index